THE WORLD OF OVID'S
METAMORPHOSES

WITHDRAWN

THE WORLD OF OVID'S

METAMORPHOSES

JOSEPH B. SOLODOW

THE UNIVERSITY OF NORTH CAROLINA PRESS

CHAPEL HILL & LONDON

©1988 The University of North Carolina Press

All rights reserved

Manufactured in the United States of America

The paper in this book meets the guidelines for permanence and
durability of the Committee on Production Guidelines for
Book Longevity of the Council on Library Resources.

92 91 90 89 88   5 4 3 2 1

Library of Congress Cataloging-in-Publication Data

Solodow, Joseph B.

The world of Ovid's Metamorphoses / by Joseph B. Solodow.

p.   cm.

Bibliography: p.

Includes indexes.

ISBN 0-8078-5434-4 (pbk. : alk. paper)

1. Ovid, 43 B.C.–17 or 18 A.D. Metamorphoses. 2. Metamorphosis
in literature. 3. Mythology, Classical, in literature. I. Title.

PA6519.M9S67   1988

873'.01—dc 19

87-24159

CIP

THIS BOOK WAS DIGITALLY MANUFACTURED.

MEMORIAE

RAVL ALFREDO PATRVCCO

CONIVGIS MEAE FRATRIS

MEDICI ATQVE HOMINIS PRAESTANTISSIMI

PRAEMATVRA MORTE EREPTI

SACER

CONTENTS

ACKNOWLEDGMENTS

I have received much help in writing this book, for all of which I am sincerely grateful. I cannot mention here everyone who has advised, warned, or encouraged, but I do want to record my particular thanks to the friends and colleagues who generously aided me with the manuscript: to James Coulter, Michael Maas, William Wilson, and Valerie Wise, who read portions of it and offered criticism that was as kind as it was valuable; to George Goold, who, subjecting it to his customary scrutiny, improved it greatly; and especially to Robert Hanning and Daniel Javitch, two friends who read the book and in whose company, moreover, so many of its formative ideas grew up that they might be considered theirs as well as mine. I am grateful too for the helpful suggestions made by the readers for the University of North Carolina Press, Sara Mack and Gordon Williams, and by the editor, Laura Oaks. The American Academy in Rome, with the support of the National Endowment for the Humanities, awarded me a Rome Prize Fellowship for 1980–1981, which provided a wonderful year of freedom to work on the book. I want to express my thanks to the Academy, to the Director of its School of Classical Studies for that year, Lawrence Richardson jr., and also to Leon Botstein, the President of Bard College, who eased the accepting of the fellowship. *Necnon tibi, carissima coniunx.*

New Haven
February 1987

INTRODUCTION

The Propoetides and Pygmalion

In Book Ten of Ovid's *Metamorphoses* we read the following tale:

sunt tamen obscenae Venerem Propoetides ausae
esse negare deam; pro quo sua numinis ira
corpora cum forma primae vulgasse feruntur,
utque pudor cessit sanguisque induruit oris,
in rigidum parvo silicem discrimine versae. (10.238–42)

Nonetheless, the lewd daughters of Propoetus made so bold as to deny that Venus was a goddess. It is said that in return, because of the goddess's anger, they were the first women to sell for money their bodies and their beauty, and as modesty ceased and the blood in their faces grew hard, they changed into unmoving flint: the difference was slight.

These few verses raise at once some of the principal questions about the poem. What are we to make of the metamorphosis? Is it right to assume, as many have, that the change is punishment exacted by Venus? The mere sequence of events (girls' denial, Venus' anger, their prostitution and change) suggests this: a principle implicit in most story-telling is *post hoc, ergo propter hoc*. This rationale is not altogether secure, though, particularly in Ovid, and the linking phrase "in return" (*pro quo*) is perfectly neutral and gives no clue to the relation between events. And what does Ovid mean by saying, "as modesty ceased and the blood in their faces grew hard"? Why, moreover, does he say this? The run of the passage makes it seem that the words offer an explanation for the change into flint. Again the conjunction provides little aid: *ut* ("as") can be temporal or modal as well as causal, with the result that the exact relation between the clauses is left unclear. Finally, why is the difference between the women and the rocks slight (*parvo discrimine*)? Do we not ordinarily consider animate and inanimate very separate, not to say opposite, states of being?

If we bring in the more well-known story immediately following, we come upon still more questions. It concerns an artist who, in revulsion at such lewd behavior, shuns women altogether and falls in love with a statue of his own making. This is Pygmalion, who at the end succeeds in converting marble into the living flesh of a woman. The two tales appear linked one with the other by the themes of chastity and stone and flesh, which they share, yet at the same time they move in opposite directions and each is the reverse of the other. What is the meaning of this far from casual juxtaposition? That hardness is always an element in a woman's nature? That art originates in a combination of eroticism with unworldly morality?

What I argue in this book is that the thematic link between the stories in the *Metamorphoses* is deceptive and any grand scheme of significance in their arrangement is illusory. The emphasis in Pygmalion's story, for instance, is concentrated on the sculptor rather than the stone. The poem regularly invites us to look for patterns of order but then frustrates our search. It almost takes pride in not allowing itself to be structured. As for the puzzling remark about modesty and hardness in the Propoetides, Ovid means by it that the women's faces were proof against blushing, and so they were but a single step away from stoniness. The play with figurative and literal hardness is an instance of the poet's wit. It serves to remind us of him as the narrator. Far from being an impersonal transmitter of the mythological material, he calls attention to himself so that we are ever aware of his mediating presence. In the end it is he himself more than anything who holds together the world of the poem.

Most important in the episode of Propoetus' daughters is the treatment of their metamorphosis. It is not in fact represented as a punishment. Angered at the women's lack of respect, Venus causes them to become prostitutes, but with that her effect on them ends. Only afterward does the transformation take place, and it does so by itself; it simply happens. Ovid even draws our attention to the ease of the metamorphosis. However improbable, in ordinary realistic terms, this ease suggests an intimate connection between the before and after states. Metamorphosis in the poem, as I try to show, is a process by which character is made manifest in appearance: the "hardness" of these women now becomes clear to all, the metaphoric is made literal. Furthermore, as a means toward realization and clarification metamorphosis plays the same role in the world as does art. Art and the artist are Ovid's special interests in the poem. A crucial document here, we shall see, is the story of Pygmalion, who has the supreme artistic gift of bringing his creation to life.

Argument and Method

My argument, which proposes these issues as several of the chief questions and answers, rests primarily upon the analysis of narrative style, the way in which Ovid tells the stories. This method seems almost dictated by the poem and by the history of the literary criticism it has produced. The general interpretations so far offered have been based either upon analysis of the thematic content of the stories or upon formal considerations. Yet the extraordinary multiplicity of possible thematic and formal analyses which the poem permits—and I suggest that a kind of deliberate vacuum is responsible—casts doubt on any single one of them and raises serious obstacles to either of these approaches. It seems best therefore to take into account this riotous confusion, which is recognized as an outstanding quality of the poem, and to look for "order," which means sense, instead in the common elements that lie beneath the diversity. These elements are, in my view, the devices of narrative through which that diversity is represented. They are the steadiest phenomena, and the best clues to what is going on. Hence this study is directed chiefly towards them, and analyzes individual stories only briefly and in those terms. It is certainly a sweet temptation to write at length about this favorite tale or that, but it is a temptation that ought to be resisted, I believe, for the sake of a larger understanding.

Analysis of the narrative style is undertaken from different angles in the sequence of the first four chapters. Chapter One, "Structures," deals with the question of the poem's overall unity, including its varying tones and genres and the shifting relationships between one story and the next. The deliberate disorder and exuberant chaos of the poem's world are described, as well as its sense that traditional narrative structures, carrying their own sets of expectations, do not aid the reader in comprehending it. What remains constant is the presence of the narrator and the theme of metamorphosis: every story includes a metamorphosis. Chapter Two, "The Narrator," takes up the role of the story-teller and examines the ways he obtrudes himself. Not only does he alone give some unity, if not meaning, to the world of the poem, but he also obtrudes most notably when expressing skepticism towards the truth of his own stories. The poet's treatment of his material is the subject of Chapter Three, "Mythology." Ovid retells the myths playfully, rendering them contemporary. While making mythology lively he also criticizes it for its claims to make sense of the world. The chief mode of imaginative literature in the ancient world, mythology in his eyes informs mostly about itself; it is self-reflective. In the following chapter, "Aeneid," two lines of argument culminate in comparisons between Ovid's poem and Virgil's. The narrative style is studied no longer in isolated features but in continuous passages, and Ovid's account of Aeneas, when compared with Virgil's, shows that he handles the most important historical mythology like the rest of his material. Virgil is not only criticized but also answered. Chapter Five, "Metamorphosis," the climax of the argument, defines the central event of the poem and explores its relation to narrative style and content. That definition is extended in the final chapter, "Art," where metamorphosis is equated with the process through which art is created. And since in Ovid's view art provides the means by which the world is comprehended, metamorphosis is ultimately important for perception as well.

Ovid is compared to Virgil not only in the fourth chapter, but throughout the book. Comparison is generally a helpful mode of presentation: qualities stand out better in some relief. Yet Virgil offers more than a convenient text for bringing out the distinctive features of Ovid. He wrote the greatest narrative poem of the Latin language, in the generation just before Ovid's. The latter, moreover, reveals in his poetry a steady, conscious engagement with the language and the episodes of his predecessor, as well as with the view of the world which they presuppose. And with all of these presuppositions Ovid disagreed radically. Virgil serves so well as a foil in part because he is nearly Ovid's opposite.

This study is entitled *The World of Ovid's Metamorphoses* because that is what it aims at describing.[1] Like perhaps any other sufficiently large work of the imagination, the *Iliad* or Machiavelli's *History of Florence* or *Our Mutual Friend*, the poem constitutes a kind of world or universe; it includes a wide field of experiences in which we come to recognize as characteristic certain phenomena and certain guiding principles. At the center stands a vision informing all the elements. My approach, an attempt to portray the world of the poem from such a center, explains some features of this study.

Many of the observations overlap with one another. The coincidence or kinship of two phenomena is pointed out. Often the same one is taken up several times, in different connections. Transitions between stories, for example, are studied in relation both to the poem's structure and to the presence of the narrator. The tendency towards personifications and "allegorical" figures bears not only on the static quality of the story-telling but also on the poem's striving towards clear embodiments. One chapter discusses the portrayal of the gods; another, their representing no large principles; a third, their role in metamorphosis. Such an arrangement of the material, recommended by the line of argument, also provides support for the argument.

As evidence for the informing vision small phenomena can be as valuable as large. Some things are readily observed, as it were, with the naked eye, such as the links between stories, the tendency toward epigram, and the handling of particular episodes. Others less conspicuous reveal themselves only under a microscope: Ovid's distinctive use of the future participle, for instance, or contrary-to-fact conditions, or the signature phrase *nunc quoque*, regularly applied to the results of metamorphosis. Minute features perhaps provide even better clues to the larger workings of the imagination in that, their origins more hidden, they are probably less subject to conscious choice. A Greek writer's employment of *kai toinun* in a work aids in its relative dating, and choices made between *upon* and *on* in certain English idioms decide a question of authorship: cannot such matters also be turned to the task of defining the qualities of a writer's vision?

Since I sometimes study rather subtle features, a procedure which may appear questionable, let me add a further word about it. The method of analysis can be represented schematically as consisting of three stages: observation of a distinctive feature in a passage, demonstration that it is typical of the poem, and interpretation of it. Each stage has its own pitfalls and each its own checks. The possibility that a feature is not distinctive we can guard against by means of philology: we can see whether other writers do the same or not. We can indicate that the instance is not unique in the poem by citing other examples. Both of these steps have sometimes been taken by other scholars, who have made some of the same observations. I refer to their work, when possible, for fuller discussion; sometimes I merely outline an argument which would require a monographic treatment. In moving from observation to interpretation we usually need to make a leap; granting the one does not necessarily entail assenting to the other. There is danger that the confidence acquired in the philological analysis may breed an unwarranted confidence in the literary conclusions. Here, especially, judgment enters, fitting interpretation not only to observation, but also to other interpretations in what is, it must be admitted, a circular fashion.

One advantage perhaps to such a form of literary criticism is that it is easy to focus on. The argument starts with a small, readily identifiable feature, and if at its conclusion it is persuasive it contains a peg on which to hang the memory of it. These features of narrative style are, to be sure, linked with consideration of larger matters, to which they often serve as an introduction. They can be the thin end of a wedge, a sharp way of gaining entrance to broad questions. In the book as a whole, as well as in its parts, this is in general the mode of working I have preferred: to move from what is specific and more clear and sure out into what is larger, less easy to describe, less certain. In Chapter Three, for instance, to illustrate a cardinal feature in Ovid's handling of his material, I take up first anachronism and Romanization and then the more general ways in which he transposes mythology into the familiar world of the reader. Similarly a general might conduct a campaign by first securing the high ground and then descending from there to attempt the conquest of the remaining territory.

One risk here lies in taking a part for the whole. To what extent, it may be objected, can a particular passage or feature, or collection of such, legitimately serve to define the poem's qualities? As example is not proof, so hint or tendency is not full description. Yet it is not evident what would constitute proof or full description in such matters. Perhaps literary criticism is always a form of synecdoche. And apart from that consideration we still may ask of a critic, which parts does he take to represent the whole? How aptly are they chosen? Are they representative?

Scholarship on Ovid

Despite the welcome wave of recent work on Ovid, especially on the *Metamorphoses*,[2] this study needs no apology. For a long time the poem was discussed chiefly from the point of view of literary history. Books and articles investigated the sources of the stories, earlier treatments of metamorphosis, models for the poem's form—was it epic?—and features of its narrative: here may be mentioned Lafaye's *Les Métamorphoses d'Ovide et leurs modèles grecs*,[3] the title of which gives in fact an unjustly narrow idea of its contents, and Martini's essay "Ovid und seine Bedeutung für die römische Poesie," which views Ovid as the fulfiller of neoteric tendencies. Literary history, however, does not determine the qualities of a poem. Yet it can help to define them, and earlier versions and techniques can provide a measure for what is distinctive in the *Metamorphoses*. That is the use made here of literary history: not to circumscribe the poet's imagination through dwelling on its models, but to illustrate it by highlighting its departures from them. Moreover, at certain important points the argument can be strengthened by reference to the ancient traditions of literary and rhetorical criticism, as found, for instance, in Cicero, Seneca, Quintilian, and Servius.

As is widely recognized, a new era of scholarship on Ovid opened in the middle years of this century. Kraus's monograph for the *Real-Enzyklopädie* (1942) and Fränkel's Sather Lectures (1945) offered fresh and unusually sympathetic readings, the one solid though penetrating, the other highly imaginative. These provoked an abundance of stimulating work, which has not yet abated. To confine ourselves to a pair of very different studies on the *Metamorphoses*, we may cite the books of Otis and Bernbeck. Today the position seems to me to be this. On the one hand, we now have excellent essays on individual tales or narrative traits, often concluding with suggestive remarks about the poem. Such work, however fruitful, has certain natural limitations. Its conclusions tend to remain unelaborated, and they run the risk of misrepresenting the whole. The majority of critics "seek the thematic importance of the work in the actions and images of specific stories, and by that effort privilege certain stories as central to the meaning and leave others as fillers."[4] Full-length studies of the entire poem, on the other hand, have not yet succeeded in giving an overall interpretation. Otis's challenging book perhaps comes closest, but his complex scheme for the poem has not persuaded many. The name of Galinsky's *Ovid's Metamorphoses: An Introduction to the Basic Aspects* suggests the somewhat piecemeal nature of its approach. The book contains useful observations about Ovid's tones, humor, and implicit criticism of Virgil and other mythologists, yet they are not formed into anything very constructive. Nearly the same is true of Wilkinson's fine pages.[5] What is lacking is a comprehensive and general literary interpretation of the poem which finds something positive in it. This I believe the present study offers, for it discovers in the phenomenon of metamorphosis important truths about perception, understanding, and art. Especially influential upon my views of Ovid is a book that deals principally with a much later period, Lanham's *The Motives of Eloquence: Literary Rhetoric in the Renaissance*. No more profoundly sympathetic account of our poet has been given than at the opening of this work, where two fundamental strategies for the literary representation of man are laid out, with Ovid the paradigm of the "rhetorical ideal of life" as Plato is of the "serious" ideal that has always prevailed. Lanham's book is fascinating to read as well as acute.

As I have often felt my own views shaped and confirmed by what others have shown me about the readings which later literary and visual artists have given of the *Metamorphoses*, so I should like this study to be accessible not only to specialists but to nonclassicists also, for instance, to students of Chaucer and Ariosto and Titian. For this reason translations are supplied for all the Latin, in the text at least, and places, events, and figures from the ancient world are identified more fully than would otherwise be appropriate. The translations are all my own. When, as happens, the same verse is translated differently at various points, this is not neglect but a desire to bring out now this, now another, quality of the Latin. I quote the original text a good deal on purpose. Paraphrase does less justice to the *Metamorphoses*, I dare say, than even to the *Aeneid*, and my argument is often based on close examination of stylistic features. A reader soaked in the text will be in a better position to weigh the claims made about it.

In the matter of the text I have not followed any one edition, but have consulted several, in particular Ehwald's edition with commentary, Anderson's Teubner text, Lee's edition of Book One and Hollis's of Book Eight. Pending the appearance of Tarrant's Oxford Classical Text, the best available is the revision of the Loeb edition carried out by Goold.[6] At every place where the textual reading might affect my argument I have noted this.

CHAPTER ONE

STRUCTURES

The Search for Structure

Since the mid-1940s Ovidian scholarship has paid great attention to the structure of the *Metamorphoses*. Sometimes at book length, sometimes in essays, critics have sought to identify the elements which articulate and unify the poem. Our age is perhaps characteristically interested in such questions. But there is also a special quality about the poem which provokes the interest. It is so extraordinarily varied, so ample, so free from obvious schemes of arrangement, that critics have repeatedly searched for designs which will be able to show the sense and purpose of the whole. I agree with this enterprise, though not with the particular results most have arrived at. We may begin our study of the poem by considering its structure as we work our way from large, external features in towards the heart of things.

Good clues about the arrangement of a work may be given by the beginning and the end. Stephens found that two philosophical passages, set at the extremities of the poem, suggested the significance of the whole.[1] According to him, Ovid's account of how the world was created out of the primeval chaos (1.5–88) is Stoic but also includes much that derives from Empedocles. The corresponding passage just before the end is the long speech of Pythagoras (15.75–478). Both of these are linked with Orphism, which celebrates Eros as the supreme deity. On the basis of this, and of other arguments as well, Stephens concludes that Love is the principal subject of the poem. We do not need to assess this idea here. I shall simply say in passing that, though the prominence of love in Ovid's stories is undeniable, the series of equations involved in this view seems to me weak, and too much of the poem is omitted. What we want to notice is how structure is a tool of interpretation.

The opening and close of the poem have been used to construct a different interpretation. In a valuable essay Buchheit has pointed out matching references to Augustus as Jupiter at the beginning (in the assembly of gods held about Lycaon, 1.200–205) and the end (in connection with Caesar's apotheosis, 15.858–60, 869–70).[2] He uses this, together with other evidence, to demonstrate that in the *Metamorphoses* the meaning of the universe is to be viewed in relation to Rome and her history. In comparison to Stephens's, Buchheit's observations on the two key passages are more firmly made, but the interpretation fits the remainder of the poem less well: the vast bulk of the work has almost nothing to do with Rome.

We may take this pair of essays as a first indication of the difficulties which beset attempts to determine the poem's structure. Both critics find in the first and last books what might be called framing elements and from them draw conclusions about the poem's subject. But the two choose to focus on different passages. What are we to do in this situation? Decide which of the two views is superior? This is not easy, since there is something to be said in favor of each. Then accept them both? But they are at odds with one another. Better than either of these courses, it seems to me, is to recognize that still other framing structures could probably be found and, moreover, that the poem calls out for such schemes and at the same time suggests so many of them as to baffle the reader.

The structures described by Stephens and Buchheit are simple, and proposed rather than demonstrated, in that they each involve but two passages. Far more extensive and detailed are the analyses of Ludwig and Otis, which bring us closer to the problem of the poem's entire structure. Ludwig finds the poem articulated in twelve sections, the first one belonging to prehistory (1.5–451), the next seven to mythical time (1.452–11.193), the last four to historical time (11.194–15.870).[3] For Otis the poem falls into four principal sections, which he calls The Divine Comedy (1.5–2.875), The Avenging Gods (3.1–6.400), The Pathos of Love (6.401–11.795), and Rome and the Deified Ruler (12.1–15.870).[4] Both, while insisting on these divisions, also recognize the continuities from one to the next. To see clearly the differences between the two let us take as a fair sample their analyses of Books Three and Four.

Ludwig analyzes the passage from 3.1 to 4.606 as a series of frames (see Figure 1). The outermost frame consists of Cadmus and his wife Harmonia. To one part that deals with Cadmus' arrival in Boeotia, slaying of a dragon, and founding of Thebes (3.1–137) corresponds another that tells of the couple's departure from Thebes and their metamorphosis into snakes (4.563–606). Inside this is set a second frame: 3.138–255 concerns Actaeon, son of Autonoe, one of Cadmus' daughters; 4.416–562 concerns another daughter, Ino, together with her husband, Athamas, and their sons, Learchus and Melicertus. These frames surround four parts devoted to Bacchus, who emerges therefore as the central subject of the passage: (1) 3.256–315, Jupiter's love for Semele and the birth of Bacchus; (2) 3.316–512, Tiresias and the intertwined stories of Echo and Narcissus; (3) 3.513–733, Bacchus' opponent Pentheus, with a long inset on those other unbelievers, the Tyrrhenian pirates; (4) 4.1–415, the daughters of Minyas, who chose to spend their time in weaving rather than in worshipping Bacchus—this last part consisting chiefly of the tales told by the sisters, which are disposed, says Ludwig, in a symmetrical set of three.[5]

Ludwig's full analysis includes observations regarding the section's tone and rhythm: love in the Tiresias and the Minyades episodes contrasts with the tragic and hymnic Bacchus theme; the section rises to a climax in Bacchus' double triumph, over the pirates and Pentheus, and his epiphany to the Minyades. He also cites details which further support the proposed structure, pointing out that Cadmus, as he leaves Thebes, is represented as thinking of the dragon, which strengthens the link between the opening and closing parts of the section; similarly, among the stories of Minyas' daughters the first and third groups begin with a *praeteritio*. Several objections can be raised against this structure, among them that whereas Actaeon is a grandson of Cadmus and Harmonia, Ino and Athamas, the principal actors in their episode, are daughter and son-in-law, so the parallel between the two stories making up the inner frame is not very close; also that Bacchus is out of sight and out of mind in much of the section.

But let us be aware of the questions such an analysis raises. To what extent does the frame shape or govern or determine or even represent its contents? Can an inset by its size take precedence over the material in which it is embedded? In other words, if we find one story set within another, as happens very often in the *Metamorphoses*, does this arrangement imply that the outer one is more important in some way? Perhaps "border" would sometimes be an apter word than "frame." Or, again, between successive stories, which kinds of links or other articulating features ought we to pay attention to? Identity of characters or place? Parallelism or other similarity of subject? General theme? What do we include in analysis, what exclude? (And in those cases, how do we decide what the subject or theme

FIGURE 1. Ludwig's analysis of *Metamorphoses* 3.1–4.606

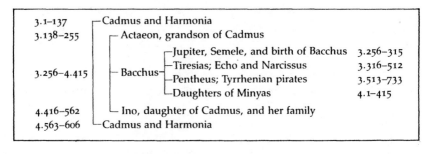

3.1–137	┌ Cadmus and Harmonia
3.138–255	├ Actaeon, grandson of Cadmus
	┌ Jupiter, Semele, and birth of Bacchus 3.256–315
3.256–4.415	├ Bacchus ┤ Tiresias; Echo and Narcissus 3.316–512
	├ Pentheus; Tyrrhenian pirates 3.513–733
	└ Daughters of Minyas 4.1–415
4.416–562	├ Ino, daughter of Cadmus, and her family
4.563–606	└ Cadmus and Harmonia

FIGURE 2. Otis's analysis of *Metamorphoses* 3.1–6.400

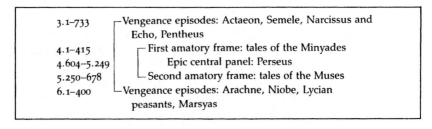

3.1–733	┌ Vengeance episodes: Actaeon, Semele, Narcissus and Echo, Pentheus
4.1–415	├ First amatory frame: tales of the Minyades
4.604–5.249	│ Epic central panel: Perseus
5.250–678	└ Second amatory frame: tales of the Muses
6.1–400	└ Vengeance episodes: Arachne, Niobe, Lycian peasants, Marsyas

is?) Rhetoric of presentation—for example, beginning two sections with the same figure of speech? Comparable size in balancing units? These are quite different matters and may conflict with one another.

These questions are sharpened if we compare Otis's analysis of the same passage. His is more consistent in that it relies almost exclusively on theme. In tracing out the variations in the theme it is also more intricate and subtle, hence more difficult to summarize accurately. It too is grounded in symmetry (see Figure 2). What Otis perceives to be the fundamental unit of structure is much larger, stretching from Book Three through the middle of Book Six. Ludwig's third section of the poem, comprising the stories from the foundation of Thebes through Cadmus' and Harmonia's metamorphosis (3.1–4.603), is here seen as matching another one, comprising the tales of Minerva and the Muses, Arachne, Niobe, the Lycian peasants, and Marsyas (5.250–6.400); these two sections surround Ovid's account of Perseus (4.604–5.249). According to Otis, Perseus constitutes the epic central panel (both the preceding and the following large divisions of the poem also have epic central panels). Flanking this are two frames in which the subject is love: the tales of the Minyades, and those which the Muses recount to Minerva. Flanking these in turn are stories of divine vengeance. Jupiter, not Bacchus, dominates this quarter of the poem, and its overall theme is vengeance.[6] Structure provides meaning.

Again the analysis contains elements that are persuasive. Otis points out parallels between the Song of the Minyades and the Song of the Muses, and between Actaeon and Pentheus, who open and close the first group of vengeance stories; he also notes the heightening of Juno's vengeance from Tiresias to Pentheus to Ino. Yet, again, his analysis has lapses and omissions: for instance, the second erotic frame directly follows the central panel, whereas between that panel and the first frame intervenes an unexplained section on Ino and the metamorphoses of Cadmus and Harmonia (416–603); moreover, the tales of the Muses which center on the rape of Proserpina are not all erotic.

The point here, however, is not to praise or criticize in detail these or other particular schemes that have been proposed for the poem, but rather to allow them to draw our attention to several important features. The number and earnestness of the analyses attest the size and the incredible variety of the poem, which tend to baffle interpretation. The remarkable lack of agreement among the analyses points to the poem's extraordinary productiveness of structures. It abounds in parallels and contrasts, symmetries and variations, with links of every sort, thematic as well as formal. If critics fail to agree (and on this poem critical agreement is minimal), it is not solely because criticism is a subjective enterprise, each critic holding his own view and there being no way of deciding among them, but rather because the poem is continually throwing out hints of structure which are neither all consistent with one another nor, if taken severally, adequate: something is always overlooked or given special emphasis. It is not that the critic was altogether mistaken; in each case he was responding to something he found in the book. None of these schemes is based on nothing; rather, hints of structure were picked up and exaggerated. The poem at the same time invites and repels attempts to interpret it through its structure.[7]

We can see these two sides in a pair of further observations. On the one hand, the "shapelessness" of the poem is reflected in the relation between its material and its book divisions. Occasionally the end of a book coincides with the completion of a story; ordinarily, however, the story spills over from one book to the next, and the division comes to seem arbitrary as a result. The opportunity for structure is neglected. Ovid sometimes seems to flaunt this too. Book Two ends with the disguised Jupiter carrying off Europa, but the poet saves for the start of Book Three Jupiter's laying aside of the bull disguise and revealing himself; as if almost to deny any break, the new book begins with the word *iamque* (3.1, "and already").[8] Though the story of Cephalus has come to an end with the close of Book Seven, his departure is postponed to the opening verses of Book Eight—and the following story is tacked on with a casual *interea* (8.6, "meanwhile"). Ovid also introduces a new character or situation right before the end of a book. Phaethon appears at the end of Book One, anticipating his visit to his father. At the end of Book Eight the river god Achelous groans over his missing horn; he is questioned about it only in the following book. And though the council of Greek heroes is summoned at the very end of Book Twelve to hear the debate over Achilles' armor, Ajax and Ulysses do not deliver their speeches until Book Thirteen. The practice of Virgil is very different: he gives to all books of the *Aeneid* a thematic compositional unity, marks them off clearly from one another, and structures his poem around their distinct groupings (the easiest example is the beginning in Book Seven of the second half, set in Italy now and comprised of war rather than travel).[9]

On the other hand, a curious instance shows us just how endemic schematizing is to critical reading of the *Metamorphoses*. In a distinguished essay on the poem's humor von Albrecht discerns patterns in the presence or absence of humor and also in the different types of humor: thus he finds a long crescendo and swift decrescendo in the humor of Book One; Book Nine contrasts with Book Eight by beginning in a humorous vein; and so forth.[10] So rampant is the desire to find principles of structure. My claim is not that these patterns are fictions of scholars' imaginations, but that they lead to nothing beyond an appreciation of Ovid's feeling for rhythm, variation, counterpoint, and the like. The soundest analysis of large sections of the poem is by Guthmüller, who in fact offers no interpretation and therefore distorts less than others.[11]

Organizations

METAMORPHOSIS

Structural analyses like those of Ludwig and Otis, which rely of course on abstraction, run aground on the uncapturable exuberance and variety of the poem. Several more concrete, recurring features give greater promise of indicating where the poem's unity lies and are more likely to point us towards the book's central concerns. Let us start with the most obvious, which gives the book its title: the diverse stories are linked by the fact that each includes a metamorphosis.[12] Ovid announces his subject in the very first words of the poem: *in nova fert animus mutatas dicere formas / corpora* (1.1–2, "my mind is moved to sing of forms changed into new bodies"), and carries it out everywhere. In Book Three, for instance, we read of the transformation of the dragon's teeth into the first men of Thebes, of Actaeon into a deer, of Tiresias into a woman, of the girl Echo into the natural phenomenon, of Narcissus into a flower, and of the Tyrrhenian pirates into dolphins. All told, about two hundred fifty metamorphoses are narrated or mentioned. This strikes me as not only the most obvious but also the most important unifying feature of the poem. Astonishingly, some critics have urged us to ignore this as trivial.[13] This flies in the face of common sense. Moreover, a self-conscious remark carefully placed by Ovid should banish any lingering doubts. In Book Eight, the very midpoint of the whole, Pirithous, after hearing of how a girl was changed into an island, declares to the assembled company that he refuses to believe in the possibility of metamorphosis (8.612–15). Of course he is wrong, as his companion Lelex undertakes to prove with another story. To describe what metamorphosis is ought to be a crucial move in interpreting the poem.

NARRATIVE LINKS

A second regular feature is that every story is joined to the one before it through some narrative link. Ovid never just says, "Now let me tell another tale." Some character or action or place always ties successive stories together, making of the whole an unbroken series. This is one of the meanings of the phrase with which the poet describes his enterprise at the start: *perpetuum . . . carmen* (1.4, "a continuous poem").[14] The series of tales beginning with Io offers a good example of this connected form of narrative. Io's son Epaphus has a playmate Phaethon, who, challenged by Epaphus about his lineage, goes to make inquiry of his father, the Sun. Thus do we move from Io to Phaethon. Phaethon's driving of his father's chariot sets the world on fire and precipitates his own death. Thereupon his sisters, weeping over his death, are changed into trees, while because of the same grief his cousin Cygnus is changed into a swan. Jupiter, when making a tour of inspection through the damaged world, catches sight of the nymph Callisto, subject of the next tale. And so it continues, one story leading to the next in unbroken succession. The only exceptions to this rule are the numerous stories which characters within the poem relate to one another, either singly (as when Vertumnus tells Pomona about Iphis and Anaxarete, 14.698–771) or in numbers (nearly all of Book Ten is sung by Orpheus), either in contest (the Muses compete with Pierus' daughters, 5.307–661) or in the course of ordinary conversation (as when Theseus and his companions stop off at the cave of the river god Achelous and spend an evening exchanging stories, 8.577–9.88). These exceptions are only apparent, however. Their narration is well motivated within the poem, where story-telling, significantly, is a popular activity. It remains true that all the parts are linked in narrative. This gives to the whole an impression of linear connectedness and coherence. The reader is made to feel that he is launched not on a series of discrete tales but a solid, continuous whole. The narrative advances with the logic of time itself.

THEMATIC LINKS

Many of the stories are joined to one another by thematic links. Successive or neighboring tales contain similar situations, characters, props, and other features. The sculptor Pygmalion, who out of stone creates a living woman, is juxtaposed with the Propoetides, women who become stone (10.238–97): one is the inversion of the other. In Book One Daphne and Io suffer nearly identical experiences. Each one's beauty attracts the immediate love of a god (Apollo and Jupiter, respectively); each flees and is pursued; each hears the divine lover boasting, almost comically, of his status (512–24, 595–97); both undergo metamorphosis, after which only their whiteness remains from their former selves (552, 743).[15] The parallel seems too strong to be accidental. Book Eight presents the tale of the aged couple, Baucis and Philemon. They are the only people to offer hospitality to Jupiter and Mercury, who have come to earth in human disguise. Though very poor, they serve the gods an appetizing banquet. Later, at the end of their lives, they are rewarded by being changed into sacred trees. The following story is that of Erysichthon, who for having dared to cut down a grove of sacred trees is punished with insatiable desire for food. The themes of food, hunger, and sacred trees, strangely combined, run between the two stories. In Ovid's rehandling of the Erysichthon legend there is some evidence of his attempt to emphasize the thematic connection with the preceding one. Callimachus, whose version of that story in his *Hymn to Demeter* served as Ovid's model,[16] had Erysichthon cut down the sacred grove because he wanted the timber in order to construct a banqueting hall. This human, practical motive has been removed by Ovid, who makes him act without any stated motive at all.[17] Consequently his Erysichthon is more purely impious, and so the tie (contrast, not parallel) to Baucis and Philemon is strengthened. We catch the poet, as it were, in the act of forging the link.

Similarly, between Books Thirteen and Fourteen he builds a kind of bridge by the parallelism of two stories. Polyphemus, who wants to be Galatea's lover, kills Acis, whom she prefers (13.750–897). Then Circe, who wants to be Glaucus' lover, transforms the woman he loves, Scylla (14.1–67). Set still further apart, the stories of Orpheus and Eurydice (10.1–77) and of Aesacus and Hesperia (11.751–95) also appear to recall one another and, because of their position, to enframe two books of the poem. In each case, at the moment of union (Eurydice's marriage, the rape of Hesperia) the woman is bitten by a snake and dies; the man renounces the world; and the gods take pity on the bereaved lover (10.40–48, 11.784–85). Moreover, a verse from the latter tale echoes one from the tale of Daphne and Apollo, all the way back at the beginning of the poem (11.774, 1.539). This is provocative. Such thematic links, which are a staple of literary composition, invite the reader to compare the stories. The similarities urge him to note the differences. He expects that the stories will shed light on one another and he will gain insight into the human problem which is being thus examined from two points of view. What are we supposed to make, he wonders, of the parallels between Daphne and Io or the contrasts between Erysichthon and Baucis and Philemon? Do not Orpheus and Aesacus define the borders of a section dealing with the theme of sorrowful love? Though not affecting all stories, these thematic links are numerous; critics have been much occupied in pointing them out.[18] Taken together, they hint that the poem can be ordered as a mosaic of developed themes.

COMPREHENSIVENESS

The last regular feature of the *Metamorphoses* is its several forms of comprehensiveness, which, singly and combined, are so strong as to be deliberate. The poem is comprehensive in chronology, in subject matter, and in literary genres. In time the book goes from the creation of the world to the recent past, from the metamorphosis of cosmic chaos into order at the beginning of time all the way down to the metamorphosis of Julius Caesar into a god, which took place a year before the poet's birth. No era falls outside the boundaries of the poem. Ludwig has rightly compared the work to the universal histories which became especially important in the first century B.C.: on the Greek side, Timagenes and Nicolaus of Damascus may be mentioned; Varro with his *De Gente Populi Romani*, on the Latin.[19]

In subject matter too the poem embraces virtually everything. It touches upon all the major stories of ancient mythology, the two large groups (the Theban cycle and the Trojan war, together with the episodes that lead up to and follow each) as well as stories of the early heroic age, of Athens and its royal family, of Rome's founding (somewhat skimpy, to be sure), and many others. It is so complete that it might serve as a mythological handbook. (That in fact it came to do so is ironic.)

Less often observed is the poem's comprehensiveness of literary genres. Lafaye draws up a list of all the poetic genres found,[20] but the poem includes much more. At one place or another it handles the themes and employs the tone of virtually every species of literature. This deserves study in some detail, since not only the number of genres but also the way they are introduced helps us to understand Ovid's intention. Epic naturally predominates. The hexameter verse and the primarily narrative character of the material alone would suffice to suggest this.[21] But the poem abounds in those small features distinctive of epic: similes (such as Apollo's pursuit of Daphne: "as when in an empty field a Gallic hound sees a hare . . . ," 1.533–39), catalogues (Actaeon's hounds, 3.206–25; hunters of the Calydonian boar, 8.301–23; and others), ecphrases, or descriptions of works of art (the tapestries of Minerva and Arachne, 6.70–128; the mixing bowl which Anius gives to Aeneas, 13.681–701). And it includes familiar heroic scenes such as a storm (11.480–572) and, of course, battle (the battle of Perseus against Phineus and his allies, 5.1–235; of the Lapiths and Centaurs, 12.219–535).

The poem also includes the epyllion, a Hellenistic substitute for epic. The epyllion was short, usually no more than several hundred verses, and complete in itself; by Ovid's day it tended to treat erotic themes, often a woman's strange or problematic love. The *Metamorphoses* has, of course, many self-contained stories; in the narrower sense we may cite as an epyllion the story of Scylla, the girl who betrayed her father and country to their enemy Minos in the hope of winning his love, but who was then rejected by him anyway (8.1–151). The subject was also treated in an independent, nearly contemporary epyllion, the *Ciris*.

Second only to epic comes tragedy, and among tragedies none were closer to Ovid than those of Euripides.[22] His account of Hecuba

(13.399–575) closely follows, up to a certain point, the Attic original, even translating some of its verses. The confrontation between Bacchus and Pentheus (3.511–733) and the career of Medea (7.1–403) are obviously indebted to Euripides as well. Many other stories in the *Metamorphoses* may have been treated on the stage in tragedies which are now lost to us. Aeschylus, for example, wrote an *Oreithyia* (cf. *Met.* 6.675–721); Sophocles, a *Tereus* (cf. 6.411–674) and a *Niobe* (cf. 6.146–312); Euripides, a *Phaethon* (cf. 1.748–2.400); both Accius and Pacuvius, early Roman writers of tragedy, an *Armorum Iudicium*, on the dispute between Ajax and Ulysses for the arms of Achilles (cf. 13.1–398). The nurse who panders to Myrrha's passion for her father (10.298–502) is a figure that can be traced back to Phaedra's nurse in the *Hippolytus* of Euripides. Elsewhere a cowherd rushes in to announce to Peleus that a monstrous wolf is ravaging his cattle by the shore (11.349–78). His language is very high-flown, and although, as he himself declares, there is no time to lose, he spends more than twenty verses elaborating the scenery. As a result "the whole speech reads like a parody of the traditional messenger-speech of tragedy."[23] As for the familiar literary elements of a tragedy, no trace is found of chorus or dialogue, but examples abound of dramatic monologues, especially those of women in distress. On the model of Euripides, who was famous for them, Ovid composed such monologues for Myrrha (10.320–355), Scylla (8.44–80), Althaea (8.478–511), and others.

These remind us that rhetoric is not excluded from tragedy, and indeed it is present in the poem in all its forms. The speeches of the women are all of the deliberative variety: Scylla, for instance, debates with herself whether to remain loyal to Megara, the city over which her father rules, or by betraying it to ingratiate herself with Minos, the captain of the besieging forces, with whom she has fallen in love. The speech of Pythagoras, on the theme of universal change, is an instance of the demonstrative type (15.75–478). The contest between Ajax and Ulysses at the beginning of Book Thirteen, in which each delivers a full speech before the assembled Greeks, provides a brilliant example of forensic oratory. Mere mention must suffice for the ingenious and varied arguments heaped up by each side and for the epigrams and other figures of speech employed in presenting them. The precepts of the orators are illustrated in more subtle matters also: each speech is perfectly suited to the character of the man delivering it, Ajax blunt and soldierly, Ulysses wily and deceptive; and at one point the latter resorts to an effective gesture—he wipes away a feigned tear (132–33). At the end Ovid announces Ulysses' success thus: *quid facundia posset, / re patuit* (382–83, "the power of eloquence was made perfectly plain"). He tells us that the subject of this oratorical contest has been oratory itself, that Ulysses has not only gained the arms of Achilles but also shown the superiority of rhetorical power.[24] A pregnant remark is found in an earlier episode of the Trojan War, when the heroes are relaxing and exchanging stories. Ovid says: *virtusque loquendi / materia est* (12.159–60). In its context this should mean "heroism is the topic of conversation." But perhaps, if *loquendi* is taken with *virtus*, it might also suggest "rhetorical ability is the topic"—which would be a very Ovidian thought.

The *Metamorphoses* also includes a pair of hymns. In the singing contest between the daughters of Pierus and the Muses, the representative of the latter begins her entry like this:

Prima Ceres unco glaebam dimovit aratro,
prima dedit fruges alimentaque mitia terris,
prima dedit leges: Cereris sunt omnia munus.
illa canenda mihi est; utinam modo dicere possim
carmina digna dea! certe dea carmine digna est.   (5.341–45)

Ceres was the first to cleave the soil with curving plow, the first
to give the earth ripe fruits and grains, the first to give men
laws: all these are the gift of Ceres. Her must I sing. May I only
be able to sing songs worthy of the goddess! For surely the goddess is worthy of song.

The list of the goddess's benefactions and the statement of her worthiness as a subject of song immediately imply the form of a hymn, and so too does the language with its anaphora and other repetitions. And, as one expects, this is followed by a story about the divinity, here the rape of Ceres' daughter Proserpina (346–661). These prefatory verses turn the whole of the Muse's song into a hymn to Ceres.

The other hymnic passage is remarkable for the ingenuity with which it is worked into the poem. Instead of giving it to a character to deliver, the poet sings it himself, creating a brilliant transition into it from the narrative. He describes the worship of Bacchus by the women of Thebes, who "lay aside their weaving, offer frankincense, and call the god Bacchus and Bromius and Lyaeus . . ." (4.10–11). Ovid then dedicates several verses to a catalogue of ten more names and appellations; this is a regular feature of the hymnic style. The list concludes, as usual, with an open-ended clause that is designed to safeguard the worshiper from any accidental omission: "and the other many names which you, Liber, hold amongst the Greeks" (16–

17). The apostrophe becomes a pivot on which the discourse turns in a new direction. Now follows a series of anaphoric clauses all including the word *tu*, another distinctive mark of the hymn: "your youth is unconsumed, you are the eternal lad, in the height of heaven you appear most lovely . . ." (18–20). Ovid then starts to move back to his narrative by picturing Bacchus' train: "wherever you go, the cries of women echo" (28–29). This brings him smoothly to the Theban women again, with whom he contrasts the impious daughters of Minyas. Now the narrative can proceed once more. This is an extraordinary tour de force, a bravura performance. Ovid has woven the hymn into the rest of his text without a seam showing.

The lesser, or lighter, genres are also represented. Among the many passages dealing with love a certain number unmistakably call to mind Roman erotic elegy because of the situation and the language. Apollo pursuing Daphne closely resembles the lover familiar to us from the elegiacs of Propertius, Tibullus, and, of course, Ovid himself. Though the god pleads his case movingly, he is spurned by the maiden. He admires her fingers, hands, and arms. Ovid adds the shrewd observation: *si qua latent, meliora putat* (1.502, "whatever is concealed, he thinks better"), which echoes what he had said earlier in one of his elegies:

> *suspicor ex istis et cetera posse placere,*
> *quae bene sub tenui condita veste latent.*   (*Am.* 3.2.35–36)

From these [the exposed parts of her limbs] I suspect that the rest, well concealed under her thin garment, are also lovely.

In Apollo's speech the adjectives *miser* in the phrase *me miserum!* (508, "unhappy me!") and *vacuus* in *vacuo . . . pectore* (520, "an unattached heart") are both standard, almost technical, terms used of the elegiac lover.[25] The story of Iphis and Anaxarete is drawn from the same world (14.698–761). Nearly the whole of this tale of unrequited love consists of a paraclausithyron, the familiar set piece of elegy in which the lover camps outside the door of his hard mistress, entreating, in vain, to be admitted.[26] Among many other passages of a similar nature we might single out the letter which Byblis writes to her brother Caunus, with whom she is in love (9.530–63). This represents an extension of the elegiac genre in a new direction, and the pioneer had been none other than Ovid himself, who earlier, in his *Heroides*, had created a series of epistles addressed by unhappy, love-struck women to the objects of their passion.

Pastoral too finds its place within the poem. In Book One Mercury disguises himself as a shepherd, steals[27] some she-goats to enhance his performance, and equips himself with a panpipe—all in order to fool the monster Argus and so liberate Jupiter's paramour Io, whom Argus is guarding (1.676–84). In its setting, characters, situations, and activities the passage is bucolic, and as if to underline this the poet echoes a verse from Virgil's *Eclogues*.[28] More extensive and more impressive for its pastoral quality is the plaint which Polyphemus makes to Galatea (13.789–869). Polyphemus of course is the one-eyed giant who traditionally (since the *Odyssey*) had appeared in poetry as a kind of monstrous shepherd. In portraying him as a love-sick swain Ovid is following the lead not so much of Virgil as of *his* master Theocritus, who established the pastoral genre. Elements found in the eleventh idyll of Theocritus, where Polyphemus sings of his love for Galatea, Ovid takes up and reemploys, exaggerating them greatly. Theocritus' four pastoral comparisons for the girl are now multiplied to fifteen; the series begins: "Galatea, whiter than the leaf of the snowy privet, more blooming than the meadows, taller than the lofty alder . . ." (13.789–90). In a typically Ovidian fashion, the shepherd follows this immediately with an equally long list of rustic comparisons expressing his displeasure with the maid's rejection of his suit: "Galatea, also harsher than unbroken bullocks, harder than aged oak, more treacherous than the wave . . ." (798–99). Similarly Ovid amplifies the Cyclops' description of his own wealth. In Greek he had claimed to pasture a thousand sheep; in Latin, after remarking that his sheep abound in vale, glade, and cave, he adds wittily:

> *nec, si forte roges, possim tibi dicere, quot sint.*
> *pauperis est numerare pecus!*   (823–24)

Should you ask, I couldn't tell you how many there are. Only the poor man counts his flock!

With these exaggerations and other references Ovid both re-creates and plays with pastoral.[29]

Another genre of literary composition that Ovid weaves into the poem is the epigram. Poets were called upon to write verses that would be engraved on monuments or other objects open to public view; in Hellenistic times the occasion seems often to have been feigned, and the epigram, losing its connection to a real object, became purely literary. Two of the commonest kinds of epigram are the sepulchral and the votive, and both are found in the *Metamorphoses*. Phaethon's sisters inscribe upon his tomb an epitaph beginning with the formulaic words "Here lies Phaethon . . ." (2.327–28). Aeneas' nurse also receives a commemorative epigram:

HIC · ME · CAIETAM · NOTAE · PIETATIS · ALVMNVS
EREPTAM · ARGOLICO · QVO · DEBVIT · IGNE ·
                                        CREMAVIT
                                        (14.442–43)

Here am I, Caieta, nurse of the man famed for his piety. Having
rescued me from the fire of the Greeks, he cremated me with
the fire of dutifulness.

(At the corresponding point in his narrative, *Aen.* 7.1–4, Virgil refers
to an epitaph for Caieta but does not report it.) A votive inscription
is recorded in the story of Iphis. Having been transformed, as she
wished, from a maiden into a lad, she dedicates thank-offerings to
the goddess Isis with these words:

DONA · PVER · SOLVIT · QVAE · FEMINA · VOVERAT ·
                                        IPHIS
                                        (9.794)

The vow of gifts which Iphis had made as a woman Iphis dis-
charges as a man.

This kind of inscription we also meet in the *Aeneid*, when the hero
dedicates a Greek shield during his travels:

AENEAS · HAEC · DE · DANAIS · VICTORIBUS · ARMA
                                        (3.288)

Aeneas dedicates these arms taken from the victorious
Danaans.

Ovid is more prone to include epigrams, and he also gives them a
different quality, as we can see by comparing the last two. His are
epigrams not only in the sense of "inscribed verses," but also in the
other, developed sense of "witty sayings." The play on the word
"fire" in Caieta's epitaph and the antithesis of "man" and "woman"
in Iphis' dedication—contrast the pedestrian dedication in Virgil—
make the epigrams stand out in greater relief.[30]

Several other forms of writing, held to be nonliterary today, were
literary genres in antiquity, and so also make their appearance in
Ovid's pages. History would have been represented, at least to Ovid's contemporaries, by the string of stories about Rome, from Aeneas down to Julius Caesar. The last two books of the poem comprehend a number of more or less historical episodes: the founding of
the nation, the Alban kings who ruled it after Aeneas, the apotheosis
of Romulus and his wife Hersilia, the tales of Numa and Egeria, the

arrival at Rome of the god Aesculapius (which includes, recounted in detail, his itinerary through the southern half of Italy, 15.701–28), and finally the triumphs and deification of Augustus' adoptive father. As the geographical survey belongs to historical writing, so too does an ethnographic observation such as Ovid makes in regard to the Thracians: *pronumque genus regionibus illis / in Venerem est* (6.459–60, "in those parts the people are prone to sexual desire")[31]—note the characteristic subject of the observation. At the beginning of Book Fifteen Pythagoras delivers a lengthy speech urging vegetarianism (15.75–478). Insofar as it purports to give instruction on the proper conduct of life, it is didactic and philosophic, very much like Lucretius' *De Rerum Natura*, the language of which, not coincidentally, it often echoes. At the same time, because most proofs of the basic propositions are drawn from the physical world, the speech is a piece of natural philosophy also. It takes up in turn the celestial bodies, the seasons, human physiology, the elements of the universe, geology, and zoology (187–417). Similarly, the brilliant depiction at the beginning of the poem of how the world was changed from chaos to its present form (1.5–150) falls under the heading of science. It is not surprising then that in Book Three of his *Naturales Quaestiones* Seneca often quotes from Pythagoras' speech in the *Metamorphoses* (four times in chapters 20–26) and from the description of the great flood (three times in chapter 27).

It is necessary to remind ourselves that these literary genres sometimes appear in Ovid combined, or at least not easily separable from one another; the poem is a kind of medley. To some extent, epic *is* history. Oratory and rhetoric play a part in almost everything. The erotic is not confined to elegy but extends to many other genres: Polyphemus is a shepherd *and* a lover. Moreover, the mixing of genres did not originate with Ovid; it was first a phenomenon in the Hellenistic era. Theocritus had inserted into a collection of pastoral poems an encomium (*Idyll* 17), an epithalamium, or marriage song (18), a hymn (22), and a pair of epyllia (13, 24),[32] and Callimachus made epigram prominent in his narrative of aetiological tales. To be sure, in the former the poems are discrete, and it is the collection which embraces different genres. Of the latter's four books of *Aetia* the first two (now lost) were unified, we know, through the format of a dialogue conducted between the poet and the Muses, whereas in the last two this format is given up and the individual stories simply follow one another without any attempt at linkage. Under such conditions, where the overall unity was questionable or dim and the parts more distinct than the whole, what mingling of genres there was must have been less remarkable. And the epic, except insofar as it had been replaced by the epyllion through the taste of some writers, remained untouched by this movement: however different from the Homeric poems, the *Argonautica* of Apollonius is still thoroughly epic. The mixing of genres at Rome is more evident, and perhaps more extensive. Ennius' epic of Roman history, the *Annals*, includes features that suggest lyric poetry.[33] Satire is present in Lucretius' poem (for example, 3.894–930). In the *Aeneid* too one may recognize genres other than epic: the description of Evander's Rome smacks occasionally of pastoral poetry (8.175–78, 359–61); philosophy is found in Anchises' exposition of the soul's fate after death (6.724–51); a hymn to Hercules appears amid the celebration of the Ara Maxima (8.293–302); and the story of Dido, it has often been remarked, much resembles a tragedy.

Nonetheless, the mixing of genres goes much further in the *Metamorphoses* than in any earlier literary work known to us.[34] The intrusions of non-epic passages are, first of all, longer, therefore more noticeable. The hymn to Ceres, the exchange of speeches between Ajax and Ulysses, and the teaching of Pythagoras—each fills nearly half a book. More important is the number of genres which are included. We hear clear strains of epic, epyllion, tragedy, oratory, hymn, love elegy, epistle, pastoral, epigram, history, philosophy, and science. This farrago is unmatched anywhere else. The playfulness, finally, with which Ovid handles the genres also implies that he is extremely self-conscious about them and that the comprehensiveness is not an accident. The rhetorical duel between the heroes is a kind of staged performance. The hymn to Bacchus is introduced and ended with conspicuous ingenuity. Mercury is merely disguised as a shepherd. The epigrams are well polished. Pythagoras' lecture becomes a joke.[35] The poem is comprehensive, therefore, not only of time and subject, but also of literary genres, and this too becomes a principle of organization.

Dis-organizations

At the same time, each of these principles of organization that we have just recognized is in its execution somewhat askew or incomplete, neglected or violated. The drive to unity is nearly matched by the force working in the opposite direction.

METAMORPHOSIS

All the stories do contain a metamorphosis, but sometimes the metamorphosis, far from being the center or the climax, is incidental to the main line of the story. The long narrative of Phaethon's winning permission to drive the chariot of the Sun and his disastrous ride is justified, so to speak, only by the metamorphosis of his weeping sisters into amber at the end (2.340–66). Very similar is the close of Meleager's story: his bereaved sisters are changed into birds (8.542–46), and theirs is the sole metamorphosis. And the extensive account of Orpheus ends not with his transformation, but with that of the Bacchants, who, after tearing him apart, become trees fixed in the forest (11.67–84). In these instances Ovid has contrived the metamorphosis of some group on the margins of the story. Elsewhere he attaches a metamorphosis to a story only through a tale inserted into it. The important tale of Pentheus lacks one, though within it Acoetes, who seems to be the disguised Bacchus, describes how the Tyrrhenian pirates were changed into dolphins (3.670–86). In these cases the metamorphosis is tangential to the chief episode.

NARRATIVE LINKS

All the stories are linked to one another in succession, but the link is often extremely artificial. After the story of Apollo's slaying of the monstrous Python, Ovid continues like this: the god founded the Pythian games to commemorate the event, and each victor there "received the honor of an oak wreath: the laurel did not yet exist, and from any tree whatever did Phoebus gird his own temples, lovely with their long locks" (1.449–51). By this ingenious, circuitous route he passes to the story of Daphne, who became the laurel tree. The link between the accounts of Theseus and of Minos is forged by a contrast: although the whole city of Athens rejoiced at Theseus' return, nonetheless (*tamen*) his father did not feel a joy unmixed with anxiety, because Minos was preparing to wage war on them (7.451–56). The particle *tamen* is used again when Ovid moves from Aesculapius, whose worship was imported to Rome from Delphi, on to Julius Caesar: "Nevertheless, he arrived at our shrines as a stranger: Caesar is a god in his own city" (15.745–46).[36] A similarly *recherché* contrast joins Memnon to Hecuba. Even the gods who were the implacable foes of Troy considered Hecuba's sufferings unmerited, with one exception:

non vacat Aurorae, quamquam isdem faverat armis,
cladibus et casu Troiaeque Hecubaeque moveri.

cura deam propior luctusque domesticus angit
Memnonis amissi. (13.576–79)

Although she had supported the same side, Aurora had no leisure to be moved by the destruction and fall of Troy or Hecuba.
The goddess was vexed by a closer concern, a domestic grief,
over her lost son Memnon.

Thus the reader is moved along to the next story. More examples
are given later, but these should suffice to show how the impression
of a connected narrative is undermined by a self-consciously artful
transition.

Quintilian noticed this feature of the poem too. When discussing
how the orator should handle the proem to a speech he stresses the
importance of a smooth transition from there into the next part, making his point clear by means of a contrast: "In the schools, to be sure,
we find that frigid, childish affectation whereby the transition itself
forms some kind of clever saying (*sententia*) at any cost and seeks to
win applause for this, so to speak, sleight of hand. Ovid is prone to
this self-indulgence in the *Metamorphoses*. Still, he can be excused on
the grounds of necessity, since he was attempting to give the appearance of a continuous whole to the most varied subjects. But what
need does the orator have to glide over this transition?" (*Inst.* 4.177–
78). Quintilian perceives a difficulty for Ovid in composing the *Metamorphoses*, that of unifying very varied material, and on that basis is
willing to excuse a feature which he obviously does not otherwise
approve of (clever transitions). The difficulty, however, was not imposed on Ovid. He chose to seek the appearance of unity for his
poem (as Callimachus in the later books of the *Aetia* chose not to).
Quintilian also observes that Ovid does not merely make transitions:
he makes ones that "seek to win applause for themselves," that draw
attention upon themselves. Quintilian has pointed out, in other
words, what will prove to be opposing strategies for winning unity—
narrative linkage and authorial presence. His moralizing prevents
him from making a more positive evaluation of Ovid, and also from
seeing the deep kinship between him and the orator. Altieri, a modern critic, is far more sympathetic. As he felicitously describes the
significance of Ovid's transitions, "There is no logic, no divine order
or destiny which promises either a unified eternal story or a pattern
for the recurrence of particular stories. Ovid's solution to the problem of continuing his tale may be makeshift, but it's the only one
available in a world without a God or other underlying patterns of
meaning."[37] The feature which Quintilian objects to (as others have)
is in fact the sign of a world perceived in a different, liberating way.

Critics like Otis and Ludwig would perhaps claim that the actual transition is trivial and would draw attention rather to the relations that obtain between successive stories: this panel balances the previous one, the theme of that section anticipates the following, and so on. But such schemes, I feel, are invisible to the reader working his way through and can be glimpsed, if at all, only from a lofty, large-scale survey. The reader's primary (and perhaps single) experience is of the narrator's leading him by the hand, as it were, from one tale to the next. Events do not cohere of their own accord.

THEMATIC LINKS

Many of the stories are joined to one another by thematic links, but these thematic links regularly prove to be red herrings. Similarities between stories may invite the reader to see in them the examination of some human problem from varying perspectives; but on closer look he discovers little substance behind the similarity. Ovid makes the situations of Daphne and Io parallel. What does he show us thereby? Nothing in particular. Pygmalion's statue, changed from stone into flesh, represents the reversal of the Propoetides, yet the contrast does not teach us anything about the nature of stone or flesh or about chastity or art. The themes of sacred tree and food/hunger may tie Erysichthon's story to that of Baucis and Philemon, but only in a superficial way, since neither is illuminated by the other.

For a contrasting example of how a poet capitalizes on a thematic relationship, or rather creates such a relationship for expressive purposes, we may turn to the *Aeneid*. Virgil portrays Dido and Aeneas as resembling one another in character and situation. Each, an exile who has lost a beloved spouse, is engaged in founding a new city alone and far from home; both are strong leaders and also compassionate and generous persons. This parallel affects in turn our understanding of the poem. Placed in similar circumstances and confronting the same decision between personal affection and sense of duty, Dido chooses the one, Aeneas the other; and to the extent that our sympathy lies with her—and Virgil creates much sympathy—we are enabled to measure the difficulty of Aeneas' course and the price he pays for continuing with his mission. This is the kind of "added dimension" which is missing from Ovid's thematic links. The connections suggested between his stories are in the end decorative; the parallels, balances, and antitheses are rhetorical in the narrowest sense. They convey no conclusions, no morals, no illuminations. Like the forced narrative links, they remind us that the world does not conveniently arrange itself thematically. This is not a merely discouraging notion, or a sobering one, but aims at liberating us from a constricting (and unacknowledged) point of view and heading us towards another which honors more the individual experience as unique in itself.

The poem's various forms of comprehensiveness are also all undermined. In time it does begin with the creation of the universe and end with, as it were, the day before yesterday. Nevertheless, it gives no sense of embracing a vast expanse of time. Consistency in the chronology of the stories is flagrantly violated in several places. The twin constellations of the Bears are mentioned as never touching the water, that is, never appearing to set (2.171–72), before Callisto and her son Arcas are transformed into these constellations and forbidden to sink into the ocean (2.530). In the same book Atlas is already a gigantic mountain holding up the sky (2.296–97), although not until afterwards are we told how Perseus changed Atlas from a king into a mountain (4.657–62).[38] If, as seems likely, the reference at 7.358 is to the snake who is metamorphosed at 11.56, that constitutes another instance of violated chronology. And similarly we read about Memnon's death only after the end of the Trojan War (13.576–622), and also about an exploit of Hercules (11.212–15), though he has been dead for two books (9.272).

Although the examples are neither few nor inconspicuous, broken chronology dulls the reader's sense of temporal movement less than do certain pervasive features of the narrative. The numerous inserts and the several story-telling parties also have the effect of making it unclear which event followed which. Thus Helenus' prophecy to Aeneas, an episode from the *Aeneid* which ought to have found its place in Book Thirteen, is recalled by Pythagoras in Book Fifteen (439–49), well after the time of the event. Meanwhile in Book Thirteen a mixing bowl presented to Aeneas depicts a pair of stories from the Theban cycle (13.685–99), which had been related all the way back in Books Three and Four. Ludwig, who analyzes the poem in terms of three ages, admits that in the central age, the mythical (1.452–11.193), on account of the various inserts, "the reader does not so much have the impression of a deliberate forward motion, but rather imagines himself lingering in a large and uniform time period."[39] The sense of timelessness extends beyond these bounds to the entire poem, however, and it is created by something still more basic to the poem. From beginning to end all the stories are told as if

they were taking place in contemporary Rome. Thus an assembly of
the gods closely resembles a meeting of the Roman Senate, Pentheus
speaks of siege-engines, characters know the triumph and the census, Diana with her maids might easily pass for a Roman matron,
and a pet deer is even found wearing the *bulla*, the locket symboliz-
ing free birth.[40] Since everything is portrayed as happening "now,"
there is no feeling of temporal progression as the poem unrolls.

In subject matter the poem does touch upon all the major stories of
ancient mythology. But many of them it *merely* touches upon. The
more well-known a story is, the slighter or more oblique Ovid's version of it becomes. Sometimes a story is even rendered conspicuous
by its absence. The most famous episode in Medea's life after the
adventure of the Golden Fleece, the episode which forms the center
of the most popular tragedy in antiquity, Euripides' *Medea*, is utterly
slighted. Ovid fills 250 verses with accounts of Medea's magic-work-
ing and of her subsequent flight over Greece (7.159–403), which are
narrated at the expense of her more well-known deeds in Corinth:
a mere four verses, and those very allusive, suffice to recount how
she killed Jason's new wife and then her own children (394–97).
If the weight or focus of a story is not shifted, it is often told in a
new setting or from an unusual angle. No other account of Hercules' mighty labors is offered but the one of the hero himself, who
reviews them while lying upon his funeral pyre, wrapped in a poisonous mantle which is consuming him with fire. The language
again is allusive: *saevoque alimenta parentis / Antaeo eripui* (9.183–84,
"from savage Antaeus I took away the nourishment of his parent")
is the way Hercules describes his defeat of a wrestler-king who re-
cruited his strength through contact with the Earth, his mother, and
who needed therefore to be lifted up and strangled. The speech includes anaphora (181, 187–88, 197–98), other repetitions (184–85),
apostrophe (176–80, 185, 186–90), and paradox: *nec profuit Hydrae /
crescere per damnum* (192–93, "nor did it boot the Hydra to grow
through loss"), and the catalogue of labors closes with an epigram:

> *defessa iubendo est*
> *saeva Iovis coniunx, ego sum indefessus agendo!*   (9.198–99)

Jove's cruel wife is weary of giving orders: I am not weary of
carrying them out!

These all serve to sharpen the point he is making. Hercules recalls
his feats of prowess solely as a foil, to give the contrast to his present
situation:

sed nova pestis adest, cui nec virtute resisti
nec telis armisque potest.   (9.200–201)

But a new source of ruin [the fiery cloak] is at hand, which can
be resisted neither with courage nor with arms and weapons.

The Labors of Hercules then are introduced into the poem allusively
and obliquely, not recounted for their own sake but referred to as
part of a rhetorical argument.

Such dramatic shifts in weight or angle are also exampled in Ovid's
handling of the *Odyssey*. Though Ulysses himself appears in the contest over the arms of Achilles at the beginning of Book Thirteen, the
first mention of his voyage home occurs only later in the book, when
Ovid, like Virgil before him, has Aeneas sail past several sites where
the Greek hero had stopped (13.711–13, 719–20). The remainder of
what we are given from the *Odyssey* is told to us not by the poet, but
by one or another of his characters. The episode with the Cyclops
Polyphemus, one of the most memorable of the Greek epic, is approached twice in the *Metamorphoses*. The nymph Galatea narrates
Polyphemus' love for her as a kind of counterpart to the story familiar from the *Odyssey*, and a pair of details invite this view. Galatea
says that the giant, once he had fallen in love, was so busy grooming
himself—using a rake, for instance, to comb his hair—that as a result
he gave up his usual ferocity and thirst for blood, and ships could
come and go in safety (13.768–69). Then, told by a prophet that Ulysses will take his one eye, Polyphemus laughs and replies: *"o vatum
stolidissime, falleris," inquit. / "altera iam rapuit"* (774–75, " 'O most
blockheaded of seers, you are wrong,' he said. 'Another, a girl, has
already taken it.' "). In the next book when Achaemenides, one of
Ulysses' companions, begins to speak, we might expect him to give
an account of the adventure. In fact, however, he tells only of its
consequence, of what befell him when he was stranded on the island
with the Cyclops (14.167–222).[41] Thus Ovid touches twice upon this
episode without ever recounting it. The *Odyssey* appears in the *Metamorphoses* for the last time when Macareus, replying to Achaemenides, relates the adventures with the Laestrygonians and with Circe.
The former he abridges very greatly: no one unfamiliar with the Homeric original is likely to understand immediately that the words
Laestrygonis inpia tinxit / ora cruore suo (14.237–38, "he stained the impious lips of the Laestrygonian with his blood") indicate that one of
Ulysses' men was eaten for dinner by Antiphates, king of that region. The latter adventure Macareus recasts so as to emphasize the
homey quality of the scene (Circe surrounded by her maids and tame

animals), the preparation of the magical herbs and drugs, and his own metamorphosis into a pig and then back again (248–307).[42]

As a last instance of how Ovid treats literary classics we may consider his version of the *Iliad*. Though Books Twelve and Thirteen concern chiefly the Trojan War, Homer's poem is more evidently absent than present. Nestor's campfire tale of the battle between the Lapiths and the Centaurs, which fills two-thirds of a book (12.146–535), acts as a substitute for the extensive fighting around Troy. The only actual fighting Ovid describes is the duel waged by Achilles and the almost invulnerable Cygnus—an episode which, though embellished by clear Homeric reminiscences (cf., e.g., 96–97 with *Il.* 7.219–23, 245–48; 140–41 with *Il.* 3.369–72), is unknown to Homer. The material which does derive from the Greek original is reported to us indirectly, not by Ovid but by one of his characters. All the familiar incidents come up exclusively in the debate between Ajax and Ulysses, who refer to them while conducting their suit for the arms of Achilles: the near departure of the Greeks (13.216–35), the nighttime scouting expedition (15, 98, 243–52), Ajax' duel with Hector (85–89, 275–79), Ajax warding off fire from the Greek ships (8, 91–94), Patroclus wearing the arms of Achilles (273–74), to mention but a few. For the *Metamorphoses*, Homer's epic exists as ammunition to be used in an oratorical duel.[43] Ovid's relation to the *Iliad*, near yet utterly removed, is most aptly expressed in his mention of the confrontation between Hector and Achilles:

> *perque acies aut Cygnum aut Hectora quaerens*
> *congreditur Cygno (decimum dilatus in annum*
> *Hector erat).*   (12.75–77)

Ranging the battlefield in search of either Cygnus or Hector, Achilles meets Cygnus (Hector was put off until the tenth year).

The climactic event of the *Iliad* is relegated to nothing more than a casual parenthesis. Not only does Ovid recount familiar stories only through a displacement or from a novel perspective which makes it his own, but he even contrives to call attention to this. This is a recognized feature of Alexandrian literature too, though, as it seems to me, less significant than in Ovid. It is true that those writers shared his questioning of literary authority; in this sense Ovid is the fulfiller of neoteric tendencies.

The poem, to be sure, does embrace all literary genres. But the very variety of genres, and of their concomitant styles, produces a kind of inconcinnity. The epic battle surrounding the death of Achilles (the end of Book Twelve) directly precedes the oratorical duel

between Ajax and Ulysses (beginning of Book Thirteen). The intimate, even homely story of Baucis and Philemon (8.618–724) contrasts with the broad, nearly heroic narrative of Erysichthon (8.738–
878), in the retelling of which Ovid has stripped from the Callima-
chean original a whole series of domestic details. The switching of
styles does not always wait for the end of a story, but may take place
in the middle of its course. In Book One the scene of the dispatch of
Mercury and his journey and arrival comes straight from epic (668–
75); when he puts on different clothing he enters the world of pastoral (beginning at 676). Mercury needs to be a quick-change artist:
so abrupt is the shift of generic scenes. Ovid makes no attempt to
soften the contrasts; the result is cacophony rather than symphony.
Particularly instructive is the mixing of genres within the story of
Daphne and Apollo. The elegiac elements we have already noted.
The evocation of epic is most notable in the simile for Apollo's pursuit of Daphne, which begins: "as when a Gallic hound spots a hare
in an empty field, and with their feet the one seeks its prey, the other
its own safety . . ." (1.533–34).[44] Insofar as the narrative is elegiac, it
represents the point of view of Apollo, for whom the whole is a lark,
a love adventure, with nothing much at stake. Insofar as it is epic, it
represents Daphne's—and for her it is a matter of life or death. Here
the clash of genres reveals its most important meaning. Each genre
carries with it certain presuppositions and a certain way of looking at
the world, and the styles which point to the different genres can thus
signal opposing interpretations of the same event.[45]

Ovid does not aim at providing several interpretations from which
we are to select the one that appeals to us, as on a multiple-choice
test. There is no right answer, nor a pair of right answers. His goal is
more profound, to shake us from the very habit of thinking in terms
of genre and to stir us to an awareness of what such thinking means.
Lanham has described this effect produced by the works of Ovid and
other genre-mixers, including Lucian, Rabelais, and Sterne:

> They seem to war on the stable orientations literary genres en-
> shrine. They think narrative coherence a sham, not because it is
> unreal but because we impose it on the world without acknowl-
> edgment. They seek to make us self-conscious about the imposi-
> tion, about literary form at all points. Their narratives are always
> posing; their style aims always for effect. They keep faith with
> their own pleasure, not with a reality somewhere "out there."[46]

In regard to the poem's chief organizing features, then, we find on
the one hand a large number of overlapping schemes and structures,

which hint at an ordered, coherent world. On the other hand, all of these are undermined and undercut; they all prove to be inadequate.

Altieri relates this to the contents of the poem and the one subject it does have: "the theme of flux, like the multiplicity of stories, by its very nature asserts both the absence of all informing structures or principles of form and the equality of all present moments."[47] The poem invites us to look for structures within it and makes a number of proposals, and then it systematically defeats them all. What we read is not the result of a plan that failed, a design that went awry in the execution, nor does it represent mere chaos or randomness. It clearly strives for order, and in many different ways, but it never consistently achieves it: the poem might claim as a motto its own phrase, *discors concordia* (1.433, "an inharmonious harmony"). Instead it conveys a sense of dis-order, of orderings undone. This is not the Euripidean perception, found for instance in the *Hercules Furens*, that there is a metaphysical disorder in the universe, but rather the more commonsense observation that things are so uncertain and unstable as to elude the schemes set to catch them. People and things change from moment to moment (the poem gives a very lively sense of this), relations among them are many-sided and ever in flux, generalization is impossible, and the observer is always bound by his own subjectivity. From no single, fixed point of view is everything seen to fall into place, certainly not from that of any god. As no god brought Ovid's universe into existence,[48] so none directs its course. These are the notions that Ovid renders artistically. Every aspect of the poem's arrangement tells us to beware interpreting structures which must, necessarily, falsify the riotous diversity and changeableness of reality. The *Metamorphoses* does not simply reveal an awareness of this notion: one of its central concerns is to demonstrate the inadequacy of schemes and structures for making sense of the world.

Story-telling

The premise of the poem is that story-telling is a fundamental means of comprehending the world. It is the most popular activity in the poem. Again and again, when a character wants to describe or explain something, he resorts to a story. Bacchus, going by the name of Acoetes, shows Pentheus his power through the story of the Tyrrhenian sailors rather than through direct statement or any other means (3.582–691). Lelex proves the possibility of metamorphosis with his account of Baucis and Philemon (8.618–724). Anaxarete's harshness towards Iphis is used by Vertumnus as a cautionary tale to Pomona (14.698–764). The drive to tell stories is revealed no less clearly when people are taking their leisure than when they are acting purposefully. The daughters of Minyas whiling away the time of Bacchus' festival, Theseus' companions spending the evening *chez* Achelous, the Greek heroes sitting about the campfire before Troy, all turn naturally to narrative. There is nothing peculiar in this; the poem only reminds us forcefully of how basic an activity story-telling is. This remains true for us, but it must have been all the more so in a society which scarcely relied on the abstractions of social science to provide understanding of human behavior.

The poem, moreover, does not deal with mere story-telling; it is not concerned with casual or carelessly told anecdotes. The highest form of story-telling is found in literature, for writing offers the opportunity of employing language for utmost effect. Furthermore, the ripest (by far) of literary subjects is mythology; this material, potent since Homer at least and worked and reworked through the centuries, allows the ancient writer the maximum in variety and nuance. The *Metamorphoses* thus focuses on story-telling at its acme of content and expression. And no one has ever hesitated to agree that Ovid's stories *are* superb![49]

Implicit in narrative (at least the narrative of the ancients) are certain features which we may overlook because we take them for granted but to which Ovid was alert and wished to draw our attention: linear movement, variety combined with unity, and (often) thematic repetition. That these are all proper to literature can be seen by comparison with the visual arts, from which they are perforce absent. These features, which might well be termed "structures" since they support the narrative and make it possible, the *Metamorphoses* deliberately calls into question.

The chief expectation created by narrative is of linear movement, starting with one situation at moment X and going to another at moment Y; as time can be neither stopped nor reversed, so the action of a story moves in one direction. This expectation is assaulted in the poem, with its occasionally impossible chronology and its refusal to allow us to sense any sweep of time between the Creation and Caesar's assassination. The inset stories, more complex, extensive, and baffling than, say, Books Two and Three of the *Aeneid*, fuel the assault, not only in the poem as a whole but in many individual stories as well. And, as we shall see, the essential narrative technique militates against a sense of movement. Because there are bound to be several scenes or episodes between points X and Y, another expectation arises, of variety combined with unity: the distinct parts ought to form a larger unity; the whole ought to be articulated. This too the *Metamorphoses* strives to defeat. At the same time that it includes immense variety, it raises questions about boundaries (what belongs with what?) and decorum (what suits what?). It keeps us off balance. The poem counters, furthermore, our expectation that the various parts of a story will be grouped about a theme, that they will treat, in however complex a manner, a single subject or a closely related group.

By the way he composes his poem Ovid undermines our reliance on story-telling. He reminds us of its conventions and artificialities and exposes them to view, suggesting that they do not need to be accepted. His aim is to liberate us from whatever trust we place in literature, or at least to make us aware of this trust. But he does more than attune our consciousness. As an alternative to story-telling he presents us with another form of understanding: the visual picture. The stories strive towards a kind of pictorial realization, which is usually found in metamorphosis. There is something paradoxical in a story-telling which, while reveling in itself and the manifold opportunities open to it, looks beyond itself to a fundamentally different mode. The poem, we may say, moves from narrative towards image, from story towards icon. Ovid delights in exploring the relationship between the two, as we shall see. Here let it suffice to note that the structures implied and undone in the *Metamorphoses* amount to a commentary on story-telling and, with it, on mythology and literature.

CHAPTER TWO

THE NARRATOR

The conclusions so far may seem mostly negative. No single narrative line draws the whole poem together, no thematic link (except metamorphosis itself), no evident unity of subject or style. The conspicuous absence of the structures that ordinarily support a literary narrative calls into question the adequacy of those structures for making sense of things. Yet all is not utter chaos either; the world of the poem does not altogether lack a point of focus. One thing does stand out, dominating and informing the whole: the narrator himself, the poet Ovid. His distinctive voice we learn to recognize as we read the poem, we feel him present everywhere mediating the transmission of the stories, we rely on him as a kind of guide through the vast confusion of the world. He alone unifies the poem. Here is the positive counterweight to the falling structures. And like them the strong presence of the narrator reflects on the nature of story-telling. Ovid recalls and holds up to scrutiny the convention that the narrator is impersonal and objective. He may be the center of this world, but he represents himself as no godlike creator, rather a man who is fallible and has doubts even about his own narrative.

How Many Narrators?

Of the poet's imposing presence we have had some indication already. Before going further into this, however, we need to deal with the question whether there is one narrator or more than one. The *Metamorphoses*, unlike any other ancient narrative poem, raises this question because of a certain peculiarity in technique. One conspicuous feature of the poem is the large number of stories told by the characters themselves. Thus Pan, to put Argus to sleep, tells him the story of Syrinx (1.689–712); a citizen of Croton recounts to Numa the founding of his city (15.12–57); and so forth. We have already noticed the tales exchanged by Alcmene and Iole, the account given by Orpheus of the Propoetides, Pygmalion, and others. Often Ovid describes in effect story-telling parties, at which characters swap tales: Minerva, visiting the Muses, hears a full account of their singing contest with the daughters of Pierus, the entries of both contestants plus two other stories thrown in for good measure (5.269–678); the river god Achelous and the traveling heroes who have stopped off at his cave try to top one another with stories of incredible metamorphoses (8.547–9.92); and, gathered around a campfire before Troy, the Greek warriors listen to a set of stories, all recounted by Nestor, of course (12.168–579). A considerable proportion of the poem reaches us at second hand, as it were.

It cannot be denied that the multiplicity of narrators serves several practical ends. A narrative of this sort is more varied, in that it allows for direct discourse and for interplay between characters. (This possibility, hardly developed here, is greatly elaborated by Chaucer in *The Canterbury Tales*.) It also permits some stories to be fitted in without pains being taken over linking them: the natural turns of ordinary conversation provide an adequate motive. Moreover, if the conversation is focused, it makes possible a sequence of stories which have some theme in common, for instance, as in Achelous' cave, where the night's topic of discourse is whether or not metamorphosis is possible. Still, we may wonder if the apparent changes in narrator indicate anything more than the practical difficulties of a poem conceived like this one. How many narrators in fact do we hear? Are the different speakers—Ovid, his characters, those whom they quote in turn—distinct from one another? Do they have separate voices like Chaucer's pilgrims? And if so, do they signify changing points of view, like other features of the poem?

It has been asserted that the poem does include multiple voices, and this is not surprising today when we are keenly conscious of the persona who inhabits a poetic or other fiction. Nonetheless, I believe there is basically a single narrator throughout, who is Ovid himself. The introduction of other speakers is more formal than consequential; the words are heard as those of the poet. The most important general reason for thinking this—the uniformity of tone maintained through the poem—does not, unfortunately, lend itself to ready demonstration. It is true that the tone of the narrative varies greatly. Still, this itself amounts to a kind of uniformity over a long enough stretch, in that the variation is constant and not linked to change in speakers. The mixture of tones and all the other features that characterize Ovid remain the same when he yields the floor to one of his own characters. Other figures in the poem are characterized by their speech—Deucalion is shown by his words to be pious, Niobe arrogant, Ulysses clever—but no narrator is.

We can test this question further by examining a particular passage. Nearly the whole of Book Ten is recounted by Orpheus. Can we distinguish his voice from Ovid's? At the beginning of the song, when he declares his two themes and we recognize that one of them (pederasty) touches his own life, we are led to expect a well-focused section reflecting the concerns of the teller and illustrating a certain moral as well:

> puerosque canamus
> dilectos superis inconcessisque puellas
> ignibus attonitas meruisse libidine poenam.   (10.152–54)

Let us sing of boys loved by the gods and girls smitten with unlawful passions, and of how lust earned its punishment.

In the event, however, Orpheus' performance diverges from his promise. Only some of the stories fall under the announced rubric. Anderson says that the lengthy story of Myrrha (298–502), a girl who committed incest with her father, is "the only one which accurately carries out Orpheus' theme,"[1] but this is not quite fair. Orpheus begins with two brief tales of pederasty, Ganymede and Hyacinth (155–219), and Adonis is a lad loved by a divinity (503–739). But none of these except Myrrha appears to deserve his fate: on the contrary, they are blameless victims. Moreover, the Cerastae, the Propoetides, and Pygmalion (220–97) are unrelated to the main themes, and the greater portion of the story of Venus and Adonis is occupied by the goddess's narration about Atalanta and Hippomenes (560–707)—a tale within a tale within a tale.

It has been noticed that other inserted stories are also told in a way that fails to correspond to their ostensible purpose. Thus when Vertumnus, urging Pomona not to spurn love, recounts to her the tale of Iphis and Anaxarete, he ought to emphasize the girl's harshness and the punishment which follows it; instead he shows more interest in the young man's sufferings and fate (14.698–761).[2] Why does Vertumnus' version not suit his purpose well? Because the narrator is not really Vertumnus at all: it is Ovid.

To return to Orpheus, a pair of further details also suggest there is little or no separation between him and our Roman author. His ac-

count of Myrrha he prefaces with a long apology for its immoral
nature (300–10). Anderson notes some discrepancy here between Orpheus the pederast and Orpheus the puritanical critic of a scandal-
ous story; besides a mere slip from consistent characterization, might
we not see in this a sign that Orpheus is not altogether distinct from
his creator? A small problem of geographical reference hints at the
same. Orpheus' performance is set, we know, in his native Thrace
(77, 83).[3] He begins by dwelling on the enormity of Myrrha's crime:

> *si tamen admissum sinit hoc natura videri,*
> *gentibus Ismariis et nostro gratulor orbi,*
> *gratulor huic terrae, quod abest regionibus illis,*
> *quae tantum genuere nefas.*   (10.304–7)

If nature allows this offense to be seen, I felicitate the Thracian
peoples and our region, I felicitate this land, because it is far removed from those parts, which produced so great an abomination.

It may be that Orpheus is contrasting Thrace alone with Myrrha's
homeland. In that case "Thracian peoples," "our region," and "this
land" would all refer to the same place—an abundance that Ovid is
certainly capable of. Yet to say the same thing three times is somewhat unusual,[4] and the repetition of the verb makes me wonder
whether the reference in all three is in fact the same. *Orbis* can mean
"region" (as at 8.100) but also "world." And I think, like Haupt and
Ehwald and Fränkel, that with "this land" Orpheus has Thrace no
longer in mind, but Italy. The last observes that verse 309 echoes
Georgics 2.139, part of Virgil's famous praise of Italy.[5] As the passage
goes along then, the land contrasted with Myrrha's seems to shift
from Thrace (which in fact was notorious for its libidinousness, not
its sexual restraint; cf. 6.459–60) to Italy. Here too therefore we may
feel that Ovid is peeking out through the figure of Orpheus.

A later passage also deserves to be examined in this connection.
Venus is describing the climax of the footrace between Atalanta and
Hippomenes:

> *neve meus sermo cursu sit tardior ipso,*
> *praeterita est virgo.*   (10.679–80)

And so that my speech not be drawn out longer than the race
itself—he overtook the girl.

A witty remark, in a complex setting—three narratives placed one
inside the other, like a series of Chinese boxes: Ovid tells the story of

Orpheus, within that Orpheus tells the story of Venus and Adonis, and within that in turn Venus tells the story of the athletic couple. Ovid is self-reflective here: by repeating the basic story-telling situation to the point of exaggeration, he reminds us of the tralatician nature of mythology and the subjective quality of each telling. And yet the remark quoted denies as much as it acknowledges the fictive situation. For to whom is it best suited—Venus, who has been speaking only since verse 560? Orpheus, speaking since 148? Or Ovid himself, now in his tenth book? The question cannot be answered really, but the fact that we can reasonably entertain it suggests that the boundaries between the poem's narrators are blurry.

One final possibility for multiple narrators remains. The voices of the characters cannot be distinguished from that of the poem's narrator, but is that narrator Ovid himself or is he instead a persona, a sovereign figment of the poet's with his own character, interests, and view of the world? Many may be inclined toward the latter view. I cannot bring myself to agree, however. I can find no sign of distance between narrator and poet. Never does the one permit us to see through him to his maker. Nothing he says betrays him as ignorant, mistaken, naive, or foolish. Still, he might be an all-encompassing fiction, as completely the manufacturer of the narrative as Ovid is of him. In that case I wonder what the worth is of assuming such a persona; I do not see that it is in any way fruitful. Not only does the hypothesis gain us nothing, but it needs to answer several difficult questions, such as why the "signature" at the end of the poem is so personal, or why the voice here is so similar to that in Ovid's other poetry. Only one narrator then is present, so far as I can hear.

Transitions

The central importance of the narrator, the fact of his ubiquitousness, is indicated by the multiplicity of ways in which his presence is felt. Reserving some of the subtler and more pervasive of these for a discussion of subject and style, we can take up here those which are more easily isolated. We may conveniently begin with a feature already noticed, the frequent evidence of the narrator in the transitions from one story to the next. We often are moved along through the poem not by the consequence of action but only by some extraordinary manipulation or act of cleverness on the poet's part. Without his personal intervention, as it were, we would never have heard this new story. The narrative does not follow any kind of natural course.

On the contrary, the poet seems almost to flaunt his own directing and diverting of it.[6]

A simple example is found in Book Ten. Orpheus is singing, and the trees come to listen. After a long enumeration of the trees, the poet says:

> *adfuit huic turbae . . . cupressus,*
> *nunc arbor, puer ante deo dilectus ab illo.*   (10.106–7)

> This crowd also included the cypress, now a tree, formerly a
> boy loved by the god Apollo.

Thus he launches into the story of Cyparissus. The casualness of the transition takes the reader by surprise. No logic connects Cyparissus to the story of Orpheus, merely a chance observation, almost a whim, of the narrator. Equally contrived is his movement onward from Arachne, who was turned into a spider for challenging the goddess Minerva in weaving. Arachne's story, Ovid says, made the rounds of Lydia and then spread through the world; a childhood friend of hers who heard it, though now living across the sea in Thebes, nevertheless paid no heed; this was Niobe, who persisted in boasting that her offspring were more numerous than Leto's (6.146–51). Ovid performs a similar sleight of hand to get from Achelous to Nessus. The former's love for Deianira cost him merely the loss of one of his horns, the narrator says; but you, Nessus, he adds, apostrophizing the centaur, paid with your life for the love of Deianira (9.98–102). The comparison of these two, which forms the bridge between them, can be envisioned from only one point of view, that of the narrator.

Other instances are more intricate; the very intricacy measures the manipulativeness of the teller. Having sealed Callisto's fate (and brought her story to an end), Juno flies away from the scene:

> *habili Saturnia curru*
> *ingreditur liquidum pavonibus aethera pictis,*
> *tam nuper pictis caeso pavonibus Argo,*
> *quam tu nuper eras, cum candidus ante fuisses,*
> *corve loquax, subito nigrantes versus in alas.*   (2.531–35)

> Saturn's daughter enters bright heaven in her maneuverable
> chariot, drawn by painted peacocks. The peacocks had been
> painted just as recently, after the slaying of Argus, as you,
> o talkative raven, had been turned all at once from your former
> white into a black-winged bird.

Ovid then proceeds to tell the raven's story. This transition resembles the previous one, even down to the apostrophe, but it is still more *recherché*. One half of the comparison here, the peacocks, is not the subject of a story at all, merely a prop dragged in by the narrator. Like a good prestidigitator Ovid knows how to displace interest: he gets the reader to pay attention to one thing while busy with another himself. A passage in Book Four (604–11) is no less contrived. Cadmus and Harmonia, metamorphosed into snakes, are consoled for this change through the fame won by their grandson Bacchus, who is worshiped as a god in both India and Greece. Acrisius, the only member of the family remaining in Greece, drives away Bacchus (who is only his third cousin once removed) and denies he is the son of a god. Is this the lead-in to Bacchus' story? Not at all. The narrator, swerving in a new direction, continues: *neque enim Iovis esse putabat / Persea* (610–11, "nor for that matter did he think Perseus was the son of Jupiter"). Here begin the episodes surrounding Perseus; Bacchus' story is related elsewhere. Again we are made aware of the poet's activity in cleverly stitching the material together.

For a final illustration we may turn to a section of Book Nine in which a string of tales is assembled with attention-grabbing ingenuity (273ff.). When we begin, Hercules has just been made a god. Ovid now describes the situation of those who survive him. His children are still pursued by his archenemy Eurystheus. In Iole, Hercules' widow, his mother Alcmene has a person to whom she can confide her complaints, her pride in her son, and her own misfortunes. Iole by this time is remarried and pregnant. Having established all this, the poet is ready to move ahead. Alcmene says to her former daughter-in-law, "I hope you have an easier time than I did when I gave birth to Hercules." This licenses the telling of that story, which ends with the metamorphosis of a servant into the weasel. Iole in turn replies with an account of how her own sister Dryope became a lotus plant. The weeping of the two women which ensues is ended by the appearance of a thoroughly rejuvenated Iolaus, the nephew of Hercules, which launches another series of stories. And so forth.

TRANSITION THROUGH ABSENCE

A peculiarly Ovidian form of transition has often been remarked, which might be termed *transitio per absentem*. The narrator notes the absence of a particular person from a scene; he then tells us why that person was absent and what he was doing instead, and thus moves on to another story. This form of transition makes especially clear the role of the poet, since only from his point of view, outside the narrative, is such an observation possible. In Book One, for instance, all his fellow river gods of Thessaly gather at the house of Peneus either to console or to congratulate him for the metamorphosis of his daughter into the laurel tree—all, that is, except for Inachus, who was home bewailing the loss of his own daughter (1.583–87). Thus we pass from Daphne to Io. Elsewhere Bacchus, after punishing the Thracian women who had murdered Orpheus, deserts the scene of the crime for Lydia. All his entourage accompanies him:

> *at Silenus abest: titubantem annisque meroque*
> *ruricolae cepere Phryges vinctumque coronis*
> *ad regem duxere Midan.*   (11.90–92)

Silenus was missing, however. Tottering with years and wine, he had been captured by Phrygian countrymen and, tied with wreaths, brought to their king, Midas.

Midas releases and entertains him, in recompense for which Silenus' master Bacchus grants him a wish. There follows now the familiar story of Midas' golden touch. Similarly, a little further on, Priam, not knowing his son Aesacus has been transformed into a bird and believing him to be dead, holds a funeral for him, which is attended by all his brothers—except Paris, who is busy carrying off Helen from her husband (12.4–10).

Let us look finally at a transition made by the narrator's noting the lack not of a person but of something abstract. From Peleus, who has just become the husband of Thetis and by her the father of Achilles, Ovid shifts the focus away to Ceyx, frame for the next stories, by introducing an extraneous character, Peleus' half-brother Phocus:

> *felix et nato, felix et coniuge Peleus,*
> *et cui, si demas iugulati crimina Phoci,*
> *omnia contigerant.*   (11.266–68)

Peleus was blessed in his offspring, blessed too in his wife; everything good had come his way—if you except the crime of murdering Phocus.

After slaying Phocus, Peleus takes refuge with Ceyx. This might be called a *transitio per rem absentem*.[7] By such contrivance the narrator draws our attention upon himself.

TRANSITION THROUGH CONTRARY-TO-FACT CONDITION

Ovid often makes the transition between stories with a contrary-to-fact condition. Though at first this might seem unrelated to what we have been examining, in fact it is akin. In each case the narrator observes what did not exist—now not a person who was absent but (rather as in the last example) a situation or an action which did not take place. Again the peculiar nature of the observation refers to the narrator who makes it. In this way, for instance, Ovid passes from Byblis, a Milesian girl changed into a fountain, to Iphis, a girl changed into a boy:

> *fama novi centum Cretaeas forsitan urbes*
> *implesset monstri, si non miracula nuper*
> *Iphide mutata Crete propiora tulisset.*   (9.666–68)

The report of this new and remarkable metamorphosis would have filled the hundred cities of Crete perhaps, had not Crete produced a wonder closer to hand in the metamorphosis of Iphis.

The transition between Ganymede, brought to heaven by Jupiter, and Apollo's beloved Hyacinth, is managed like this: "You too, son of Amyclas, Phoebus Apollo would have elevated to heaven, if the grim fates had granted enough time for the elevating" (10.162–63). In each of these examples, we may note, the repetition of a word gives the sentence a slightly epigrammatic sound, which in turn reinforces the artificiality of the expression. A third instance occurs shortly afterwards. The story of Pygmalion has just ceased with the statement that his wife gave birth to a daughter Paphos. The narrator continues: "Of her was Cinyras born: had he been childless, he could have been counted happy" (10.298–99). This ushers in the tale of Cinyras' notorious daughter Myrrha.

An interesting example is furnished by Medea. She has persuaded Pelias' daughters that she will be able to rejuvenate the old man as she did Aeson (Pelias' brother and Medea's father-in-law) if they allow her to cut him up and put the parts in a pot with magic herbs; she in fact intends to kill him. Immediately after describing the butchering and boiling, the narrator continues: *nisi pennatis serpentibus isset in auras, / non exempta foret poenae* (7.350–51, "had she not taken to the air on her winged dragons, she would not have been exempt from punishment"). We notice Ovid's characteristically elliptic narrative: the murder of Pelias, that is, Medea's failure to rejuvenate him, which the preceding lines lead up to but do not mention, is merely alluded to. The contrary-to-fact sentence also moves the story onward.[8] In her flight Medea passes over the sites of several metamorphoses, which Ovid then reports.

Kraus well describes in general terms the place of the narrator: "Where relations among characters and transitions by means of spatial or temporal concurrence fail, he has recourse to the imaginary connections of analogy and antithesis, which are not always set in the consciousness of narrating characters but are expressed by the poet himself: thus in place of the usual historical connection there appears one which is merely that of discourse."[9] In the techniques of transition, especially *per absentem* and by means of a contrary-to-fact statement, we sense the presence of that figure "behind" the poem (as we are wont to say) who is in control of it.

Epigram

This voice behind the poem is a very insistent one. Another of the prominent ways it makes itself felt is through epigrammatic expression. We may understand "epigram" broadly as any saying which is brief, neat (that is, contained in itself), and marked by antithesis, repetition of words, paradox, or some other play upon the verbal surface. It is not necessary here to create a stricter definition. Naturally, the elements mentioned are often found in combination. Because of their form epigrams tend to stand out from their contexts and to be memorable and quotable.[10] And as expressions that always look studied, they are intrinsically self-conscious; more than other features even of highly stylized poetry they point beyond the narrative, beyond the verbal surface, back to the poet himself.

It has often been observed not only that this is a feature of Ovid's writing, but also that he shares it with his age. Although the effects of it have not perhaps received due attention, the tendency is well known. We have only to glance at the literature of Ovid's generation and the several succeeding ones, where we find, as prominent as studs, neat formations like Manilius' *nascentes morimur, finisque ab origine pendet* (*Astron.* 4.16, "we die at our birth, and our end follows from our beginning") or Lucan's more well-known *victrix causa deis placuit, sed victa Catoni* (*Bell. Civ.* 1.128, "the vanquishing cause was dear to the gods, but the vanquished to Cato"). The writings of the elder Seneca, Ovid's slightly older contemporary, teach us that such turns of phrase, far from being confined to verse, permeated oratory and, we know, other forms of prose composition as well. The commonness of epigrammatic expression in Latin literature of the Silver Age may make it seem fruitless to try to interpret its importance in the *Metamorphoses*. Yet I believe we can arrive at a worthwhile conclusion which fits with the distinctive features of the poem and at the same time, though its precise bearing varies, may also be valid for many of those other works. In all of them perhaps the fondness for epigram draws attention to the speaker.

PARADOX AND OTHER EPIGRAMMATIC EXPRESSIONS

Epigrams in Ovid sometimes describe unusual or paradoxical situations. The expression seems almost to arise naturally out of what is given in the story. Set as a guard over Io is the monster Argus, who is well fitted for his duties: his head is ringed with a hundred eyes. Ovid observes:

> *constiterat quocumque modo, spectabat ad Io;*
> *ante oculos Io, quamvis aversus, habebat.*   (1.628–29)

Whichever way he stood, he was looking towards Io; though turning his back, he had Io in front of him.

The repetition of the point is typical, with the second version somewhat more pungent that the first. Myrrha, the girl in love with her own father, is the subject of a fine pair of epigrams: *scelus est odisse parentem, / hic amor est odio maius scelus!* (10.314–15, "hatred of one's parent is a crime, but this love is a crime greater than hatred!"); and regarding her suitors, *ex omnibus unum / elige, Myrrha, virum, dum ne sit in omnibus unus* (10.317–18, "choose, Myrrha, one man from amongst them all, except for one amongst them all"). Similarly the situation of Narcissus is conducive to epigram. Of the young man who has unwittingly fallen in love with his own reflected image the poet says: *oculos idem, qui decipit, incitat error* (3.431, "the same mistake which leads his eyes astray leads them on"). Shortly afterwards, when Narcissus himself realizes his error, he cries out: *quod cupio, mecum est: inopem me copia fecit* (3.466, "what I desire, I have with me; abundance has impoverished me"; the second half of the verse also suggests "opportunity has left me helpless"); and then finally: *nunc duo concordes anima moriemur in una* (3.473, "now we two hearts which beat together will perish in a single soul"). In passages like these it is not so much the case that a given situation itself evokes the epigrammatic expressions as that Ovid seeks out such a situation, or, more important, in fact creates it through his language. The paradoxes do not inhere in the material, but are called into existence by the poet's bent towards epigram. Epigram is among other things a means of discovering and fixing what is unique in a situation.

A number of such expressions are likely to strike us as somewhat hollow or mechanical, as having the form of an epigram while lacking any spark of aptness or ingenuity. The phrase cited last might be judged so, like another used of Narcissus: *fuit in tenera tam dura superbia forma* (3.354, "in a soft shape there was pride so hard"). Atalanta, pained at the thought that the attractive Hippomenes, entering the footrace in order to win her hand, is doomed to forfeit his life, exclaims: *occidet hic igitur, voluit quia vivere mecum* (10.626, "therefore will he die, because with me he wanted to live"). The antithesis of *occidet* and *vivere* is as weak as it is unmistakable; it seems almost ornamental. Elsewhere Daedalion, sorrowing for the lost Chione, becomes a hawk, who savages all the other birds. His metamorphosis is closed with the sentence: *aliisque dolens fit causa dolendi* (11.345, "grieving himself, he becomes a cause of grief to others").

Yet at the same time some of Ovid's highest achievements are his perfect epigrams. Could he more brilliantly summarize the figure of Envy than by telling us that as she flies over the talented and prosperous city of Athens, *vixque tenet lacrimas, quia nil lacrimabile cernit* (2.796, "because she sees nothing to weep over, she weeps")? Marsyas, flayed alive by Apollo, is made to exclaim: *quid me mihi detrahis?* (6.385, "Why do you tear me from myself?"). The clever observation is made of Achilles: *armarat deus idem idemque cremabat* (12.614, "the same god [Vulcan] who had armed him was cremating him now"). (This playing within the realm of mythology is also typical.) As an outstanding example we may cite Ovid's extremely ingenious description of Erysichthon, who is starving to death: *ventris erat pro ventre locus* (8.805, "in place of a belly there was a space for a belly").

The chief thing to notice is not so much the quality of the individual epigrams as the tendency for them to appear wholesale in the poem. Let several more examples serve as a reminder of this fact. A race of men, produced from the dragon's teeth which Cadmus had sown, no sooner arises fully grown from the earth than they begin to do battle with each other. One dies: *exspirat, modo quas acceperat, auras* (3.121, "he gives up the life-breath which he had gotten but a moment before"). Pygmalion carves a statue so lifelike that the viewer might believe it wanted to move: *ars adeo latet arte sua* (10.252, "to such an extent is art concealed by its art"). Peleus, who is both grandson of the supreme deity and husband of Thetis, boasts: *Io-*

vis esse nepoti / contigit haud uni, coniunx dea contigit uni (11.219–20,
"while scarcely one man is lucky enough to have Jupiter for a grandfather, only one man is lucky enough to have a goddess for a wife").
An especially vicious wolf is said to be *dulcedine sanguinis asper*
(11.402, "bitter because of the sweetness of blood").[11] Contrasting
Ino with the other daughters of Cadmus (Semele, annihilated by Jupiter's thunderbolt, Autonoe and Agave, who lost their sons Actaeon
and Pentheus) Ovid reports: *de totque sororibus expers / una doloris erat,
nisi quem fecere sorores* (4.418–19, "of so many sisters only one was
free of pain—except for the pain that her sisters brought her"). This
touching epigram, which introduces Ino and her story, is a *transitio
per rem absentem*. The scene in which a storm engulfs Ceyx' ship is
illuminated weirdly:

> *praebentque micantia lumen*
> *fulmina: fulmineis ardescunt ignibus ignes.* (11.522–23)

Light is provided by the flickering lightning: with the fires of
the lightning glow the fires of heaven [the stars].

(Ovid is fond of using the same word in two different senses, as he
does here: see Murphy for a defense of *ignes*.) And so on, almost
beyond measure.

THE EFFECTS OF EPIGRAM

What are the effects of a style which tends towards epigram? For
one thing, such sentences, essentially ornamental, slow the forward
movement of the narrative. The action described comes to a halt for
a moment—or more than a moment, when the poet is inclined to
repeat himself. Another effect is humor. Humor, of course, is a no-
toriously subjective reaction. The passages that evoke a smile or
a chuckle from one may not from another. Among the examples
quoted I would single out 1.628–29, 2.796, 6.385, and 11.522–23 as
humorous. However that may be, it is hard to believe that a reader
would find humor in none of the poem's epigrams. A third, more
general effect is related to this. Epigrammatic expression, even when
not humorous, often diminishes the pathos of a particular scene. The
excessively neat, contrived phrase calls attention to itself and distracts the reader from the business at hand. Thus the horror that
might be felt at Myrrha's incestuous passion or the terror and pity of
Ceyx' plight lose their edge because of the accompanying epigrams.

Even in scenes which are light and gay or simply plain, epigrams
abound. The several effects already discerned—the slowing of the

narrative pace, humor, the slackening of emotional intensity—are but manifestations of a more general effect: Ovid's tendency to epigram concentrates attention on the narrator himself. It is as if he does not want us to become so engaged by the story as to lose sight of him; one may feel a gentle tug-of-war between the two. This is the comprehensive effect in both this poem and many other works from the Silver Age. The tale shares the limelight with the teller. Interest is focused not only on what is being said but also on the narrator, who consciously delivers the epigrams.

We can confirm this observation and also its interpretation by referring to Latin literature. Comparison of Ovid with Virgil illustrates Ovid's marked tendency towards writing epigrams and something of the quality of the epigrams. And the testimony of several ancient writers on rhetoric strengthens the conviction that such a style drew attention to the speaker.

During the capture of Troy we read the following in Virgil: *trahebatur . . . / . . . a templo Cassandra adytisque Minervae* (*Aen.* 2.403–4, "Cassandra was being dragged from the temple and shrines of Minerva"). Ovid refers to the same event like this: *a virgine virgine rapta* (14.468, "when one virgin had been carried away from another," that is, from the temple of another). The phrase is an enigmatic, somewhat playful reference, teasing the reader's knowledge of mythology. It is also a recasting of the Virgilian description in epigrammatic language. Another, keener example shows this again. Virgil describes King Anius thus:

> *rex Anius, rex idem hominum Phoebique sacerdos,*
> *vittis et sacra redimitus tempora lauro.* (*Aen.* 3.80–81)

> King Anius, at the same time king over men and priest of Apollo, his temples encircled with fillets and holy laurel.

Ovid transforms this into the following:

> *hunc Anius, quo rege homines, antistite Phoebus*
> *rite colebatur, temploque domoque recepit.* (13.632–33)

> He was received both in temple and at home by Anius, under whose kingship men were duly looked after, under whose priesthood Apollo was duly worshiped.

(What I cannot capture in English is that with both subjects in the passage from Ovid the same Latin verb is used, *colebatur*, its meaning varying with each, "look after" and "worship"; the play on the same word at 8.724 is more nearly a pun than a zeugma.) Both poets make the same double identification of Anius as king and priest. Both reinforce this by echoing it in an added detail: Virgil's Anius wears both fillets (of a priest) and laurel (of a triumphant general, says Servius); Ovid's receives his visitor both in his palace and in the temple. But Ovid tries to outdo his predecessor and give the verses a special touch through the zeugma with *colere*. A plain statement in Virgil becomes in him an epigram.

I do not, of course, mean to suggest that antithesis or repetition of words is unknown to Virgil; it is simply that such features of language are much less common and have a different place in his poetry. First, Virgil may sometimes merely imply a contrast, as in this verse: *teneras arcebant vincula palmas* (*Aen.* 2.406, "shackles held her tender palms"). He suggests an antithesis between Cassandra's tender hands and the chains, but he does not articulate it. Ovid would not have left this to our imagination; he would have added an adjective like *dura* or *saeva* to point the contrast, as in the epigrammatic phrase about Narcissus (3.354, quoted above). Moreover, when Virgil does employ an antithesis, it is rarely decorative or otiose. Of the dying Priam, for instance, he writes: *sanguine foedantem quos ipse sacraverat ignis* (*Aen.* 2.502, "befouling with his blood the fires which he himself had hallowed"). The verbs *foedare* and *sacrare* contrast with one another here—and the contrast is sharpened by *ipse*—but they are not a pair of obvious opposites like *tener* and *durus*.[12] The contrast is at the same time less obvious and more substantial. The phrase points up the horror of Priam's death and even touches the problem of belief in the gods.[13] Similar in its thematic relevance is a sentence which Jupiter speaks: *mortalin decuit violari vulnere divum?* (*Aen.* 12.797, "Was it right that a god be injured by mortal hand?"). The verse is framed by the opposing words, which do not quite face one another squarely: *immortalis* would be the precise antithesis of *mortalis*, as *homo* of *deus*.

Ovid's propensity to such expressions was recognized in his own day. Seneca the Elder recalls Cestius' saying of him that "he drummed into the ears of the present generation not only his *Art of Love* but his epigrams too" (*Contr.* 3.7); Cestius deplores the poet's influence over an orator. Elsewhere Seneca faults Ovid for heaping up epigrams instead of being content with one (*Contr.* 9.5.17, citing as an example *Met.* 13.503–5). A pair of ancient writers can guide us to a proper appreciation of this. Cicero and Quintilian, for us the two chief Latin exponents of rhetoric, both remark on the effect which elaborate care over words has upon oratory. The former tells us: "A suspicion of careful preparation, of an attentiveness which is artificial . . . very greatly deprives the speech of credibility, the speaker of authority" (*Inv.* 1.25). The latter writes: "When one has to fight by evoking powerful emotions like brutality or jealousy or compassion, who could tolerate a speaker who waxes wroth, weeps, or pleads in antithetical phrases, matching rhythms or sounds, and so forth? For in these matters excessive care over words detracts from the credibility of the feelings: truth appears to be wanting wherever artificiality is paraded" (*Inst.* 9.3.102). The two authors agree that excessive attention to language diminishes the credibility of the representation. Applying this to the *Metamorphoses*, they would claim (I imagine) that the epigrams, a particular form of care over words, make us feel as if Ovid is not concerned solely to convey the material to us, to make us experience pathos, joy, or whatever.

The positive interest that such a style does convey is suggested once again by Seneca. He puts into the mouth of Votienus Montanus an explanation of why he did not prepare declamations ahead of time: he who does do this "is content to charm his audience with epigrams and descriptive passages: he wants them to approve of *him*, not his case" (*Contr.* 9.praef.1—is not this itself an epigram?). Here then an ancient author expresses precisely my own view, that language studded with epigram deflects attention away from the material to the speaker.

The Narrator's Point of View

We have at hand more, and more vivid, evidence of the narrator's omnipresence. The texture of the poem is marked with comments that can be made only from his point of view and from nowhere else. This is hardly a matter of interpretation, rather of fairly simple observation. Such remarks are constant reminders to the reader that someone is *telling* this story. It does not exist independently, on its own; it does not reach us unmediated. The narrator frequently breaks in on the story with his own voice. These interruptions, as is natural, often take the form of a parenthesis or an apostrophe; they are often expressed epigrammatically. But the manifestations of the narrating voice are legion. I begin by suggesting the range.

The most obvious examples are remarks which the narrator makes to the reader directly in the first person. We can leave aside here passages in which the poet announces his own subject, on the grounds that the first person singular is traditional: Virgil's *arma virumque cano* finds its counterpart in Ovid's proem. But there is nothing traditionally epic in the first-person discourse at the close of the

Metamorphoses. The passage which ends the poem (15.871–79) is a lengthy statement of the poet's own immortality, more closely resembling personal lyric—Horace *Odes* 3.30 is the chief model—than anything familiar from more "objective" narrative.

Even apart from this the poet is not shy of speaking in his own voice. In Book Two, after describing some of the destruction visited upon the earth by Phaethon's fall, Ovid pauses for a moment before picturing still greater catastrophes. In that pause he says: *parva queror* (2.214, "I utter but small complaints"). Who is this "I" who suddenly intrudes but the narrator himself? The effect, unparalleled by anything in Virgil, is very striking. We were reading about the burning of the fields with their crops, and perhaps were being drawn into the story, when out pops the narrator to announce that *he* has greater woes to speak of. Near the opposite end of the poem, when comparing Augustus with Caesar, he gives other instances of sons who were greater than their fathers: Agamemnon and Atreus, Achilles and Peleus, and so on. His last instance, Jupiter and Saturn, he introduces thus: *ut exemplis ipsos aequantibus utar* (15.857, "so that I may use examples which are equal to the subjects"). That a character in the poem should say "I" is not surprising. It is remarkable, however, when the narrator does so. And the alternation somewhat blurs the difference between the two.

Ovid's presence is felt less directly, but clearly nevertheless, in other novel ways. In Book Nine he is bringing to a close the story of Iphis, who, though born a woman, has now been changed to a man; Iphis and his mother are thankful to Isis for bringing about the change. First Ovid addresses Iphis: *nam quae / femina nuper eras, puer es!* (9.790–91, "for you who were recently a girl are now a lad!"). The apostrophe is hardly remarkable. At once, however, it nearly turns into an exchange between narrator and character: *date munera templis, / nec timida gaudete fide! dant munera templis* (791–92, "Offer gifts to the temples and rejoice in your sturdy faith! They do offer gifts to the temples"). The plural imperatives must be addressed to Iphis and his mother. The echoing of the command in the statement that follows it makes it seem that the two hear Ovid's words and harken to them. The poet strikes an extremely personal note. He expands the apostrophe to the point of breaking its usual bounds: where else does a character respond to the teller? and does not that response affirm the existence of the teller? The narrator has an easy entrance into his story.

On several occasions he steps in to finish speeches for his characters. During the battle between Perseus and the supporters of Phineus he reports in direct discourse the boastful words of Lycabas but then adds, "he had not yet said all this" (5.65–66). Conspicuously he rounds out his account. A passage about Syrinx is far more remarkable. To lull Argus to sleep, Mercury has begun telling him the story of that nymph, which proves to be so powerful a soporific that long before it is over the hundred-eyed monster is fast asleep. At this point, his goal achieved, Mercury abruptly stops speaking—but then the narrator himself steps in to pick up the thread and finish the story, telling us what Mercury was going to say (1.700–12)! The transition is handled in a surprising way. Equipped with the clarities of modern punctuation, the lines run as follows:

> *"Pan videt hanc pinuque caput praecinctus acuta*
> *talia verba refert"—restabat verba referre*
> *et precibus spretis fugisse per avia nympham . . .*   (1.699–701)

> "Pan sees her and, his head girt with pointy pine needles, he speaks the following words"—it remained to speak the words and say that the nymph, spurning his entreaties, fled over the trackless wastes . . .

The last words of Mercury's direct discourse, *talia verba refert* ("he speaks the following words") are a familiar enough phrase for introducing direct discourse. What follows, however, is not Pan's words, nor those of Mercury, but rather those of Ovid: *restabat verba referre* ("it remained to speak the words").[14] Moreover, the indirect discourse which now follows, six main clauses spread over twelve verses, stands in an odd syntactic relationship to the rest: these infinitives, though they appear parallel to *referre*, cannot be so, but must depend in a different and very loose way on *restabat*.[15] The unannounced double shift of voice, so abrupt as to be deceptive, and the varying constructions with *restabat* reinforce our sense of the narrator's interruption.

Sometimes we are reminded of the teller behind the tale through a parenthetic quip inserted in the narrative. Perseus, intent on rescuing Andromeda from the monster which is about to devour her, asks her parents whether they will betroth her to him if he succeeds: *accipiunt legem (quis enim dubitaret?)* (4.704, "they accepted the terms (indeed, who would have hesitated to?)"). Of similar effect is a parenthesis in Book Ten. Eurydice, because Orpheus has turned to look at her, slips back to the Underworld:

> *iamque iterum moriens non est de coniuge quicquam*
> *questa suo (quid enim nisi se quereretur amatam?).*   (10.60–61)

And dying now for the second time, she uttered no complaint
against her husband (indeed, what could her complaint have
been, save that she had been loved?).

With remarks like these the narrator brings his story to a halt and
addresses to the reader a brief aside, a comment delivered, as it
were, with a knowing wink.[16]

Such hints about the range of ways in which the narrator manifests himself should enable the reader to recognize the many other
examples there are in the poem. Once the ear is attuned, that voice
can be heard almost everywhere. In order to sharpen this faculty let
me describe several particular, peculiarly Ovidian features of language which introduce the narrator's perspective. Others could be
found, no doubt.[17]

SIMILE

The simile is a hallmark of epic narrative style. Ovid several times
employs similes which are marked by an unexpected personal note.
One begins: *sic ego torrentem . . . vidi* (3.568–69, "just so I myself once
saw a torrent which . . ."). This represents a bold, unparalleled interjection on the part of the teller. What has happened to epic anonym-
ity? No less arresting is the passage where Ovid describes the chief
gods as Roman nobles, their residences located in the choicest quarter of town:

> *hic locus est quem, si verbis audacia detur,*
> *haud timeam magni dixisse Palatia caeli.*   (1.175–76)

This is the place that, if the boldness of the phrase were to be
permitted, I should hardly be shy of calling the Palatine of great
heaven.

Though lacking the regular identifying tags, such as a *sicut* or *veluti*
or *ceu*, this is in effect a simile—and a sly and playful one, since the
narrator offers it tentatively in the form of a future-less-vivid condition. This paves the way to a full-blown simile shortly afterwards,
applied to the outcry arising from the assembled gods when Jupiter
reveals to them the treachery of Lycaon:

> *sic, cum manus impia saevit*
> *sanguine Caesareo Romanum exstinguere nomen,*
> *attonitum tantae subito terrore ruinae*

humanum genus est totusque perhorruit orbis;
nec tibi grata minus pietas, Auguste, tuorum est
quam fuit illa Iovi.   (1.200–205)

In the same way, when the unholy band was raging to extinguish the Roman people by shedding Caesar's blood, the human race was smitten by the sudden fear of awful destruction, nor was the loyalty of your supporters less pleasing to you, Augustus, than that was to Jupiter.

Instead of a universal, familiar experience like a storm or a forest fire this simile appeals to a recent, time-bound, unique event, an attempt on Augustus' life. It reverses the working of the usual simile and has a personalizing effect. This is reinforced by the apostrophe of the emperor, who is not a character within the narrative but a contemporary figure present only in the simile. The grand first simile of the *Aeneid*, in which Neptune calming the stormy waters is compared to a statesman calming a crowd, is similar—and this not by chance either. Both passages compare an event to human political activity; but whereas Virgil's is presented as timeless, something that could happen at any time, Ovid's is specific. The simile thrusts upon us both the poet and the contemporary world.

The poet is more in evidence in a very interesting simile from Book Six:

ecce venit magno dives Philomela paratu,
divitior forma, quales audire solemus
naidas et dryadas mediis incedere silvis,
si modo des illis cultus similesque paratus.   (6.451–54)

Look! here comes Philomela, rich in her splendid dress, richer in her beauty: just like her, so we are wont to hear, are the naiads and dryads who parade through the middle of the forest—provided you give them similar dress and adornment.

(We might note the epigrammatic quality of the description, *dives . . . divitior*, the adjective shifting its meaning from literal to figurative.) Philomela's entrance into the narrative—"Look! here she comes"—is dramatic in the sense that it is unexpected and arresting, and also in that it resembles the technique with which new characters are often introduced in a play. In a play, however, such words are spoken about one character by another; see, for example, Plaut. *Pseud.* 693, *Per.* 543. In bringing Philomela on by speaking the words himself, Ovid for a moment makes himself appear to be one of the figures on the stage: again the barrier between creator and creature is lowered.

This prepares the ground for the simile that follows, with the highly personal expression *audire solemus* ("we are wont to hear").[18] This is just like the *sic vidi* simile from Book Three, cited above. Here the effect is reinforced by two details. With this same phrase the narrator implies the possible fictiveness of the naiads and dryads in his own simile, as if to say, "Well, at least that's what we're always being told." Then, after making the comparison, he adds that it is valid only if you dress up the naiads. Strange simile, in which the poet nearly undoes his own comparison! (Compare 10.515–18, quoted in Chapter Six.) All this leads us to feel vividly the presence of the narrator in his simile.

Ovid has several more on-again, off-again comparisons. He likens the beautiful Adonis to the Cupids we see in paintings—but only on condition: "either give a light quiver to him, or take it away from them!" (10.518). Elsewhere he describes the metamorphosis of the lad Hyacinth:

> Tyrioque nitentior ostro
> *flos oritur formamque capit quam lilia, si non*
> *purpureus color his, argenteus esset in illis.*   (10.211–13)

A flower arises which is more brilliant than Tyrian purple and looks like a lily—if the one were not purple and the other white.

Ovid even has a do-it-yourself simile. Of the party thrown for the marriage between Perseus and Andromeda, which will end in a battle royal, he says: *inque repentinos convivia versa tumultus / adsimilare freto possis* (5.5–6, "the festive celebration that turned to sudden tumult you might liken to the sea"). The roundabout, self-conscious form of the simile perhaps advertises its literary ancestry: it recalls a simile from the *Iliad* (2.144–46). It invites the reader to join the author in making the comparison.

CONTRARY-TO-FACT CONDITIONS

Another recurring feature of the narrative which draws attention to the poet because it is a remark that can be made only from his point of view is a certain kind of contrary-to-fact statement. These are found not only in the transitions between stories but throughout the poem generally. Ovid is not the only poet to write contrary-to-fact sentences, of course; rather, many of his are different from those of earlier narrative poets. By grasping the difference, which is subtle, we can come to see how these sentences remind us of the narrator.

The contrary-to-fact statements made by other authors invariably follow the description of an unfolding action and represent the action as continuing if only some unexpected force had not checked it. In Ovid, far from arising out of the progress of the narrative, they break upon the reader unexpectedly; only the narrator could introduce so unforeseen an event. The peculiar quality of such conditions in the *Metamorphoses* can be illustrated by a comparison with Homer and Virgil. Typical Homeric examples are (I paraphrase): "Then the Greeks would have captured Troy, had not Apollo made a stand on the Trojans' behalf" (*Il.* 16.698–701), and "Then, Menelaus, you would have been slain by Hector, since he was far stronger, had not the kings of the Achaeans rescued you" (*Il.* 7.104–6; the apostrophe is rare in Homer). In these and in every single other example the narrator merely represents the natural tendency of an action already under way as being checked or blocked somehow: the Greeks were already doing well in their attack on the city and would have continued it to the point of success, had not Apollo intervened; and so forth. The form of expression does not deviate from the line of narrative, but is only an extension of it—a hypothetical extension, to be sure. Precisely the same holds true for the contrary-to-fact sentences in Apollonius' *Argonautica* (e.g., 1.492–95), as well as in the *Aeneid*, for instance, in the passage where Turnus, having forced his way into the Trojan camp and then been shut inside alone, attacks the Trojans so ferociously that he forgets to open the gates to his own men outside:

> *et si continuo victorem ea cura subisset,*
> *rumpere claustra manu sociosque immittere portis,*
> *ultimus ille dies bello gentique fuisset.*   (9.757–59)

And if at once there had come over the victorious Turnus concern to burst the bars by force and let his companions in through the gates, that would have been the last day of the war and of the Trojan race.

This is in effect a climactic statement about Turnus' battle fury, which the narrative has been illustrating for a while; it explains why, great though his fury is, it does not have the issue it might be expected to. Although contrary to fact, it still belongs intimately to the story.[19]

The contrary-to-fact sentences of Ovid with which we are concerned are fundamentally different. They represent not an extension or continuation of the narrative but an interrupting of it and a directing of attention to the speaker himself, the only one in a position to make such a remark. They lack roots in the story and are extraneous to it. It does not seem to me coincidental therefore that they are usually found combined with some other feature which signals the presence of the narrator—epigram, apostrophe, the clever use of mythology. Scylla, for example, changed from a girl into a monster, destroys the companions of Ulysses. The text continues:

> mox eadem Teucras fuerat mersura carinas,
> ni prius in scopulum, qui nunc quoque saxeus exstat,
> transformata foret. (14.72–74)

Soon she would also have sunk the Trojan ships, had she not first been transformed into a cliff, now too extant as rock.

This sentence (which makes the transition back to the story of Aeneas) is nearly gratuitous. No spectator present at the preceding action could have witnessed the near occurrence of this one. It can only be imagined from some more remote point outside the story.

Jupiter, cheating on his wife, as often, attempts to rape the lovely Callisto; of her vain efforts to fight him off Ovid says:

> (adspiceres utinam, Saturnia, mitior esses!) (2.435)

(Would that you were witnessing this, Juno—you would be less harsh!)

Here the apostrophe and parenthesis as well as the syntactic form of the sentence point to the narrator. Apostrophe is also found in a passage about Achilles, who had been slain by Paris, the effeminate abductor of Helen. The poet says to Achilles:

> at si femineo fuerat tibi Marte cadendum,
> Thermodontiaca malles cecidisse bipenni. (12.610–11)

But if you had to fall in battle with a woman, you would have preferred to fall to Penthesilea's axe.

This is also a witty epigram.[20] Geography too can be treated the same way, as when Ovid describes a Thessalian bay: *bracchia procurrunt, ubi, si foret altior unda, / portus erat* (11.230–31, "the arms of land run out where, were the water higher, there would be a harbor"). And he cleverly observes about the maiden Andromeda, who, while chained stark naked to a rock, is spotted by Perseus: *manibusque modestos / celasset vultus, si non religata fuissset* (4.682–83, "with her hands she would have hidden her bashful face, if she hadn't been chained"). Epigram again marks what we are told about Hecuba, mother of Hector and part of the booty from Troy:

> *quam victor Ulixes*
> *esse suam nollet, nisi quod tamen Hectora partu*
> *ediderat: dominum matri vix repperit Hector!*   (13.485–87)

Victorious Ulysses would not have wanted to take her, except
that she had given birth to Hector: Hector, with difficulty,
helped find a master for his mother!

This is unusually clever writing. It cannot but lessen the pathos of
the moment—Ovid has just been deploring the fall of one who was a
queen—at the same time that it deflects attention from narrative to
narrator.

Our last example is drawn from the story of the Calydonian boar.
The fierce creature has killed several hunters already; now the narrator continues:

> *forsitan et Pylius citra Troiana perisset*
> *tempora, sed sumpto posita conamine ab hasta*
> *arboris insiluit, quae stabat proxima, ramis*
> *despexitque loco tutus, quem fugerat, hostem.*   (8.365–68)

Perhaps Nestor also would have perished, before the time of
the Trojan War; but, pole-vaulting vigorously with his spear, he
leapt into the branches of a nearby tree and watched from a position of safety the enemy he had fled from.

We can see here clearly the difference between Ovid and his epic
predecessors in this point of usage. If the statement were simply
"Nestor too would have perished, had he not gotten out of the way,"
it would precisely resemble the sentences from Homer and Virgil,
extending one stage further an action already begun, here the boar's
rampage. As it is, though, the word "perhaps," telling us this is only
a conjecture, and the phrase "before the time of the Trojan War,"
which implies a perspective that cannot be Nestor's own or any other
character's either, both serve to distinguish this from the earlier uses
of contrary-to-fact sentences. Once again, in this subtle way, the
reader is put in mind of the narrator. Let us also notice how Ovid
plays with mythology in this passage. These lines are a wonderful
joke on the Nestor of the *Iliad*. Homer's Nestor, who always boasts of
how brave he was when young, is here unmasked by Ovid as a liar.
It is worth observing the coincidence of the narrator's personal voice
with untraditional treatment of the material.[21] The coincidence both
reminds us that the usual narrating voice is impersonal and implies
that a personal voice is bound to treat mythology in an iconoclastic
way.

FUTURE PARTICIPLES AND *NONDUM*

The contrary-to-fact sentences mark out the narrator as one who knows what never happened. Similarly, a pair of recurring constructions, one the obverse of the other, mark him out as knowing what (to his characters) lies in the distant future. This perhaps does not seem remarkable. A narrator after all may speak freely of what has already happened before the time of the present action: upon introducing a character or a piece of armor Homer does not hesitate to report its previous history. Yet this license does not extend, symmetrically, into the future. It is a convention of epic narrative that the teller reveals through himself virtually no knowledge of the future; the occasions when he does are few and carefully circumscribed. Ovid breaks with this convention, and thereby reminds us of his special position. One of the ways he refers to coming events is through a certain distinctive use of the future active participle. In the *Metamorphoses* he employs this form of the verb often and with a great freedom. To realize what is remarkable in this we must keep in mind that before Ovid's day the participle had occurred only in very restricted situations. The attributive use of the participle, with which we are concerned, narrowly confined before, had been extended somewhat by the lyric and elegiac poets of the previous generation. Narrative, however, remained more conservative. Again comparison with the *Aeneid* shows most clearly what is distinctive in the *Metamorphoses*.

Virgil employs the future participle as an attributive not rarely, but he always does so in one of only two ways. First, he uses it of actions which are very close to happening and the imminence of which is evident to the characters within the narrative. Thus when Aeneas says to Anchises near the end of Book Two: *perituraeque addere Troiae / teque tuosque iuvat* (*Aen.* 2.660–61, "you want to add both yourself and your family to Troy, which is about to perish"), he is certain that Troy *is* about to perish; for not only has he witnessed its near destruction himself but he has been vouchsafed a vision of the gods' completing the task. Later the Sibyl in describing Tartarus to him mentions the boulder which hangs over Ixion and Pirithous: *atra silex iam iam lapsura* (*Aen.* 6.602, "the black rock which even now, even now is on the verge of falling").[22] Second, Virgil uses the participle of future actions which are foretold by the gods, oracles, seers, and others granted special precognition. Apollo, for instance, addresses Iulus as *dis genite et geniture deos* (*Aen.* 9.642, "thou who art born of the gods and will have gods born of thee"). As a god himself, he cannot be mistaken in his prediction. In the Underworld Anchises, pointing out to Aeneas their future descendants, claims:

                    hic Caesar et omnis Iuli
progenies magnum caeli ventura sub axem.   (*Aen.* 6.789–90)

Here is Caesar and all the progeny of Iulus which is to arise beneath the vault of heaven.

The divine scheme of the universe, which he has already unfolded,
justifies his prophecy.[23] Virgil, then, uses the future participle at-
tributively only for events which are completely certain from the
point of view either of the gods or of the humans within the story.

Against this background we can see the novelty of Ovid's usage. A
rather recent innovation in the language, handled by other writers
with hesitation and restraint, the future participle develops in Ovid's
hands a very extended, free use. Let us look at several examples.
Among the rivers set ablaze by Phaethon's downfall Ovid mentions
arsurusque iterum Xanthus (2.245, "the Xanthus, which is going to
burn for a second time"). He refers of course to the episode in Book
Twenty-One of the *Iliad* where the Trojan rivers, trying to overwhelm
Achilles, are attacked by the fires of Hephaistos. In another passage
Ovid says that once upon a time crows were so white they rivaled
geese: *servaturis vigili Capitolia voce / . . . anseribus* (2.538–39, "geese
which were to save the Capitoline with their watchful cry"), he adds
by way of description—a reference to the famous event of 390, in
which the Gauls would have captured the citadel of Rome had their
stealthy approach not been thwarted by the honking of Juno's sacred
geese. Still another instance occurs when Hercules' weapons are
placed upon his funeral pyre: *regnaque visuras iterum Troiana sagittas*
(9.232, "his arrows, which once again would see the kingdom of
Troy"). Next time Philoctetes will be carrying them. And so on.[24]

Whereas the participle in the *Aeneid* described an event that either
was immediately evident to the human characters within the story
or, if distant, was foreseen with certainty by a divinity or someone
who shared the divine knowledge of what is fated, in the *Metamorphoses* it most often represents an observation that can be made from
a single point of view, that of the narrator himself. Phaethon does
not know nor does any god report that the Xanthus is going to burn
once more—only Ovid himself makes the connection between the
present event and the one to come. Moreover, the point of view from
outside the narrative is rendered all the more evident because the
information which the participle adds is wholly irrelevant to the narrative. It affects not a bit either the course of the story or our understanding of it that the river will burn again, the geese save the
Capitoline, or Hercules' arrows revisit Troy. Again, the opposite is

true of the *Aeneid*, in which the phrases quoted are affective. In Ovid the phrases with the future participle are extraneous; they are side comments, mere interruptions made by the narrator. For a moment at least they direct attention away from the narrative to the man who is telling it. In them one can hear the voice of Ovid intruding upon the tale.

Such participial phrases are matched by a set of phrases with the adverb *nondum* which refer to the future by stating not what will happen, in positive terms, but what has *not yet* happened. These are only a roundabout form of the other, and they equally signal the existence and the detachment of the narrator. A fine example is the reference to Castor and Pollux as *gemini, nondum caelestia sidera, fratres*[25] (8.372, "the twin brothers, not yet stars in the firmament"); had it scanned, Ovid might have said *futura caelestia sidera*. Others include the mention of *gramen / nondum mutato vulgatum corpore Glauci* (7.232–33, "grass not yet brought to renown by the metamorphosis of Glaucus' body") or *nondum torvae Calydon invisa Dianae* (6.415, "Calydon, not yet hated by savage Diana"; Diana's hatred later unleashes the Calydonian boar).[26]

Once again a comparison with Virgil is helpful. Both poets refer to the fact that the port of Caieta in Latium was named for Aeneas' nurse, who was buried there. Virgil's lines combine aetiology with a moving epitaph:

> tu quoque litoribus nostris, Aeneia nutrix,
> aeternam moriens famam, Caieta, dedisti;
> et nunc servat honos sedem tuus ossaque nomen
> Hesperia in magna, si qua est ea gloria, signat.   (*Aen.* 7.1–4)

Caieta, nurse of Aeneas, you too in your death have given eternal renown to our shores; even now your fame keeps its abode, and in great Hesperia your name marks the resting place of your bones, if this be any glory.

Ovid touches upon the same fact in passing:

> litora adit nondum nutricis habentia nomen.   (14.157)

He came to the shores which did not yet bear the name of his nurse.

In its phrasing the latter version is allusive, even coy. Virgil presupposes in his readers a knowledge of toponymy; Ovid, who does not name the nurse, presupposes a study of Virgil.[27] The two versions also fix the narrator in a very different relation to the narrative. Virgil stands in his own day and looks back to the thread which continues from the past down to the present, linking the one with the other. He cherishes the link, we feel, and appreciates the value of history as a memorial (though in characteristic Virgilian fashion he mutes his appreciation with the phrase "if this be any glory"). Ovid by contrast appears to stand outside of time. A disinterested, perhaps uninterested, observer, he remarks for the reader's benefit that at the moment of one event (Aeneas' arrival) the other had not yet taken place (the naming of the port). He shows no sense of history, only of the simple logic of temporal sequence. And by couching the observation in a negative way he contrives to call even more attention to himself, the figure outside the narrative who makes the observation.[28]

Self-doubt and Self-criticism

The poet of the *Metamorphoses* never makes himself more evident than when he turns on his own narrative and criticizes it. Not only does he remind us again and again that *he* is telling the story; he also frequently hints that it is not altogether reliable, but instead is *merely* a story that *he* is telling. By wondering aloud about it, the poet calls into question the truth of mythology. At least he seems to deny its literal truth. And when he does this repeatedly he reinforces the implicit, unspoken assumption that literal truth is the only kind, as if there were no symbolic truths, and once one has cast doubt on whether a reported event took place it is robbed of the values traditionally ascribed to it. Such literalization is characteristic of Ovid. It is not coincidental that he appears before us prominently as both narrator and critic at the same time. His skepticism is linked to his artistic self-consciousness: aware of his own role in manipulating the story, he is bound to be aware of others' as well, and correspondingly distrustful of them.

He may be signaling this in a passage from Book Eight. The setting ought to be recalled first. We are in the middle book of the poem, and a group gathered in Achelous' cave is discussing the possibility of metamorphosis. Lelex has just finished the tale of Baucis and Philemon. Intent on proving his point, that metamorphosis does in fact take place, he vigorously affirms the reality of the couple's change into a pair of sacred trees.

> *haec mihi non vani (neque erat cur fallere vellent)*
> *narravere senes; equidem pendentia vidi*
> *serta super ramos . . . recentia.*   (8.721–23)

This was recounted to me by old men who were not unreliable
(and there was no reason why they should wish to deceive); I
myself saw fresh garlands hanging upon their boughs.

In a central passage regarding the central phenomenon of the poem,
a story-teller mentions deceit. Lelex, as it seems to me, occupies the
same position as Ovid. To mention deceit, even while denying it, is
to call attention to it and to raise, willy-nilly, the issue of the story's
veracity. Within its context Lelex' "I myself saw them" sounds almost
defensive, as does the litotes in "not unreliable" and in a phrase he
employed when introducing the tale: *quoque minus dubites* (620, "so
that you have fewer doubts"). This passage brings into relation matters of theme and vehicle; it appears to link the question whether
metamorphosis is possible with whether the mythology recounting it
is reliable. The narrator's alertness to deceptive story-telling here receives expression which is effective because oblique, and is especially
significant because of the juxtaposition.

TELLER DETACHED FROM TALE

The range of ways Ovid reveals his skepticism is wide. Certain characteristically Ovidian turns of phrase suggest a fussiness on the part
of the poet. He conveys to readers the sense that he picks and
chooses among the materials at his disposal—and might well have
chosen differently, had he wanted to. Thus he says of Hecuba: *plura
quidem, sed et haec laniato pectore dixit* (13.493, "from her tormented
breast she uttered more words, to be sure, but also the following").
In other words, he declares he is giving us but a partial report, breaking the illusion of epic fullness and objectivity. With this casual, unmotivated phrase he recalls his own act of selection. More remarkable is a phrase that he uses to describe Ceyx' progress on a sea
voyage: *aut minus, aut certe medium non amplius aequor / puppe secabatur*
(11.478–79, "with his ship he had traversed less than half the sea—or
certainly not more than half"). The narrator permits himself to mention alternative versions of how far Ceyx had traveled when the
storm struck his ship. Here is no historian debating a crucial question of variant traditions—only a story-teller momentarily uncertain
what exactly happened. The triviality of the matter throws into relief
the narrator's pickiness as well as presence. At the end of the story
he invents an anonymous character—*aliquis senior*, he calls him (749,
"some old fellow")—who praises the love Ceyx and Alcyone have
retained as kingfishers in metamorphosis. There follows in direct discourse a comparison between them and the bird who was formerly

Aesacus; this forms the transition. The narrator is not sure, however, who precisely spoke the words: *proximus, aut idem, si fors tulit, . . . dixit* (751, "one who was nearby, or, if so it chanced, the very same old man, said . . ."). Though it is of the smallest importance, the narrator makes a point of revealing his uncertainty.

The story of the kingfishers offers a more complex example of critical distance between teller and tale. The corpse of Ceyx, who was shipwrecked in the storm, has floated back to the shore, where his wife Alcyone has been awaiting him. Transformed now, she flies to him and "kisses his cold lips with her hard beak." Then we read:

> *senserit hoc Ceyx, an vultum motibus undae*
> *tollere sit visus, populus dubitabat; at ille*
> *senserat.*   (11.739–41)

The people were uncertain whether Ceyx had felt this kiss or, because of the movement of the waves, had only appeared to lift his face; but he *had* felt it.

First Ovid offers two explanations for what was seen (here he sets them in the minds of the observers), one supernatural, the other rational; then he himself, unusually, opts for the more fantastic of them. The stand that he ultimately takes is less important than his raising the possibility of a rational explanation for the event. A passage like this makes us wonder about the reliability of what we read, and it is the narrator himself who induces this skepticism.

Ovid sometimes marks more distinctly the variations he knows of, as with the conjunctions *sive . . . sive* ("whether . . . or"). The ordinary context of this construction is illustrated at 15.324–28, where Pythagoras gives two explanations of why a certain spring causes those who drink from it to shun wine: the tone is cool and dispassionate, the doubt that of an honest, inquiring scientist (note also the triple example at 342–51). Yet when the poet speaks in the same way about the events he is narrating himself, he is withholding the traditional sanction of his authority. Thus he introduces with *sive . . . sive* his varying explanations of why man was created with greater moral and mental powers than other animals (1.78–81) and why Orpheus shuns women (10.80–81). Appropriate to certain writing, the construction is foreign to narrative.

Elsewhere the poet talks about Circe's love for Glaucus:

> *neque enim flammis habet aptius ulla*
> *talibus ingenium, seu causa est huius in ipsa,*
> *seu Venus indicio facit hoc offensa paterno.*   (14.25–27)

No other woman has a heart more susceptible to the flames of
love, whether the cause of this lies in herself, or Venus is the
one responsible, offended by her father's informing.

(Circe's father is the Sun, who had tattled about Venus' adultery with
Mars: this is an example of the ingenious connections the poet makes
among mythological characters and tales.) The separate and incompatible explanations introduced by *seu . . . seu* again imply some distance between Ovid and his story.[29] At first glance this may not seem
remarkable, since similar constructions are found in Virgil:

> *primusque Thymoetes*
> *duci intra muros hortatur et arce locari,*
> *sive dolo seu iam Troiae sic fata ferebant.*   (*Aen.* 2.32–34)

Thymoetes was the first to urge that the horse be brought
within the walls and set upon the citadel, whether by guile or
because Troy's fate was already leading in that direction.

These words, however, are delivered by the character Aeneas, not by
Virgil himself (and Virgil should not be considered the narrator of
inset stories). It would be inconceivable in the *Aeneid* for the poet to
speak as if uncertain of what happened or why.

Another comparison with Virgil points to the same difference. In
Book Six of the *Aeneid* the hero, while visiting the Underworld,
thinks he has caught sight of Dido, *obscuram, qualem primo qui sur-
gere mense / aut videt aut vidisse putat per nubila lunam* (*Aen.* 6.453–
54, "who was dim, like the moon at the beginning of the month
which a man sees, or thinks he sees, through the clouds"). With
similar words Ovid describes what happens when Althaea, Meleager's mother, throws into the fire the log which represents her son's
life: *aut dedit aut visus gemitus est ipse dedisse / stipes* (8.513–14, "the log
itself gave a groan, or seemed to give one"). We might note first of
all the personification in the groaning log, which is characteristic of
Ovid. (*Ipse*, however, is Bentley's emendation of *ille.*) This extends
into the following verses. In the phrases *invitis conreptus ab ignibus*
(8.514, "seized upon by the reluctant fire") and *flamma . . . ab illa /
uritur* (8.515–16, "is burnt by that flame") the preposition *ab* personifies as agents the fire and the flame. (The personification may be
especially appropriate here, since in some sense the log *is* Meleager.)[30] Yet the expression of alternatives, "groaned or seemed to
groan," in a self-conscious way questions the personification, for it
evokes the thought that maybe the log did *not* really groan.

As for content, although both the Virgilian and the Ovidian passages convey in similar language a difficulty of discernment, they are essentially different. In Virgil the difficulty lies wholly within the narrative; it is Aeneas who is uncertain whether it is or is not Dido whom he glimpses. Moreover, in the passage which was Virgil's model, Apollonius too was describing the uncertainty of one of his characters (*Argon.* 4.1479–80). Ovid may similarly be referring to Althaea's uncertainty about the noise issuing from the log which she has just thrown into the fire. But in the context he seems rather to be expressing his own uncertainty whether what he has just said is true or not. Playfully the narrator induces skepticism about his own narrative. The phrase in Virgil reflects in the end upon Aeneas, in Ovid upon himself.

In another passage as well Ovid draws attention to a possible disparity between what actually happened and what appeared to happen. Hercules is wrestling with Achelous: *captat, / aut captare putes* (9.37–38, "he grapples with his limbs, or you might think he grapples"). The distinction is unmotivated and gratuitous—all the more so since it is made by Achelous himself, who was in a position to know! By reminding his audience vividly that we often rely on deceptive appearances, the narrator casts doubt over everything he reports.

EXPRESSIONS OF DISBELIEF

But Ovid often indicates much more directly that the stories he tells have been handed down to him and therefore may not be reliable or even believable. Like the Hellenistic and earlier Roman poets, he writes his share of phrases such as *dicitur, fertur, ferunt, ita fama ferebat, memorant,* meaning "it is said," "they say," "so the story goes," and so on. He is not unique in using these phrases. Nevertheless, it would be inadequate to label this simply an "Alexandrian feature," for Ovid differs markedly from his predecessors in the extent and the intensity of his use, with the result that he much more strongly suggests the conventional, and suspect, nature of mythology.[31]

Even when he employs traditional language, he often applies it in unusually personal and critical ways. *Fertur* ("is said") occurs commonly in Latin poetry. Ovid uses it in the passage from Book Six where he recounts how Tereus raped his sister-in-law and then cut out her tongue, to prevent her from telling:

hoc quoque post facinus . . . fertur
saepe sua lacerum repetisse libidine corpus.   (6.561–62)

Even after this crime . . . he is said, because of his lust, to have
attacked her mutilated body again and again.

If this were all, it might seem no more remarkable than any one of a
score of phrases in Catullus or Virgil. But into the middle of the
sentence (after *facinus*) Ovid inserts the parenthetic comment: *vix au-
sim credere* ("I should hardly dare to lend it credence"). In this context
the word *fertur* takes on special weight, because the secondhand reporting which it denotes is set in opposition to personal belief.

A second example is strikingly clear in that it lends itself to a comparison with Virgil. Ovid reports the unusual gestation of Zeus' son
Bacchus, snatched from his dying mother's womb: *patrioque tener, si
credere dignum est, / insuitur femori* (3.311–12, "the tender babe is sewn
into his father's thigh, if this deserves to be believed"). The phrase *si
credere dignum est* could have been lifted directly from Virgil, who
employs it in speaking about Aeneas' trumpeter Misenus, killed because he had challenged a divinity to a contest:

*aemulus exceptum Triton, si credere dignum est,
inter saxa virum spumosa immerserat unda.*   (*Aen.* 6.173–74)

His rival Triton took the man by surprise, if this deserves to be
believed, and drowned him in the foaming wave, amongst the
rocks.

The ancient commentators remark on the connotation of "ambush"
in the word *exceptum*.[32] It is about this, and nothing more than this,
that Virgil expresses the reservation. Like the famous *tantaene animis
caelestibus irae?* (*Aen.* 1.11, "can heavenly spirits be so angry?"), this
phrase refers to the difficulty of attributing "low" behavior (anger,
stealth) to the gods. In Ovid, however, the very same phrase questions the likelihood of a well-known piece of mythology.

We catch the poet criticizing his own material, and thus bringing
himself squarely before us, in many another phrase, most of them
unparalleled in earlier literature.[33] The Sun mourns his son Phaethon, and, Ovid adds: *si modo credimus, unum / isse diem sine sole ferunt* (2.330–31, "one day, so they say, went by without daylight—if
only we believe it"). *Quis credere possit?* (15.613, "who could believe
it?"), remarks Ovid parenthetically of the Romans' unwillingness to
look upon a citizen whose forehead has sprouted horns; and *credere
quis posset?* (6.421, "who could have believed it?") of Athenian failure
to participate in a pan-Hellenic war. (The latter is marked by apostrophe and is a *transitio per absentem*.) About Scylla, a monster with the
head of a girl, we are told:

> *virginis ora gerens et, si non omnia vates*
> *ficta reliquerunt, aliquo quoque tempore virgo.* (13.733–34)

She had the looks of a maiden, and, unless the poets have left
behind nothing but fiction, she also *was* a maiden at some time.

The piquancy of this remark is enhanced by a literary echo: the expression *virginis ora gerens* ("had the looks of a maiden") had been
applied by Virgil to Venus, Aeneas' mother, on an occasion when she
appeared to him in disguise (*Aen.* 1.315).[34] At the very end of his
poem Ovid writes a similar phrase:

> *perque omnia saecula fama,*
> *si quid habent veri vatum praesagia, vivam.* (15.878–79)

If the presages of poets have any truth to them, I by my fame
shall continue to live through all the ages.

There might be a touch of modesty here. (If so, the rest of the epilogue suggests it is false modesty.) Be that as it may, in the closing
lines of the *Metamorphoses* Ovid hints that not everything said by
poets is reliable.[35]

The effect is similar when instead of the narrator himself one of his
characters expresses similar notions. Indeed the effect may be all the
sharper when a mythological figure is made to suggest the possibility that mythology might be false. Thus Orpheus, pleading before
Pluto and Proserpina for the return of his beloved Eurydice, argues
that Love is known even in the Underworld. The proof:

> *famaque si veteris non est mentita rapinae,*
> *vos quoque iunxit Amor.* (10.28–29)

If the story of that long-ago rape is not a lie, you too were
brought together by Love.

This is an ingenious form of argument, by which the judges themselves are introduced as witnesses for the prosecution. To be sure,
the phrase in question is perhaps merely a polite form of expression:
Orpheus, one feels, does not necessarily doubt that Pluto carried
off Proserpina. Still, the expression resonates with much else in the
poem. Further along, when Pythagoras calls mankind's fictitious images of the Underworld *materiem vatum* (15.155, "the stuff of poets"),
we should recognize that he is influenced by a particular philosophic
tradition. But this is not the case when to the fantastic explanation
of why the river Anigros is poisonous he appends the remark: *nisi
vatibus omnis / eripienda fides* (15.282–83, "unless, that is, all trust-
worthiness is to be withdrawn from poets").

Still more directly critical are several other expressions which we read in Ovid's pages. Cadmus sows in the ground the teeth of the dragon he has slain: of the clods of earth which now begin to move about (they are to become men in a moment) the poet says: *fide maius* (3.106, "an event too great to be believed"). Could there be a blunter statement than this? Similarly Ovid terms the transformation of the Minyads' looms into vines "a thing that goes beyond belief" (4.394). Nor are we surprised to hear Nestor claim about the labors of Hercules, *ille quidem maiora fide, di! gessit* (12.545, "By heaven! his deeds *are* too great to credit"), or Anius say about the gifts Bacchus gave his daughters, *voto maiora fideque / munera* (13.651–52, "gifts greater than could be hoped for—or believed"). How could we be surprised, when we are likely to feel the same ourselves? Ovid does retell mythology, with all its incredible episodes, but at the same time he encourages our skepticism through the expression of his own.

This stance towards mythology is encapsulated in a last example. Near the very beginning of the poem, as virtually the first of the hundreds of metamorphoses to follow, Ovid describes how after the Flood the earth was repopulated. The sole survivors, Deucalion and Pyrrha, tossed stones behind their backs, and the stones, he reports, grew soft and took on human form. Of the stones' losing their hardness he observes in a parenthesis: *quis hoc credat, nisi sit pro teste vetustas?* (1.400, "Who would believe this, were it not vouched for by antiquity?"). This is a remarkable, ingeniously double-edged comment. Ostensibly it supports the truth of the narrative, yet it has precisely the opposite effect.[36] In the very act of affirming the episode the poet succeeds in casting the gravest doubt on it. In fact, as I believe, he is indifferent to the truth of it, but here we particularly want to notice how he steps forth and comments on his own narrative.

Haupt and Ehwald compare a verse from the *Aeneid*. Virgil apostrophizes Lausus just as he is about to die at Aeneas' hands: the poet will not pass over in silence the doomed young man or his outstanding deeds. To this statement he adds the phrase cited by the editors: *si qua fidem tanto est operi latura vetustas* (*Aen.* 10.794, "if some antiqueness will bring credence in so great an achievement"). The word *vetustas* and, still more, the very personal intervention of the narrator recommend the comparison. The differences, however, are no less striking than the similarities and help to define the special quality of Ovid as a narrator present in his own poem. Such an appearance of the narrator in Virgil is rare. Moreover, Virgil introduces himself *qua* poet, speaking only of the power of his own poetry to survive and so to commemorate the heroic young man.[37] The note struck is elegiac rather than doubting.[38] Ovid expands the role of the narrator. He does not confine himself to mournful reflections about his own poetry (in fact, he never in the *Metamorphoses* hints at any such thought), but instead allows himself even to criticize the very material that he is offering. And this is but the most dramatic way that he is present in his own narrative.

The norm of decorous behavior for narrative poets had been defined by Homer. Aristotle singles out for mention his relative absence from the poem: "Homer deserves to be admired on many grounds, particularly because he alone of the poets knows what he ought to do: the poet himself ought to speak as little as possible" (*Poetics* 60a5–7).[39] Aristotle's prescription, no less than Homeric practice, was probably responsible for the endurance of this doctrine. The doctrine survived intact, so far as we can tell, until Roman times, when we find first Virgil and then Ovid violating it. Certainly Virgil is very much a presence in the *Aeneid*; this is what Otis called "the subjective style." And yet the two Latin poets are not at all like one another. The narrator of the *Aeneid* is felt as participating in the poem, engaged with its subject, concerned for his characters and what they represent as if they were independent of their creator. The foundation of Rome is important to Virgil, as is—such is the poet's sympathy—even Dido, who threatens to obstruct it.

Ovid, by contrast, not only is more prominent but also stands in an altogether different relation to his narrative. He tends to be withdrawn from the narrative, not plunged into it. He remains separate from it and is not to be confused, much less identified, with it. We are aware of him and his story, and some gap between. The story is always and evidently seen from his point of view. He creates the consciousness that it reaches us only through him. In this way he renders the narrative "subjective" in a new way, in the sense of "arbitrary" and even "unreliable."

Ovid does not really criticize the literal truthfulness of mythology. Instead he reminds us that it is a human product, mediated to us by a person, not handed down from a god on tablets of stone. He conspicuously eschews the role of authoritative story-teller. He manifests himself differently from Virgil. As Altieri says, "All writers participate in their materials in some sense, but Ovid calls attention to his involvement, and he does it by attending to immediate surface phenomena, not by calling attention to deeper meanings in the text."[40] The concerns of the two poets are not on the same plane. Questioning the material, Ovid thematizes the narrator's involvement in it.

Spitzer well describes the place of the narrator in *Don Quixote*:

> For, let us not be mistaken, the real protagonist of this novel is not Quijote, with his continual misrepresentations of reality, or Sancho, with his skeptical half-endorsement of quixotism—and surely not any of the central figures of the illusionistic by-stories: the hero is Cervantes, the artist himself, who combines a critical and illusionistic art according to his free will. From the moment we open the book to the moment we put it down, we are given to understand that an almighty overlord is directing us, who leads us where he pleases.[41]

The novel is akin in many ways to the *Metamorphoses*, and these words suit the narrator of the one as well as the other. The hero Ovid is active in several fields. As he himself continually reminds us, he has created the world of the poem, he has brought it into existence and shaped it. He is also one of the chief elements holding it together. And at the same time he maintains a certain distance from his creation. This is a remarkable series of roles. Missing from all of them is any sense of derived authority. Instead, the poet appears before us on his own as a refreshing, liberating, fruitful spirit. Who desires the steady seriousness of a Virgil? Why should every antithesis be significant? How much more real seems a world at the center of which stands a fellow human! More than anything else Ovid represents the freedom and the power of the individual. By his candor he may give a new life to poetry.

CHAPTER THREE

MYTHOLOGY

We have seen Ovid linking the stories of the *Metamorphoses* together and reminding us that they are all told through him and from his point of view. He brings his presence to our attention. But we have also seen him criticizing the truthfulness of his own stories, and in this he is doing something more than highlighting his own existence as author. He is commenting on his chosen material as well, which is mythology. He conveys his view of mythology not only by his direct remarks but also, and more importantly, by the manner of his narration. This will remain our theme for a while. We are aware of Ovid in his treatment of mythology, and at the same time his treatment forms a comment upon it. This may seem self-evident and equally true for literary compositions on all subjects. Are we not aware of the poet Catullus, for instance, in his presentation of the events of his life, while we interpret his form of presentation as reflecting on those events? Nonetheless, the space which can be opened between the narrator and the material, a space in which the narrator's treatment of the material arises as a theme, is perhaps special to mythology. Mythology was the oldest, most handled, most popular subject matter of literature, and at the same time was recounted in the least personal manner: traditionality and impersonality had become fused. Thus when Ovid recounts the stories from an ostentatiously personal, subjective point of view, by that very fact he raises questions about the nature and the place of mythology.

Mythology in ancient literature may best be considered a form of language, a common mode of discourse on the topics of human life. The *Metamorphoses* employs that language—to talk about mythology itself. The poem is so self-conscious that it turns upon its own subject. This point distinguishes the work from others of Ovid's. In the poems of love, in the didactic poetry, in the *Fasti*, mythology is the means for expressing some of the poet's thoughts; it does play a role. In the *Metamorphoses*, however, it steps into the center of the stage. The question, therefore, of how Ovid handles mythology becomes important in its own right. My argument is that he takes it as a free space in which to play, in which to mock and extend, embrace and reject, invent and foreclose as he sees fit. He transposes it to the most familiar terms by removing that which is distant, divine, or supernatural and making the stories purely human and contemporary instead: his mythological world is very matter-of-fact. He turns mythology away from its concentration on the general and the generic, toward the illumination of unique moments in the life of the individual.

In studying Ovid we have no need to take up the thorny questions about the origins of mythology or of particular myths. (A knowledge of his direct literary sources is sometimes helpful, though.) For him all myths were the same. He does not distinguish between Greek and Roman and eastern, between historical myths and local legends and tall tales. For him myth is not related to cult, as it was still for Callimachus. Myths are stories found in literature (and, to some extent, in painting and sculpture). Moreover, they occupy so large a space in the field of literature that mythology is virtually synonymous with fiction.

Anachronism

One of the most obvious ways of rendering myth matter-of-fact is to collapse differences of time and space. By transferring the stories from the remote, legendary past to his own day, Ovid makes them seem familiar. Some of the devices through which he does this lend themselves to ready description and classification; others are more subtle and more pervasive. The most well-known is anachronism, by which an object or person or institution or name is projected back into a time when it had not yet come into existence. Thus the past takes on the coloring of the present.

RECOGNITION

Though familiar to us and recognized already in antiquity, anachronism is not easy to identify in all cases. To guard against error, we may briefly consider the questions of what constitutes anachronism and how it is recognized. First of all, the narrator's similes may be excluded, on the grounds that they refer not to the time of the story, but to that of the narrator, who speaks *ex sua persona*.[1] Thus it is a true (and very striking) anachronism when Achaemenides, recounting his adventures on the way home from Troy, reports that he saw the Cyclops "hurling huge stones, which were driven as if with the force of a siege catapult" (14.183–84), for no one in the heroic age could have known siege engines, which were not invented until the early fourth century. The following simile, however, ought not to be considered an anachronism, since Ovid himself (speaking as the narrator) invents the comparison for the Calydonian boar attacking its hunters: "as when a mass of stone shoots forth, hurled by the tightened cords and aimed at walls or at towers crammed with soldiery" (8.357–58). Similes, then, we may dismiss from consideration.[2]

Except in similes, the appearance of any invention or institution before its time is, strictly speaking, anachronism.[3] There remains, however, the problem of recognition. It may be inadequate merely to point out that Ovid attributes to the age of legend something which we know came into existence in, let us say, the fourth century. Which ones struck Ovid's readers as anachronisms? How often did they (or he himself, for that matter) realize that things were depicted with historical inaccuracy? Moreover, what range was allowed to poetic license? That is, how far might anachronism go without drawing attention to itself? Despite the currency of the *Iliad* and the *Odyssey* we are entitled to wonder, for instance, how remarkable it seemed to Ovid's readers that the besiegers of Megara live in tents rather than huts (8.43), that heroes recline on couches for dinner instead of sitting at tables (8.566, 12.155), or that when Ulysses addresses his fellow Greeks as *cives* (13.262, "fellow citizens"), he implies political systems which lay centuries in the future: the *polis* (in which for the first time men could be said to hold citizenship) and, since he is addressing not merely the Ithacans but the entire Greek host, some larger organization besides, such as one of the Hellenistic leagues or a state like Rome with an extensive franchise.

Doubts about these or other particular instances are reasonably entertained. Still, they ought not to prevent us from realizing how pervasive anachronisms are in the *Metamorphoses*. That we are not likely to be too prone to finding them in classical texts is suggested by the evidence of the ancient commentators on Virgil, who show high awareness of them.[4] It is true that these men were pedants, but they were the sort of pedants who taught the appreciation of literature to Roman youth. Thus I suspect that the ordinary, educated

reader shared their attentiveness to such matters. In the case of
Ovid, moreover, a propensity for anachronism fits with other features of his narrative through which mythology is made both human
and contemporary. Furthermore, in a given passage the sheer quantity of anachronism is sometimes persuasive. It is so dense that it
leads us to recognize examples which might otherwise remain doubtful. Thus Ulysses' addressing the assembled Greeks as *cives* may not
seem a startling anachronism, yet it is surrounded by other contemporary touches. For example, arguing in a speech that he, not Ajax,
deserves to receive the armor of Achilles, Ulysses refers to Rhesus'
tents (249); mentions a chariot such as is used in the triumph (252), a
characteristically Roman institution; and accuses Ajax of being an
uncultivated boor who, because he is unfamiliar with great art, does
not even know what the scenes chased on Achilles' shield represent
(290–95). The discernment and discrimination of Ulysses hardly belong in the heroic era; rather, they represent the cultural refinement
of the Augustan age, in which Ovid took such great pleasure. The
poem is filled with such anachronisms.

TECHNIQUES OF PRESENTATION

Sometimes the mere use of a technical term creates an anachronism.
For example, in the battle between the Lapiths and the Centaurs
Ovid arms one warrior with what he calls a *Macedonia sarisa* (12.466).
The *sarisa* is the huge thrusting lance which was characteristic of the
Macedonian phalanx. The term, taken over from Greek, is an unusual one,[5] and the oddity of the weapon's employment in legendary
times is underlined by the adjective. In choosing this word instead of
one of the dozen or so that Latin possesses for "spear" Ovid introduces an anachronism into his account of the battle.

Commonly, the anachronism shrieks at us from the page. Contem-
plating the capture of Thebes by the effete Bacchus and his train,
Pentheus wishes that at least there were a real war and real opponents. He puts it thus:

> si fata vetabant
> stare diu Thebas, utinam tormenta virique
> moenia diruerent!   (3.548–50)

If the fates forbade Thebes to last, would that its walls might
fall to men, to artillery!

He also refers to the trumpet (535), a post-heroic invention. Pentheus' importation of siege engines and trumpets into the era of

Greek mythology is not more remarkable than the reckoning in
Olympiads carried out by one of Circe's maids, who expresses the
fact that Picus could not be even sixteen years old like this: *nec adhuc spectasse per annos / quinquennem poterat Graia quater Elide pugnam*
(14.324–25, "not yet did his age allow him to have witnessed four
times the contest held every fourth year at Elis in Greece"). The
Olympic games were traditionally considered to have begun in 776
B.C., long after the day of Troy's fall. The anachronism in reckoning
by Olympiads here is perhaps rendered more evident by the circum-
locution.

Explaining how Iphis and Ianthe fell in love, Ovid tells us that
they were the same age, they were equally good-looking—and they
went to elementary school together: *primasque magistris / accepere artes, elementa aetatis, ab isdem* (9.718–19, "from the same teachers they
learned the first arts, the fundamentals of education for youth"). Not
only is communal instruction (not to speak of coeducation!) itself a
stark anachronism, but so too is the implied division of it into stages,
presided over in turn by the *magister*, the *grammaticus*, and the *rhetor*.
These Roman institutions have their roots in the Hellenistic age, but
go back no further.[6]

One of the most amusing and most extensive examples of anachronism is the cave of Achelous, a river god in whose abode Theseus
and his companions stop for an all-night banquet. The banquet scene
itself is painted with a number of anachronistic touches: the heroes
recline on couches, are served by barefoot maids, and drink wine out
of a cup made from a jewel (8.566–73). This refinement smacks of
the age of Augustus, not Theseus. Achelous' house is especially
remarkable:

> *pumice multicavo nec levibus atria tophis*
> *structa subit: molli tellus erat umida musco,*
> *summa lacunabant alterno murice conchae.*   (8.562–64)

> Theseus entered the hall, which was built of porous pumice-
> stone and of tufa that was far from smooth; the ground was wet
> with soft moss; cockles alternating with murex formed the ceil-
> ing panels overhead.

A humorous logic dictates the decoration: it is perfectly apt that a
river god carpet his floor with moss and adorn his ceiling with shells.
Anachronism may be suggested by the word *atrium*, which, regard-
less of whether it originally meant "central room" or "entrance,"
belongs to post-epic architecture. However that may be, Achelous'
house is nothing other than a first-century grotto-nympheum, each

one of its features finding close parallels in contemporary construction. A grotto-nympheum was most often a natural formation improved by artifice, like Achelous' cave, sometimes wholly man-made so as to simulate nature.[7] (The Romans evidently enjoyed the mingling of art and nature.) Such a grotto frequently received a coffered ceiling, as does Achelous'. For further simulation clumps of pumice-stone were often applied to the walls,[8] and cockles were in common use—here the rough, spiny shells of the murex set off the smoothness of the others. The face of the real Theseus (even Callimachus' Theseus!) surely would have registered surprise at such a sight. Ovid's readers would have felt at home.

The deliberateness and the pleasure with which the poet narrated anachronistically are suggested by a pair of passages in which the anachronism is combined with learned wit. About Mercury, who is flying over Athens, Ovid says: *despectabat humum cultique arbusta Lycei* (2.710, "he gazed at the Attic soil beneath and the shrubs of the cultivated Lyceum"). Since the Lyceum, a famous place of exercise on the outskirts of the city, was not built until the time of Pisistratus or Pericles, the phrase contains a bold anachronism.[9] But it also contains a fine pun: the word *cultum*, "cultivated," refers both to the shrubs planted in the Lyceum and to the renown of the place as the seat of Aristotle's school.[10] Elsewhere Ovid refers to a mixing bowl given to Aeneas, which *fabricaverat Alcon / Hyleus* (13.683–84, "Alcon of Hyle had made"). Alcon was a well-known metal-working artist who lived probably in Hellenistic times, in any event long after Aeneas' day.[11] Here a literary joke accompanies the anachronism. This historical figure is said to be from Hyle in Boeotia, which was the home of another artisan in metal: Tychios, who, according to Homer (*Il.* 7.220), had made Ajax' famous shield![12]

CONTRAST WITH VIRGIL

As a final example of anachronism let us take the statue of Picus: *niveo factum de marmore signum* (14.313, "a statue made from snow-white marble"). Marble, however early employed, is still foreign to the period of the Trojan war, when the story of Picus is set.[13] It so happens that Virgil also mentions a statue of Picus: it adorns the old temple in which King Latinus receives the Trojan ambassadors. The passage offers a neat contrast to the undisguised anachronism of Ovid's, for there the statue is *effigies . . . / antiqua e cedro* (*Aen.* 7.177–78, "an image of ancient cedar"). In early times, it was known, men had made images of wood;[14] Virgil is aiming at historical accuracy.

In order to appreciate the role which anachronism plays in the *Metamorphoses*, we may set it in relief against the *Aeneid*. Virgil's practice in this matter is opposite to Ovid's. Customarily he is careful to avoid anachronism. Nevertheless, he does have some instances of it, and these, the exceptions to his practice, are especially instructive. Precisely because he *is* ordinarily careful, the exceptions are unlikely to be accidental. If we inquire what motivates Virgil's decision here, we find there are basically two reasons for allowing anachronism, which are quite different from Ovid's. A passage that lends itself as an illustration is Virgil's description of the ancient Italian temple, in which he mentions the wooden statue of Picus (*Aen.* 7.170–91).[15]

The larger group of anachronisms within this passage comprises customs and material objects which, though old, cannot derive from so early a period as the Trojan War. Among cedar images of the native kings is Picus (187–88), who holds both a *lituus* (the rod used by augurs) and an *ancile* (a shield of a particular type, sent to the Romans from heaven), and who is dressed in a *trabea* (a special toga worn by kings, consuls, and certain ancient priesthoods). In the temple, Virgil also tells us, an omen had bidden the kings to raise the first *fasces* (173–74), symbol of royal authority. There too were held sacred banquets at which the elders usually sat through many courses (175–76). All these institutions are ancient, probably belonging to Etruscan usage. Nonetheless, they are in a strict sense anachronisms, since contemporary scholarship recognized that they derived from the time of the Roman kings.[16] Virgil allows them, nonetheless, because they all continued to exist in his own day. Priests still wore the *trabea* and augurs still bore the *lituus*; the consuls, who had replaced the kings, were still preceded by lictors bearing *fasces*; the *ancilia* were still displayed in public processions every March and October. The effect of the passage is complex. Such customs, recognizably ancient, make Virgil's readers aware of the distance between their own time and that remote past in which Latinus and Aeneas lived. The description smacks of bygone days. Yet at the same time there is no sharp break between that past and the present. It is rather the continuity between them that Virgil makes manifest, as befits an epic which is historical and aetiological. His anachronisms, if they can be called such, are barely perceptible. Ovid's, by contrast, are prominent and noticeable.

The *Aeneid* contains another kind of anachronism. In the same passage the poet describes the temple as *centum sublime columnis* (7.170, "raised aloft with a hundred columns"). A temple of this size, rare enough in Augustus' day, was unheard of in Latinus'.[17] Virgil here allows the historical implausibility because it lends dignity and distinction to the subject.[18] In the same way, it has been shown, he violates the customs of the heroic age, as they were portrayed in the Homeric poems, by attributing to mortals a lavish use of gold: Dido's dishes and cups, clothing and ceilings, for instance, are gold (*Aen.* 1.640, 698, 726, 728).[19] This too casts a fabulous light over the heroic age. In general, then, Virgil's anachronisms either make the past seem a grand, venerable period, or they locate in it the origins of the present.[20] Those in the *Metamorphoses*, however, do not arouse wonder or admiration for mythology: they render it familiar.

Before moving ahead let us examine an interesting passage from Book Six which illustrates the close relation between anachronism and the felt presence of the narrator. While giving a list of the Greek cities which sent their kings to Thebes, Ovid makes a telling juxtaposition. On the one hand, he names among the cities *nondum . . . Calydon invisa Dianae* (6.415, "Calydon, not yet hateful to Diana") and *neque adhuc Pittheia Troezen* (418, "Troezen, which was not yet Pittheus' "). The future events he looks forward to in these phrases are Diana's anger at Calydon, which will be motivated by King Oeneus' failure to sacrifice to her (see 8.270–82), and Pittheus' accession to the throne in the next generation (the present episode taking place during the time of his father Pelops). Both these phrases are of a familiar sort. By reminding us of what is going to happen but has not happened yet, they draw attention to the know-it-all narrator. On the other hand, in naming some of the other cities Ovid gives them epithets which are directly anachronistic: *Pelopeiadesque Mycenae* (414, "Pelopid Mycenae") he calls one, although Pelops' descendants, Atreus and Agamemnon, are far from having begun to rule; *nobilis aere Corinthus* (416, "Corinth, famous for its bronze"), although the renowned bronzework of the city is probably not much older than the second century; and *Messeneque ferox* (417, "fierce Messene"), although the fierceness of the Messenians was shown only in historic times, whether exercised against their Lacedaemonian neighbors in the eighth and seventh centuries or, after the city proper had been founded in the fourth century, against the sieges maintained by Demetrius, Philip V, and Nabis in the late third and early second centuries. The collocation of the anachronisms and the phrases with "not yet" is very suggestive. Ultimately, it tells us, no great difference exists between these two phenomena of the poem. Combined, they show that for the narrator only his own present is real; everything is seen from this one point of view. The reader is reminded that both teller and tale are contemporary and accessible.

Romanization

Not always easy to distinguish from anachronism is Romanization, the narrating of mythological tales as if they were taking place in the Roman world instead of a Greek or vaguely legendary one. Ovid lays a contemporary color over his stories by references to names and institutions that belong to Roman political, social, or private life.[21] Many of these, of course, are at the same time anachronisms: since Rome evolved only after the heroic age of Greece, displacements in time and in space overlap. There is little need to distinguish between them. They are different aspects of Ovid's drive to represent myth in everyday terms.

Let us first look at some brief examples of this device with which Ovid peppers his text.

Jupiter at one point urges Venus to go consult the *rerum tabularium* (15.810, "the Archive Office of history"); the Tabularium was the building in Rome where the national records were kept. We may contrast this with the *Aeneid*, in which at an exactly similar moment the king of the gods says to his daughter that he will tell her the future, *volvens fatorum arcana* (*Aen*. 1.262, "unrolling the hidden secrets of fate"): the phrase suggests the opening of a scroll, yet it is not specifically Roman in reference.

Several times in Ovid the technical term *ambire* is applied to mythological episodes. The word, drawn from Roman political life, means "to canvass, seek the (electoral) support of." In an attempt to have her son Aeneas deified, *ambieratque Venus superos* (14.585, "Venus had canvassed the gods"); her campaign succeeded, of course. And Ulysses contrives to suggest that Thetis acquired divine armor for Achilles in the manner of a Roman politician seeking election: *pro nato caerula mater / ambitiosa suo fuit* (13.288–89, "the sea-blue mother went about canvassing on behalf of her son"). Another example with *ambire* is found at 9.432.

The term for "electoral defeat" is *repulsa*, and the Sun, telling Phaethon that he can ask for anything he wants, puts it like this: *nullam patiere repulsam* (2.97, "you will experience no rejection").

Similarly the triumphal procession, that peculiarly Roman institution, makes several appearances in Ovid's pages. Ulysses, boasting of how he had captured Rhesus' horses and chariot, describes the latter as *curru laetos imitante triumphos* (13.252, "a chariot like those used in joyous triumphs"). Issuing from the mouth of the narrator himself, this comparison would have been unremarkable; from one of his characters, it is striking. In a later passage Iphis, desperate because unsuccessful in his suit for Anaxarete, concedes victory to her thus: *laetos molire triumphos / et Paeana voca nitidaque incingere lauru!* (14.719–20, "set in train your joyous triumph, give the shout of victory, wreathe your brow with shining laurel!"). The accompanying details make it plain that here, as in the other passage, *triumphus* means the triumphal procession itself (cf. *Am.* 1.7.35–40).[22]

From public life again comes the distinctively Roman notion of *bellum iustum*, "the just war," which is twice applied to Minos' campaign of revenge. *Iusta gerit certe pro nato bella perempto* (8.58, "surely he is waging a just war on behalf of his murdered son"), someone remarks. And both the thought and the Roman form of expression are repeated in *necem iustis ulciscitur armis* (7.458, "with just arms he avenges the slaying").

Mythological figures are made to follow the customs of Roman private life also. Ovid describes a pet deer that wears not only necklaces and earrings but even a *bulla*, a drop-shaped locket:

> *bulla super frontem parvis argentea loris*
> *vincta movebatur parilique aetate.* (10.114–15)

Upon its forehead swung a *bulla*, tied by a small cord; it was made of silver and was of the same age as the deer.

The *bulla* was a sign of freeborn status among the Romans. Frequently made of precious metal, it was worn from birth until the beginning of manhood. This adds another touch of Romanness to the narrative. Ovid's model for the animal is the deer whose death sparks the warfare between Trojans and Italians in the *Aeneid* (7.483–92). It too is quasi-human: it wears garlands among its horns, allows itself to be combed, washed, and patted, even comes to table. But Ovid goes a step beyond Virgil by rendering the pet in a specifically Roman guise.

Like anachronism, Romanization is several times combined with humor in a way that makes us feel how conscious and careful the poet was in this matter. The poverty of a fisherman is described thus: *ars illi sua census erat* (3.588, "his art was his census," that is, his only wealth lay in his skill as a fisherman). The reference to the census is an instance of Ovid's Romanizing mythology. The census was the quinquennial revision of the citizen-rolls, which among other things rated each citizen's property. By extension the word *census* came to mean "wealth" or "property" as well, the sense it bears in our passage (cf. 8.846, 9.671, 15.422; *Fast.* 1.217–18). Here this amounts to an ironic joke, since the point is the man's poverty.[23]

A similar combination is found in another passage, when Nessus, ferrying Hercules' bride across the river, attempts to carry her off:

> *Nessoque paranti*
> *fallere depositum "quo te fiducia" clamat*
> *"vana pedum, violente, rapit? . . .*
> *. . . exaudi, nec res intercipe nostras!"*   (9.119–22)

As Nessus prepared to cheat him of his deposit, Hercules cried out: "Violent man, to what length does this vain trust in your feet carry you? . . . Listen to me: do not usurp my property!"

The language of Roman law is echoed in the words "cheat of his deposit," "trust," and "usurp." In this Roman touch there is also some humor, for by the standard of objective realism it is incongruous that at so critical a moment Hercules should resort to such formal language. The same is true of Orpheus' plea made before the gods of the Underworld in order to win back Eurydice: *iuris erit vestri: pro munere poscimus usum* (10.37, "she will be your possession: I ask only for the granting of usufruct"). Passages like these make it hard to believe that the Romanization of mythology is a casual feature of Ovid's presentation.[24]

As a splendid final example, and one that also offers the chance of a comparison with Virgil, we may turn to the assembly of the gods in Book One, which Ovid makes appear to be a session of the Roman Senate. He first describes the neighborhood the gods pass through on their way to Jupiter's house, where the meeting is to be held.

> *hac iter est superis ad magni tecta Tonantis*
> *regalemque domum: dextra laevaque deorum*
> *atria nobilium valvis celebrantur apertis.*
> *plebs habitat diversa locis: hac parte potentes*
> *caelicolae clarique suos posuere penates.*   (1.170–74)

Up this way [the Milky Way] lies the gods' path to the royal palace, the home of the great Thunderer. On the right and the left the atria of the noble gods, their doors flung open, are teeming. The plebeians dwell elsewhere: in this quarter the famous and powerful divinities have established their household gods.

It is hardly necessary to list the details through which the poet renders this scene Roman, and very contemporary Roman at that: the royal palace set on a hill, the atria, the society divided into classes, the marked social character of the different quarters of the city, the swarms of people flocking to the homes of the magnates (to court their favor, no doubt). And though the word *penates*, "household gods," is often used by metonymy for the house itself, its basic meaning shows through sufficiently here to spark a witty notion: even the gods have household gods! Just in case we failed to catch the reference to contemporary Rome, Ovid steps out of the narrative to make this clear:

> *hic locus est quem, si verbis audacia detur,*
> *haud timeam magni dixisse Palatia caeli.*   (1.175–76)

> This is the place which, should the boldness of the expression
> be permitted, I would not hesitate to call the Palatine of mighty
> heaven.

The coloring of the whole passage is summarized here and, let us note, again combined with reference to the narrator.

With the gods assembled, the meeting itself begins. Whether imagined as held in the imperial palace itself or in the marble temple of Apollo nearby[25]—Augustus used both places—it resembles a session of the Roman Senate. The presiding magistrate sits on a raised platform (178). At the end of his speech, which deals with the crimes and transformation of Lycaon, he offers a formal resolution (242–43). The response from the other gods is recognizable:

> *dicta Iovis pars voce probant stimulosque frementi*
> *adiciunt, alii partes adsensibus implent.*   (1.244–45)

> Some of them voice their approval of Jove's words and urge on
> his indignant complaint; others play their part by applauding.

These gods bear a close likeness to the sycophantic, dissembling Senate of the early Empire which Tacitus was to describe. Again Ovid calls attention to the parallel, this time through a simile: he compares the outcry of the gods when they heard of Lycaon's attack upon Jupiter to the outcry of all the world at the attempt once made on Augustus' life (1.199–205).[26] The notion that governs this passage recurs later when, at another assembly of the gods, Venus is said to rise from her seat *media . . . sede senatus* (15.843, "in the middle of a session of the Senate").

Ovid's tendency to Romanize mythology appears more distinctly if we contrast this same scene with an assembly of the gods in Book Ten of the *Aeneid*.[27] There the gods come not to the Palatine Hill of heaven, but *sideream in sedem* (*Aen.* 10.3, "to the starry abode"), a vague phrase. They sit down *tectis bipatentibus* (10.5, "in a hall with doors at both ends"), which is unlikely to have summoned up a definitely Roman image.[28] Later, after hearing the speeches of Venus and Juno, Virgil's gods react, like Ovid's, in different ways: *cunctique fremebant / caelicolae adsensu vario* (10.96–97, "all the divinities murmured their varying assent"). Here again there is nothing specifically Roman, and the simile that follows is drawn from nature, not recent history. Finally the meeting is over:

> *solio tum Iuppiter aureo*
> *surgit, caelicolae medium quem ad limina ducunt.*   (*Aen.* 10.116–17)

Then Jupiter arises from the golden throne; the gods conduct him in their midst to the threshold.

In escorting Jupiter the gods act very respectfully, to be sure, but, despite a suggestion made by Servius, their behavior is not specifically Roman.[29] As Romanization is basically foreign to the *Aeneid*, so it is characteristic of the *Metamorphoses*.

Modernization

Anachronism and Romanization are only the narrowest, most readily recognized forms of a general phenomenon of the poem. Many scenes from the *Metamorphoses* are made contemporary in ways less easy to notice or define. A word, a pair of stray details, or something almost intangible about the tone often creates a feeling of modernity. These little touches are found again and again, far more often than the two particular forms we have just looked at—indeed, one might say, in virtually every passage. Cumulatively they have a powerful effect: the stories of the poem seem drawn from ordinary, everyday, humdrum life, not from the distant realms of mythology.

A single word sometimes suffices. When sacrificing a cow to Pallas, Achilles, so we are told, *inposuit prosecta calentibus aris* (12.152, "placed the entrails on the burning altar"). *Prosecta*, which originally meant only "things cut off," became a technical term of Roman religion in the special sense "parts of the animal cut off for sacrifice." As such the word throws a contemporary Roman coloring over the sacrifice, which otherwise is Homeric. To similar effect Ovid employs the verb *invergere*, a technical term at Roman libations:[30] *invergens liquidi carchesia vini* (7.246, "tipping out cups of clear wine").

Sometimes it is rather the ensemble of details which makes the picture, as when Ovid describes the bath of Diana, in the course of which she will be seen by Actaeon:

> *nympharum tradidit uni*
> *armigerae iaculum pharetramque arcusque retentos;*
> *altera depositae subiecit bracchia pallae;*
> *vincla duae pedibus demunt; nam doctior illis*
> *Ismenis Crocale sparsos per colla capillos*
> *colligit in nodum, quamvis erat ipsa solutis.*
> *excipiunt laticem Nepheleque Hyaleque Rhanisque*
> *et Psecas et Phiale funduntque capacibus urnis.*   (3.165–72)

To one of her weapon-bearing nymphs Diana hands over the
spear, quiver, and bow she had been holding. Another catches
up in her arms the cloak she has laid aside. Two more remove
the sandals from her feet. Boeotian Crocale, more skillful than
these, binds up into a knot the hair that lies scattered along
Diana's neck—though her own hair is down. Nephele, Hyale
and Rhanis, Psecas and Phiale scoop up the water and pour it
out from capacious pitchers.

The emphasis here on the domestic and familiar is secured in part by
the economy of narrative: even within a rather leisurely account this
scene is relatively long. Moreover, though lacking any precise word
or reference that would more easily identify a feature of Roman political or religious practice, it yet with small touches evokes a clear
image of domestic life. Diana appears to be a grand Roman matron,
with a large number of servants in her retinue. The observation that
Crocale, though uncombed herself, does up her mistress's hair suggests the subjection of the one to the other. And to point out that
she is more skillful than the other girls is to imply a hierarchy even
among the attendants.[31] All in all, a recognizable situation. Similar is
the domestic scene (14.260–70) of the sorceress Circe, sitting among a
bevy of her maids, all intent not on spinning and weaving, but on
the preparation of magical potions.[32] The atrium of her home is marble, and, as in a large Roman household, servants conduct the guests
into the mistress's presence;[33] these details contribute to the general
effect of the scene's being set in the present, not in mythological
times. Ovid's "Circaean walls" may belong as much to Latium as to
Never-Never Land.

A description of the same sort, that scarcely calls for comment, is
of the female centaur Hylonome, who retains the love of Cyllaron in
several ways and

> *cultu quoque, quantus in illis*
> *esse potest membris, ut sit coma pectine levis,*

ut modo rore maris, modo se violave rosave
inplicet, interdum candentia lilia gestet,
bisque die lapsis Pagasaeae vertice silvae
fontibus ora lavet, bis flumine corpora tingat,
nec nisi quae deceant electarumque ferarum
aut umero aut lateri praetendat vellera laevo.   (12.408–15)

also by the care she took—as much as was possible in those
limbs! Her hair she smoothed with a comb. Now she entwined
rosemary in it, now violets or roses; sometimes she carried daz-
zling white lilies. Twice a day she washed her face with the
streams that fall from the summit of the Pagasaean wood; twice
a day she bathed her body in the river. The skins which she
strung over her left shoulder or side were only those which
came from choice animals and were becoming to her.

The description is found in the middle of the epic battle between the
Lapiths and Centaurs; immediately after, the loving pair of centaurs
are slain. The *Iliad* contains passages like this, in which bloody battle scenes are interspersed with others that remind us of peace and
domestic tenderness (e.g., 6.237–529, 11.221–30). Here too this contrasting scene is poignant. Still, as often in Ovid, the tender is tinged
with the grotesque. The poet, whose devotion to *cultus* is notorious,[34] in the opening verses calls attention to the incongruity of a
centaur whose toilet is so careful. And he stresses it more by combining obvious fastidiousness with a style of dress that is recognizably
barbarian: the historian Tacitus (*Germ.* 17) records that the women of
the Germans selected skins carefully and dressed so as to leave one
side bare. Whatever else he achieves here, Ovid is also rendering
fabulous mythology familiar.

There is no need to adduce many more examples; each reader can
find enough for himself. Bernbeck gives an unusually fine, clear
analysis of the Underworld according to Ovid (4.432–46). His is
the first Underworld to be represented as a city, complete with a
thronged forum and a royal palace. The dead, naturally enough, had
trouble finding their way down—they had never been there before,
and the path, of course, was dark! Once arrived, they engage in the
same trades as before. And indeed—Ovid throws this in at the very
end, nearly as an afterthought—some of them are punished.[35] Here
again the contemporizing of mythology provokes humor. In Nicander (apud Ant. Lib. 17) the goddess responsible for metamorphosing
Iphis into a lad is Leto; Ovid exchanges her for Isis (9.687), whose
worship was very popular in Rome during his own day. Bothe makes

an acute observation about the orations which Ajax and Ulysses deliver during the dispute over Achilles' arms. Ajax, he notes, talks like a tribune of the plebs, in a style which is plain and simple and seems to spring directly from his character; whereas Ulysses' speech is that of a senator speaking to patricians and enhancing his elevated language with every device of rhetorical art. Not surprisingly, the majority approve of the former speech, but the latter wins the votes of the chiefs.[36] No political significance is to be read into this. Ovid simply paints the two opponents to represent contrasting political, social, and rhetorical positions of his day.

Two last passages deserve special mention because they are different in form. Pythagoras is reciting a list of cities which once were great but have now declined:

> Oedipodioniae quid sunt, nisi nomina, Thebae?
> quid Pandioniae restant, nisi nomen, Athenae?   (15.429–30)

What is the Thebes of Oedipus but a name? What but a name does the Athens of Pandion remain?

The philosopher commits a stupendous error, for in his day, the late sixth century, Thebes and Athens, far from being over the hill, were nearing the acme of their greatness. Instead, the statement fits Ovid's own time, when Thebes was no longer a city worthy of mention, and Athens had sunk to a mecca for sightseers and university students.[37] Back near the beginning of the poem Ovid had made the opposite, complementary "error." In a passage there he set not Athens' decline, but its wealth and its intellectual and artistic greatness, at far too early a date: in the age of Aglauros the city was "flourishing with talent and riches" (2.795). In both cases Ovid presents his material from a strictly contemporary point of view.

Gods and Things Humanized

GODS

The poet renders mythology familiar in other ways as well. Not only does he compress the dimensions both of time and space, but he also forces all the animate creatures, gods and men, onto the same level. As everything is here and now, so everything is human. The gods, in all their higher senses and functions, are removed from mythology. By "higher senses and functions" I mean the use of the gods by earlier writers to represent anything in the universe that was greater than the individual: truth, morality, fate, reason, justice, history, society, beauty, even (as sometimes in Euripides) chance or violence. In the *Metamorphoses* the gods do not stand for any such abstractions (which are altogether foreign to the poem). When they appear, they act just like men, men who happen to have greater powers and unending lives in which to exercise them.

This negative proposition, that the gods in all elevated senses are absent, is not easily proved. Proof of it is not required here, however, since it has been recognized so often as to be a commonplace of criticism.[38] Nevertheless, it is possible, if not to demonstrate, then at least to illustrate this feature of the poem in several ways. A comparison with Virgil, to begin with, does this handily. In the *Aeneid* the hero receives from Helenus an important prophecy, in which the will of the gods is revealed as guiding the Trojans' wanderings. Characteristic of Virgil's Helenus are sentences like *sic fata deum rex / sortitur* (*Aen.* 3.375–76, "thus does the king of the gods allot the fates"), and the moving *fata viam invenient aderitque vocatus Apollo* (3.395, "the fates will find a way, and Apollo, when summoned, will be present to help"). By linking gods with fate and making them the guarantors of what is destined, namely, that the Trojans will reach Italy and become the Romans, Virgil gives to his story a tremendous importance: the "historical" adventures of Aeneas, and Roman history generally, are not simply events of local and temporary significance, but have become part of the divine scheme of the universe, indeed the central element in that scheme. At the corresponding place in the *Metamorphoses* Ovid's Helenus mentions in his prophecy neither fate nor god. For him there exists no superhuman cause but happenstance:

> . . . *donec Troiaeque tibique*
> *externum patria contingat amicius arvum.*   (15.442–43)

. . . until there befall to Troy and to you a foreign field more hospitable than your homeland.

Contingere ("befall") is the key word here. In Ovid, fate and divinity, which had formed in Virgil that upper realm of existence which gave meaning to his own, have been completely edged out of the picture.

This can also be illustrated through a series of passages in which Ovid places his gods on the same level as material objects or men. The equation, felt with greater or lesser force, relieves divinity of any higher sense. Venus at one point complains that she has seen her son Aeneas *bellaque cum Turno gerere, aut, si vera fatemur, / cum Iunone magis* (15.773–74, "wage war against Turnus, or rather, to tell the truth, against Juno"). The phrase with *aut*, which arises as an afterthought, and the little parenthetic remark give to these words the tone of ordinary, casual conversation, and the tone fits with the relation implied between man and god. In the *Aeneid* Juno had been the divinity who led the opposition to Aeneas and the Trojans. Nevertheless, neither she nor any of the other chief gods was accustomed to appear and intervene directly in the affairs of men. Gods and men dealt with one another, but were kept apart on separate planes. Hierarchy reigns in the *Aeneid*. Here, however, Ovid's Venus, in saying "against Turnus, or rather against Juno," places Juno on the same level as Turnus. There is no longer a clear distinction between the divine and the human. The gods have come to rest on earth.[39]

Elsewhere Ovid conveys the same by means of a kind of zeugma, by setting the gods into an unexpected parallelism. In Book Thirteen, for instance, Ajax recounts thus the Trojan attack on the ships:

ecce ferunt Troes ferrumque ignesque Iovemque
in Danaas classes.   (13.91–92)

Look! The Trojans are bringing sword, fire, and Jupiter against the Greek fleet.

The sense might be rendered "the Trojans attack with fire and sword, with the aid of their gods." Yet the precise phrasing "sword, fire, and Jupiter" almost suggests that Jupiter is something material and tangible.[40] Later, in his answering speech, Ulysses returns to the point and uses a similar zeugma: *arma tulisse refert contra Troasque Iovemque* (13.269, "he claims he bore arms against the Trojans and Jupiter"). Again, we are made to feel that the gods are not lofty, superior beings.

An outstanding instance of what might be called "reduction by zeugma" is found in a description of the stubborn war being waged between the Trojans and Rutulians: *habetque deos pars utraque, quodque deorum est / instar, habent animos* (14.568–69, "each side has gods and, what is equivalent to gods, it has courage"). This is especially probative because the equation of the two parallel members, gods and courage, is made fully explicit. The phrase, which declares courage the equivalent of divine assistance, hints that the latter may be merely a name covering the former. Divinity in effect is rationalized away.

We may confirm the proposition, finally, by glancing at two examples of irony which Ovid directs at the notion that the gods represent something or other significant. In Book Ten Orpheus strikes the chords of his lyre and starts to sing. "Begin my song, o Muse, with Jupiter," he says (10.148–49). The topos *ab Iove principium* is both old and widespread in classical poetry, and it is regularly a solemn one.[41] A typical instance of its use is found in Aratus' *Phaenomena*, a Hellenistic poem about the stars, the beginning of which may be paraphrased thus: "Both human life and the world of nature are full of Zeus. We always need him. We are his offspring. He gives us useful signs, which he set in heaven. All hail Zeus!" Jupiter's importance in Aratus contrasts markedly with Ovid's employment of the topos. When Orpheus asks that his song begin with Jupiter, he means it literally: he announces that his poem is going to be a series of homosexual love stories, and the first example he cites is the king of the gods himself, who once raped Ganymede. *Ab Iove principium* indeed! The ironic twist given to the topos is a clue to Ovid's revised notion of divinity. His Jupiter is no principle permeating the universe, no source of life, no benefactor of humankind—just a fellow in love.

The other passage occurs in the story of Byblis. Possessed by love for her brother, this young woman delivers herself of a monologue in which she swings back and forth between resisting her passion and yielding to it. At one moment she is pondering a dream she has had of sexual relations with her brother:

> quod autem
> somnia pondus habent?—an habent et somnia pondus?
> di melius!—di nempe suas habuere sorores:
> sic Saturnus Opem iunctam sibi sanguine duxit,
> Oceanus Tethyn, Iunonem rector Olympi.   (9.495–99)

But what importance do dreams have?—Or *do* dreams have importance, in fact? May the gods forbid!—The gods, why, *they* have had their own sisters: Saturn married Ops, who was a blood relation; Oceanus married Tethys; and the ruler of heaven, Juno.

Her thought pivoting on the colloquial exclamation *di melius!* ("may the gods forbid!"), Byblis comes to the reflection that the gods themselves justify incest.[42] As she puts it later: *sequimur magnorum exempla deorum* (9.555, "I follow the example of the mighty gods"). Such sophistic use of the mythological gods, which, to be sure, is not unknown before Ovid, bespeaks the loss of any moral content.[43] This pair of ironic comments helps us to see what Jupiter, Juno, and the others are *not*. In the *Metamorphoses* there are plenty of gods, but no divinities. Those larger spheres of meaning which the gods represented for Sophocles, Aratus, or Virgil are altogether missing in Ovid.

The remainder from this subtraction is simply figured. Shorn of their "higher" attributes, the gods become mere men. This possibility had always been implicit in the anthropomorphic representation of the gods which had characterized Greco-Roman mythology, and it had sometime before been realized, yet Ovid carries it further than previous writers. His insistence on such a representation is remarkable. Naturally, so prominent a feature of the poem has not escaped notice.[44] Since this is so and we have already seen several instances, it should be sufficient to quote just a few more examples here.

In a pretty passage from Book Two, Mercury, alighting on earth in order to pursue Herse, primps like a teenager before a big date on Saturday night:

> nec se dissimulat: tanta est fiducia formae.
> quae quamquam iusta est, cura tamen adiuvat illam,
> permulcetque comas chlamydemque, ut pendeat apte,
> collocat, ut limbus totumque adpareat aurum,
> ut teres in dextra, qua somnos ducit et arcet,
> virga sit, ut tersis niteant talaria plantis.   (2.731–36)

He does not disguise himself, so great is his confidence in his own beauty. Yet, though the confidence is justified, he enhances his beauty through the pains he takes. He combs his hair, and drapes his cloak so it hangs just so and the fringe and all the gold embroidery can be seen. In his right hand the wand with which he brings on sleep or keeps it off is polished. The wings gleam on his well-scrubbed feet.

Every brushstroke tells, as the poet portrays an Olympian deity as an eager, human adolescent.

Elsewhere the entire company of gods is moved by quite a different emotion: the desire for material honors, or rather the fear of losing them. Jupiter has just announced his intention of extirpating mankind. The other gods respond: rogant, quis sit laturus in aras / tura (1.248–49, "who, they ask, will bring incense to their altars?"). Jupiter assuages their anxieties and then unleashes the flood.

In the next book the world is in danger of being destroyed in a different way. Phaethon, falling from the chariot of the sun, has set the heavens ablaze and now threatens the earth. Jupiter decides to save the situation by intervening:

sed neque, quas posset terris inducere, nubes
tunc habuit nec, quos caelo demitteret, imbres.   (2.309–10)

But at the time he had neither clouds to cover the earth nor
rains to send down from heaven.

The king of the skies and the weather temporarily lacks two of his
chief attributes. (He uses his thunderbolt.) The reader is led to wonder whether Jupiter more closely resembles an omnipotent divinity
or a general whose supply lines have been cut.

Our last example concerns Callisto, a nymph in Diana's entourage
who has been made pregnant by Jupiter. She gives clues to her condition through her silence and her blushes:

et, nisi quod virgo est, poterat sentire Diana
mille notis culpam: nymphae sensisse feruntur.   (2.451–52)

And by a thousand signs Diana might have realized Callisto's
crime, were it not that she herself was a virgin: the other
nymphs, they say, realized it.

In other words, it takes one to know one! This piece of eminently
human psychology is transferred to Diana. Where has divine omni-
science gone? And what shall we say about the implication of the
nymphs' knowledge? Here again divinity is rendered human and
familiar. The instances of this must number in the scores.

SPLIT DIVINITY

Another feature of Ovid's representation of the gods is closely related to this; it is merely a particular form that it takes. At the same
time that his gods are men, they yet retain some measure of their
divine powers or functions, if not their majesty. By rubbing these two
sides of their existence against one another Ovid often produces humor. A classic example is found in Book One. As a divinity Apollo is
the god of oracles. As a man he is ill-starred in love: though he
desires Daphne, he does not know he is going to be disappointed.
Ovid brings these together in the wonderful phrase *suaque oracula*
fallunt (1.491, "his own oracles deceive him"). This phenomenon too,
which I call the "split divinity joke," has often been described by
others.[45] For us the important point is that this is another, common
way in which Ovid's humanizing of the gods manifests itself.

An extended example arises in the song which one of the Minyads
sings about the Sun. He is in love with Leucothoe. The poet, describ-

ing his passion, plays on his double existence as a person and a
natural phenomenon:

> quid nunc, Hyperione nate,
> forma colorque tibi radiataque lumina prosunt?
> nempe, tuis omnes qui terras ignibus uris,
> ureris igne novo, quique omnia cernere debes,
> Leucothoen spectas et virgine figis in una,
> quos mundo debes, oculos. modo surgis Eoo
> temperius caelo, modo serius incidis undis
> spectandique mora brumales porrigis horas.   (4.192–99)

Of what use to you now, son of Hyperion, your beauty, your
color, your radiant light? For you who burn the whole earth
with your flames are burned yourself with a new flame. You
who should see everything gaze at Leucothoe; you have eyes
only for one girl, instead of the universe, as you ought. Too
early you arise in the eastern sky, too late you set in the water;
by lingering to look you lengthen the winter hours.

The joke is not confined to the more important gods like Apollo or
the Sun. It is found with minor divinities as well, water nymphs for
instance: nymphae quoque flere videntur / siccatosque queri fontes (13.689–
90, "the nymphs also appear to weep and to complain that their
springs have run dry")—a delightful picture in which the existence
of naturally flowing streams is combined with the notions that divine
spirits shed the streams as tears and complain thereby that they are
being drained. Ovid rings a clever change on this idea when he elsewhere represents sea nymphs "drying their green hair" (2.12). Since
they are inhabitants of the sea, their hair is green and ever wet; since
they are women concerned for their appearance, they are drying it.
Ceres, offended at Erysichthon and eager to have Hunger punish
him, is constrained to employ a messenger: neque enim Cereremque
Famemque / fata coire sinunt (8.785–86, "for the fates do not permit
Ceres and Hunger to meet"). Ovid plays on their being both people,
governed by a code of social decorum, and abstract principles which
logically exclude one another. A similar split is indicated for Mount
Tmolus, near Sardis in Asia Minor, who is asked to judge a musical
contest between Pan and Apollo: monte suo senior iudex consedit et
aures / liberat arboribus (11.157–58, "as umpire the old man took his
seat on his own mountain and unstopped his ears by removing the
trees"). The humor here is very broad.[46] The joke even extends to a
so-called allegorical figure like Sleep, who is fast asleep, of course,

when Iris arrives at his house, but slowly awakens. As Ovid puts it: *excussit tandem sibi se* (11.621, "at long last he shook himself from himself"). Over a wide range of objects and in a great variety of tones, the split divinity joke recurs throughout the text, a constant reminder of the gods' status in the poem.

THE INANIMATE

Ovid portrays as people not only divine beings but, at the other end of the spectrum, inanimate objects as well. The same view of the world which renders gods human also is inclined to personify things which are ordinarily regarded as abstract or lifeless. Ovid tends to move everything downward or upward onto the plane of the human. It matters little, therefore, whether some of the examples just cited, which may seem only marginally divine, belong there or here. Beside the personifications of springs, mountains,[47] and sleep, we find others, such as of the trees and rivers that joined in the mourning over Orpheus:

> positis te frondibus arbor
> tonsa comas luxit; lacrimis quoque flumina dicunt
> increvisse suis.   (11.46–48)

The trees, shaving off their hair by laying aside their leafage, mourned you, and the rivers too, they say, were swollen with their own tears.

Similarly in Book Two, when Phaethon comes to visit his father, the Sun, Ovid describes among the latter's attendants the four seasons, each one a woman garbed to represent an appropriate activity: Summer is naked but wears a crown of wheat-ears, Autumn is dusky with trodden grapes, and so on (2.27–30). And later, when Phaethon, unable to handle his father's team and chariot, runs amok through heaven, the constellations react like people:

> tum primum radiis gelidi caluere Triones
> et vetito frustra temptarunt aequore tingi.   (2.171–72)

Then for the first time the cold Bears [a northern constellation] were warmed by the rays of the sun, and in vain did they try to plunge into the ocean, which is forbidden.[48]

This form of representation, which is common in Ovid, is not unique to him. Again, however, it is the *degree* to which he personifies things that marks him off from his predecessors. A comparison with Virgil makes this clear.[49] Each poet is describing the dawn.

Aurora interea miseris mortalibus almam
extulerat lucem, referens opera atque labores.   (*Aen.* 11.182–83)

Dawn in the meantime had brought forth the nourishing light for unhappy mortals, bringing back tasks and toils.

admonitorque operum caelo clarissimus alto
Lucifer ortus erat.   (*Met.* 4.664–65)

And the Light-bringer, recaller of men to their tasks, had arisen clear in the lofty sky.

In Virgil the rising of the sun leads men directly to return to their labors; the two events are bound together. Ovid puts some distance between the events: he personifies the dawn through the agent noun *admonitor* ("recaller") and makes its consequences less direct by having it *remind* mankind of tasks instead of simply bringing them on. The personification in the *Aeneid* is moderate and less remarkable.[50] Ovid's steady inclination to represent things as human constitutes an essential element of his imagination.

Intra-mythological References

As part of his program—if one can associate our poet with such a word—of making myth familiar and turning it to a new purpose, Ovid strives to block any grand claims that had been made or might be made in its behalf. A natural opponent of abstract scheme and lofty system, he takes measures to prevent us from attaching any general significance or special prestige to mythology. A conspicuous feature in the narrative works toward this end. Again and again Ovid takes two facts of mythology which ordinarily are not related to one another and joins them in some new and unexpected fashion. Circe, for instance, is the daughter of the Sun; and as a sorceress she has the traditional power of altering the course of nature. Ovid brings these together when he reports that by her magical incantations she was accustomed both to darken the face of the moon and *patrio capiti . . . subtexere nubes* (14.368, "to cover with clouds her father's face"). This I call an "intra-mythological reference." These references are often witty, of course, and indicate Ovid's irreverent stance towards mythology, but their effect extends beyond this. The accumulated instances convey the sense that for Ovid mythology as a system or network has become a kind of game in which the player is to draw as many connecting lines as possible between the given "facts." The ease of manipulation suggests that mythology can be anything you want it to be.

In Book Two, Jupiter, when dispatching Mercury on a mission, tells him that his destination is the Phoenician city of Sidon, which Jupiter identifies as *quaeque tuam matrem tellus a parte sinistra / suspicit* (2.839–40, "the land which looks up at your mother from the left"). Ovid combines here narrative requirement (Mercury has to be sent to Sidon) with the mythological fact that Mercury's mother is Maia, one of the Pleiads, a southern constellation. Given the mythological background, it is a flawless piece of logic to describe the place thus. And yet to do this is to remind the reader how much mythology can be made into a form of discourse that refers to itself.

Let us look at some further examples. Jason promises marriage to Medea, whose grandfather is the Sun, and he affirms his promise with an oath taken *perque patrem soceri cernentem cuncta futuri* (7.96, "by the all-seeing father of his father-in-law-to-be"). As wife of Jupiter, though not the mother of his children Apollo and Diana, whom he had by Latona instead, Juno is called the "stepmother" of the two young divinities (6.336). Elsewhere Neptune urges Apollo to slay Achilles; he agrees, says Ovid, *animo pariter patruique suoque / . . . indulgens* (12.597–98, "yielding equally to his uncle's wishes and his own"). It is the truth, of course, that Neptune is Apollo's uncle, and yet it is one we are never reminded of. Drowning at sea in a storm, Ceyx *socerumque patremque / invocat* (11.561–62, "invokes his father-in-law and father"): Aeolus, father of Ceyx' wife and king of the winds, might halt the storm; Ceyx' own father, Lucifer, might bring daylight and salvation. A delightful example is found near the end of the poem. When Julius Caesar is about to be assassinated, Venus attempts to cloak him in the very same cloud with which she had cloaked both Paris, when snatching him away from Menelaus, and Aeneas, when rescuing him from Diomedes (15.804–6). Ovid somewhat incongruously relates two episodes from the *Iliad* with a recent political event; the cloud which forms the link has become almost a prop of mythological action.[51]

As with epigrammatic utterances, so too with intra-mythological references many of the finest examples are given to characters within the stories. Ovid is fond of having a speaker who is arguing a case appeal to mythology himself. Since here mythological figures are

themselves bending mythology to their own purposes, these instances perhaps even more than the others make us feel that mythology is a playground open to all. When Thebes is attacked by
Bacchus and his followers, Pentheus, the king of the city, exhorts his
men to vigorous action by reminding them that they are descended
from the dragon whom Cadmus had slain:

> este, precor, memores, qua sitis stirpe creati,
> illiusque animos, qui multos perdidit unus,
> sumite serpentis! pro fontibus ille lacuque
> interiit: at vos pro fama vincite vestra!   (3.543–46)

Remember, I beg you, from what stock you have been created,
and pluck up the courage of that serpent who, though all
alone, slew many. He died for the sake of his pond and springs:
you be victorious for the sake of your fame!

Similarly, when Hercules sees Nessus about to rape his wife, he
threatens him by reminding him of his father Ixion, who, for having
made an attempt on Juno, is punished in the Underworld by being
fixed on an ever-spinning wheel:

> si te nulla mei reverentia movit, at orbes
> concubitus vetitos poterant inhibere paterni.   (9.123–24)

If you were not moved by any respect for me, still your father's
rotations might have checked your unlawful desires.

The combination of Nessus' parentage with his crime is novel and
striking. In Book Ten Orpheus pleads before Pluto and Proserpina
that Eurydice be restored to him. To emphasize the power of love
he cites as an example his present judges: famaque si veteris non est
mentita rapinae, / vos quoque iunxit Amor (10.28–29, "if the report of
that long-ago rape is not wrong, Love joined you two also"). This is
an ingenious reference to the story of Pluto's carrying off Proserpina.

Not averse to repeating a clever remark, Ovid has Medea refer to
her ancestry. Of her magical powers she boasts: currus quoque carmine
nostro / pallet avi (7.208–9, "even grandfather's chariot grows pale at
my spell"). Anius, addressing Anchises, refers to "the birds of your
wife," that is, the doves of Venus (13.673–74). Polyphemus, the son
of Neptune, while wooing the sea nymph Galatea, makes this pitch:
adde, quod in vestro genitor meus aequore regnat: / hunc tibi do socerum!
(13.854–55, "remember too that my father is king over your waters:
this is the man I'll make your father-in-law!")—an amusing (though
unsuccessful) plea, made possible by the poet's freedom of move-

ment within mythology. It recalls a point scored by Ajax in the contest over Achilles' armor: to demonstrate his superiority he reminds the audience that his grandfather Aeacus is Judge of the Underworld, whereas Ulysses' father, Sisyphus, is one of the notorious sinners punished there (13.25–26). It is curious that Ajax here follows one genealogy but shortly after employs the canonic one which makes Laertes Ulysses' father (124). Perhaps the poet has nodded. Yet it may be that he is showing us how even a blunt, plain figure like Ajax can turn mythology to his own ends.

The possibility for intra-mythological references had been present all along. A comparison with Virgil will make clear, however, how distinctive they are in Ovid. After Phaethon's bereaved sisters were changed into trees, their cousin Cygnus also came to mourn. Virgil refers to this as follows: *populeas inter frondes umbramque sororum / dum canit . . .* (*Aen.* 10.190–91, "Cygnus sings amidst the poplar leaves and the shade produced by his cousins"). Ovid's version is: *amnemque querellis / Eridanum implerat silvamque sororibus auctam* (2.371–72, "he had filled with his laments the River Po and the forest which had been enlarged by his cousins"). Both passages include an intra-mythological reference, though the difference is noticeable. Virgil does not let the phrase stand by itself but places it parallel to "poplar leaves," which makes the other less conspicuous and, by explaining it, less sharp. Moreover, though "shade of his cousins" and "forest enlarged by his cousins" point to the same fact, the latter seems more self-conscious, more arch, and more humorous. Ovid invites us to notice how clever he is, what a wonderful game mythology can be.

Another pair of examples establishes the same difference. During his wanderings Ovid's Aeneas receives an oracle from Apollo, *qui petere antiquam matrem cognataque iussit / litora* (13.678–79, "who ordered him to head for his ancient mother and kindred shores"). Both phrases for his destination clearly echo the language of the *Aeneid*, in which an oracle commands, *antiquam exquirite matrem* (*Aen.* 3.96, "search out your ancient mother"), and Aeneas terms Buthrotum (the settlement of Helenus and Andromache) and the city which he is destined to found *cognatas urbes* (502, "cities belonging to kinsmen"), since, as he explains, they will both look back to Dardanus as their source. Accordingly one might translate *cognata litora* in Ovid as "shores which belong to kinsmen." Set parallel to "ancient mother," however, the phrase appears to mean "shores which are your relatives," and this is a kind of intra-mythological reference that is foreign to Virgil. We may confirm this from another passage in the

Metamorphoses, in which Pythagoras refers to the city of Rome as *cognata moenia* (15.451, "kindred walls"). How is he entitled to claim the relationship? In a former life—for the philosopher believes in metempsychosis—he had been Euphorbus, a Trojan and therefore fellow citizen of Aeneas, who went on to found Rome. By virtue of being so very far-fetched, this well illustrates Ovid's characteristic play within the realm of mythology. His creation of intra-mythological references, by linking or inventing, deflects the reader from any attempt to turn mythology outwards.

Wit and Humor

Ovid contains any movement to broaden the significance of mythology in another, profounder way. As has become apparent during our discussion of the narrator and his handling of his material, he scatters humor, wit, and playfulness over the stories. Through making the stories familiar he also makes them funny. This too has received much attention from students of the poem, and rightly so, for it together with the narrator's voice, to which it is closely tied, creates the characteristic tone of the *Metamorphoses.* It is time now to focus on the humor and try to fix its place in the poem. My view is that humor is the universal solvent, doing away with all pretension. Let us look first at some examples.

Numerous though the examples are, they are not distributed uniformly through the text. Sometimes whole scenes, even sequences of scenes, are narrated very playfully.[52] Sometimes a single detail—a homely observation, a witty paradox—intrudes upon a passage that is otherwise straightforward or even moving. We should not attach any particular importance to this unevenness, which simply reflects the varying possibilities of the material. We should pay attention rather to the cumulative effect. Several clear examples should alert readers to the uncounted others.

We have already glanced at some verses from the story of Phaethon. The whole tale, in fact, provides a good illustration of Ovid's wit. In the first part, for instance, the interview between Phaethon and his father the Sun, the latter cautions his child to drive the chariot through the middle zones of heaven along the elliptic. Not to make it seem too difficult, he adds, *hac sit iter! manifesta rotae vestigia cernes* (2.133, "Let that be your path! You'll see the wheel-tracks as clear as can be"). Apparently the regular course of the Sun's car has worn ruts into the air! But it is in the second part, where Ovid describes the results of Phaethon's fall to earth, that he can give his imagination free rein. The heat produced as the chariot of the Sun hurtles towards the earth affects the rivers, including the Tagus of Spain, which was reputed to be rich in gold: *quodque suo Tagus amne vehit, fluit ignibus aurum* (251, "the gold which the Tagus carries with its current was melted by the fires"). The Nile too is affected:

> *Nilus in extremum fugit perterritus orbem*
> *occuluitque caput, quod adhuc latet.*   (254–55)

Terrified, the Nile withdrew to the end of the earth and buried its head, which remains hidden to this day.

A brilliant combination of geography with mythological fantasy! Even the ocean is evaporated by the heat; as a result mountains formerly under water now stick out and, Ovid adds instructively, "they swell the number of the Cyclades" (264). Later, after Jupiter has intervened and struck Phaethon with a thunderbolt, the boy's father goes into mourning, and for an entire day, we are asked to believe, there was no sunshine. Still, this was not quite the problem we might imagine: *incendia lumen / praebebant, aliquisque malo fuit usus in illo* (331–32, "light was provided by the fires: there *was* something useful in that catastrophe!"). Nevertheless, the fright which the world felt lasted for a long time. Even afterwards, when Jupiter was making a tour of inspection and assessing the damage, he had to restore rivers "which still did not dare to flow" (406). These are by no means all the humorous touches in the story, only a selection: among others, the Earth's long speech of complaint is particularly worth reading (2.279–300).

Another illustrative passage occurs in the story of Perseus and Andromeda. All the amusement here follows from the situation which was set by the basic plot: Perseus, flying about on wings, came upon the naked Andromeda, chained to a rock and about to be devoured by a sea monster. When he caught sight of her,

> *et stupet et visae correptus imagine formae*
> *paene suas quatere est oblitus in aere pennas.*   (4.676–77)

he was astounded and, seized by the picture of the beauty he saw, he nearly forgot to flap his wings.

He addressed her very gallantly. Then:

> *primo silet illa nec audet*
> *adpellare virum virgo, manibusque modestos*
> *celasset vultus, si non religata fuisset.*   (681–83)

At first she was silent and, being a maiden, had not the courage
to address a man, and modestly she would have hidden her
face with her hands—if only she hadn't been chained.

When it comes to the fight with the sea monster Ovid finds another
chance to play with the wings. Perseus battled the monster from the
air, stabbing him again and again, until "his thirsty wings weighted
down with the sanguinary spray, he no longer dared to trust them"
and began to fight instead from a handy rock (729–31). By accepting
the story together with its props as if they were drawn from the
everyday world, Ovid makes it humorous.

The terrible scene of Orpheus' death at the hands of the bacchants
is not without its lighter touches. To appreciate them we need to
keep in mind two things, that Orpheus' song was so magically powerful as to charm animals, sticks, and stones, and that bacchants as
part of their ritual used to tear apart live animals. For a while the
bacchants had been hurling their weapons at Orpheus in vain, but
then:

> cunctaque tela forent cantu mollita, sed ingens
> clamor et infracto Berecyntia tibia cornu
> tympanaque et plausus et Bacchei ululatus
> obstrepuere sono cytharae: tum denique saxa
> non exauditi rubuerunt sanguine vatis.   (11.15–19)

All the weapons would have been made gentle by his song, but
the great noise—the drums, the Berecyntian pipes with their effeminate horn, the Bacchic clapping and wailing—drowned out
the sound of the lyre: only then, when the poet could not make
himself heard, did the stones run red with his blood.

Orpheus' singing, effective only so long as it could be heard, lost its
power as soon as the usual noise of the Bacchic worshipers overwhelmed it. Ovid then builds upon this joke when he informs us
that before finally doing in the poet, the women first seized upon
innumerable animals—a task made all the easier because the animals
were still stunned by Orpheus' singing (20–22)!

Shortly afterwards, when Orpheus himself has been torn into
pieces, we come to the grotesque scene in which his head, severed
from the body, continues singing as it is carried down the River
Hebrus. The scene has a precise parallel in Virgil, and the comparison of the two shows the characteristic ways in which each deals
with an awkward piece of mythology:

> *Eurydicen vox ipsa et frigida lingua,*
> *a miseram Eurydicen! anima fugiente vocabat:*
> *Eurydicen toto referebant flumine ripae.*   (*Geor.* 4.525–27)

As the soul fled away, "Eurydice," the voice and the cold
tongue called out, "oh, unhappy Eurydice!" All along the river
the banks echoed "Eurydice."

> *et (mirum!) medio dum labitur amne,*
> *flebile nescio quid queritur lyra, flebile lingua*
> *murmurat exanimis, respondent flebile ripae.*   (*Met.* 11.51–53)

While the head glides along the middle of the stream, a wonder! something or other doleful complains the lyre, doleful
murmurs the lifeless tongue, doleful echo the banks.

The threefold repetition found in each passage, which sounds an
appropriately elegiac note, and the recurring mention of the lyre and
the riverbanks indicate that Ovid was imitating Virgil. Yet the differences are telling. Virgil called Orpheus' tongue *frigida*, "cold":
the word suggests death, without, however, being so explicit as flagrantly to contradict the picture of the still-singing head. To some
extent Virgil plays down the grotesque. Ovid, by substituting the
more exact *exanimis*, "lifeless," as a modifier of "tongue" draws attention rather to the incongruity, as he does also with the interjection
mirum! More remarkable still is his use of the studiously vague *flebile
nescio quid*, "something or other doleful," in place of the name Eurydice. This is a witty piece of rationalization, as if to say, "Who could
pretend to hear distinctly the words uttered by a floating and lifeless
head?" Ovid displays his earthbound sense of things in a similar
matter elsewhere. During his firsthand account of the battle between
the Lapiths and Centaurs, Nestor depicts the death of the centaur Cyllaron: he falls in combat, his beloved Hylonome takes him in her
arms and tries to prevent his spirit from escaping from the body,
and at this poignant moment, hero and heroine with mouths pressed
together, Nestor says: *dictis quae clamor ad aures / arcuit ire meas*
(12.426–27, "the din prevented her words from reaching my ears"). A
stunning anticlimax!

The meeting of Achilles and Cygnus in another battle offers Ovid
the chance at some varied fun. Cygnus, very much the poet's own
creation, is invulnerable. Haupt and Ehwald remark that Ovid altogether passes over the general tradition which makes Achilles himself invulnerable save in one place. It seems to me, however, that
Ovid has not neglected it but rather is teasing our knowledge of

mythology when he refrains from mentioning it, and this gives point to Cygnus' words to Achilles: *"quid a nobis vulnus miraris abesse?"* / *(mirabatur enim)* (12.87–88, "'Why are you surprised that I have no wound?' (for he was surprised)"). What he says next only expresses the logical consequence of his invulnerability (I paraphrase): "this armor you see upon me I wear merely for show—just like Mars himself!" And in his final boast to Achilles, a clever intra-mythological reference, he vaunts with mock modesty his descent from Neptune:

est aliquid non esse satum Nereide, sed qui
Nereaque et natas et totum temperat aequor.   (93–94)

It counts for something to be the offspring not of Nereus'
daughter [Thetis, Achilles' mother], but of the one who rules
over Nereus and his daughters and the entire sea.

These all come from passages in which the humor of Ovid's narrative is prominent. But more often some witty touch is found in relative isolation. What effect this has on the individual stories we shall consider later. Here we are interested rather in the cumulative impression this creates. Let us consider several examples. The daughters of Minyas, because they neglected the worship of Bacchus, have just been transformed into bats. The metamorphosis takes place at dusk, appropriately, for this is the time when these creatures begin to be active. Ovid then remarks: *nec qua perdiderint veterem ratione figuram,* / *scire sinunt tenebrae* (4.409–10, "the darkness prevented them from knowing how they had lost their former form"). Because of what they have become, they do not know what they have become. At the end of Book Six Ovid refers to the birth of twin boys to Orithyia and Boreas. Like their father, a god of wind, the sons too have wings. To these stock items from the warehouse of mythology the poet gives an amusing twist:

non tamen has una memorant cum corpore natas,
barbaque dum rutilis aberat subnixa capillis,
inplumes Calaisque puer Zetesque fuerunt;
mox pariter pennae ritu coepere volucrum
cingere utrumque latus, pariter flavescere malae.   (6.714–18)

Nevertheless, the wings, they say, were not born with the
body: so long as there was no beard beneath their tawny locks,
the lads Calais and Zetes were featherless; then simultaneously
their cheeks began to turn yellow and, as on a bird, feathers began to grow around their sides.

A remarkable puberty! Here again we find Ovid teasing the edges of mythology. Similarly Daedalus makes the labyrinth of Crete so amazingly tricky that he himself scarcely finds his way back to the threshold (8.166–68). Eurydice, dead of a snakebite on the very day of her wedding to Orpheus, is summoned back from among the shades: she comes—still limping on account of the wound (10.49)! And so on.

I have argued that the epigrams and other witty comments in the poem call attention to the narrator. Now we can see what the narrator is commenting on, what the object of his wit is. The verbal texture of the poem cannot be divided from the poet's treatment of mythology: the one expresses the other. From the present point of view it does not matter whether the witty saying emanates from Ovid himself or from one of his characters. Let us look at several fresh examples in which a figure within the poem, by the nature of his language, suggests an irreverent view of mythology. In no other kind of writing, perhaps, do we see so clearly the conjunction of Ovid's humorous stance towards mythology and his brilliant verbal ability.

During the battle between the Lapiths and Centaurs, for instance, the staunchest warrior on the side of the Lapiths is Caeneus, who, we have just been told, was born a woman and but recently metamorphosed into a man. One of the centaurs, seeing the havoc which Caeneus wreaks upon their ranks, is made to cry out:

> "*heu dedecus ingens!*"
> *Monychus exclamat, "populus superamur ab uno*
> *vixque viro! quamquam ille vir est, nos segnibus actis,*
> *quod fuit ille, sumus."*   (12.498–501)

> "Alas! what a disgrace!" Monychus exclaims. "We, an entire
> people, are bested by one man—who is scarcely a man! Still, he
> *is* a man, while we by our sluggishness prove to be what he
> was formerly."

One epigram leads to another as the speaker unfolds the paradoxes of the situation.

In Book Nine a terrific fight is recounted between Hercules and Achelous, who is a river god with the power to assume any shape he pleases. When the contest is going against him, he transforms himself into a snake. This is how Hercules greets his opponent's change (the hearer, it is assumed, is thoroughly versed in mythology and recalls that Hercules while an infant had strangled two serpents and that one of his twelve labors had been the slaying of the hydra):

"cunarum labor est angues superare mearum,"
dixit, "et ut vincas alios, Acheloe, dracones,
pars quota Lernaeae serpens eris unus echidnae?
vulneribus fecunda suis erat illa, nec ullum
de centum numero caput est inpune recisum,
quin gemino cervix herede valentior esset;
hanc ego ramosam natis e caede colubris
crescentemque malo domui domitamque reclusi:
quid fore te credis, falsum qui versus in anguem
arma aliena moves, quem forma precaria celat?"   (9.67–76)

"To overcome snakes was a labor of my cradle days," he said.
"And though you be greater than all other dragons, Achelous,
what fraction of the Lernaean hydra will you, a single serpent,
be? The hydra was fertile in her wounds: no one of her hundred heads could be cut off without the neck being fortified by
twin heirs. This creature, branching out in snakes that were
born from murder, growing by the harm that was done to her, I
tamed, and, once I had tamed her, I slit her open. What do you
think will happen to you who, changed into a *false* snake, use
weapons not your own, you who are concealed in a borrowed
shape?"

This example of Ovid's rhetoric is almost too good: the wit obstructs
the wit. The oxymoron in "fertile in her wounds," the personification
in calling the pairs of the hydra's heads that spring up "twin heirs,"
the paradoxes of "snakes born from murder" and "growing by harm"
—all this brilliance nearly obscures the argument *a fortiori* which Hercules is constructing, namely: "If I defeated a monster composed of a
multitude of real snakes, how much more easily will I defeat you, a
single, false snake." Not that the argument per se interests Ovid very
much; rather it gives a framework for the verbal fireworks.

The humor or wit of these passages, and of most of the others we
have considered, is unmistakable. Who could fail to smile at Perseus'
problems with his wings or Hercules' address to Nessus? After recognizing its existence, we should consider also the place of humor in
Ovid's treatment of mythology. Humor, it seems to me, goes hand in
hand with humanizing; the two are of a piece. A humorous, fundamentally playful conception of mythology naturally works itself out
in the sorts of details we have looked at. And the humanizing of
mythology gives the ground of the humor; a kind of logic leads from
the one to the other. The poet accepts the conventions of mythology
as premises and takes them a step further to arrive at novel conclu-

sions. Given that a creature like the centaur Hylonome exists, and that she is in love, it is logical that, to make herself beautiful, she entwines flowers in her mane. Given that the gods are like men and desire material sacrifices, it is logical that they are incensed at the prospect of losing them. Given that a spring is not only a source of water but also a divine spirit, the poet takes one logical step when he remarks that the water nymphs wept, and then a further one when he adds that they complained of running dry on account of their weeping. Directly from the conventions of mythology springs a narrative like Ovid's, and humor is its culminating quality.

Mythology so handled is brought and kept firmly within the realm of the familiar. Through anachronism, Romanization, and other forms of contemporizing, by giving life to the inanimate and rendering the divine human, Ovid makes mythology the everyday, flesh-and-blood world of his reader. Humor is one of the consequences. And at the same time it works to confine the meaning of mythology. The injection of humor inoculates mythology against excessive solemnity; it shuts out interpretations which tend to reduce man to a figure within some abstract scheme, whether moral or historical, political or theological. Ovid's version of mythology intimates that the past was not larger than life: it was like the present. There were no heroes: mankind was made up of men like ourselves. No gods preside over the course of events or represent a principle like justice. The words of a modern philosopher, Alfred North Whitehead, aptly describe the contribution which humor, or laughter, makes to such a view of the world:

> Is it that nothing, no experience good or bad, no belief, no cause, is, in itself, momentous enough to monopolize the whole of life to the exclusion of laughter? Laughter is our reminder that our theories are an attempt to make existence intelligible, but necessarily only an attempt, and does not the irrational, the instinctive, burst in to keep the balance true by laughter?[53]

(I would alter only "irrational" and "instinctive": Ovid's poem contains a large element of intellectual fun.)

Humor, then, is not a casual property of the poem. It is not a by-product of other processes in the making of a mythological narrative, nor is it a goal in its own right. It is part and parcel of the treatment of mythology. And if it tends to deny to mythology any privileged truths, it does not therefore allow it no truths, only truths of a different scale. The humor in the poem pares away the abstract and the exaggerated; it keeps things concrete, small, and human. The units of Ovidian thought are the individual and the moment. The poet does not see a person as heroic, as standing for anything larger than himself, as taking part in any grand design, as being the consequence or cause of (historical) events, as occupying a place in the continuum from divinity to inanimate life, as belonging to any group whatsoever. He sees only the particular. His interest is directed towards the individual person caught at a unique moment; this will prove to be most conspicuously the case in metamorphosis.

CHAPTER FOUR

AENEID

Upon its publication, some twenty-five years before the *Metamorphoses*, the *Aeneid* of Virgil had at once become a monument, a star in the firmament, a classic of Latin literature. Its immediate effect upon writing in Latin surpassed perhaps the effect of Michelangelo's frescoes in the Sistine Chapel upon contemporary painting or the influence of Beethoven's symphonies over the music of the day. If evidence of Virgil's towering achievement is needed, we have the direct testimony of Ovid. In the *Ars Amatoria*, where he lists literary works a knowledge of which is becoming to women, he recommends in the final place the *Aeneid*:

> *et profugum Aenean, altae primordia Romae,*
> *quo nullum Latio clarius exstat opus.*   (*Ars* 3.337–38)

> . . . and the exiled Aeneas, the beginnings of lofty Rome: no Latin work is more famous.

Virgil's national epic loomed so large over the literary landscape that a writer had to be affected by it, willy-nilly. Certainly Ovid himself was affected, indeed throughout his career, though nowhere more than in the *Metamorphoses*. Given the obvious overlap of genre and subject, that both poems are long hexameter narratives, and that Ovid includes in his a version of Aeneas' story, it is not surprising that the reader feels the presence of the *Aeneid* with special keenness.

The importance of the *Aeneid* to the *Metamorphoses* makes a double comparison possible and worthwhile. First, since both poems tell a story, we may compare their styles of narrative. We can examine not only the isolated but also the larger elements of narrative, and so come to further conclusions about the way each poet looks at the world. Then, since the content of the *Aeneid* is repeated in the *Metamorphoses*, after a fashion, and since, moreover, that content is especially important to the Romans, we may investigate Ovid's "Aeneid," his version of how Aeneas founded the Roman nation. The two inquiries are closely linked, for Ovid alters the meaning of the *Aeneid* chiefly through the characteristic ways in which he tells it. One might with profit compare Ovid to other narrative poets, Homer, for instance, or Apollonius of Rhodes, or perhaps Catullus, whose account of the wedding of Peleus and Thetis (64) is the earliest extant narrative in Latin verse. But no other comparison can be so fruitful as the one with Virgil: he is close in time to Ovid, and his direct influence is palpable, while his fundamental difference provides an illuminating contrast.

Narratives Compared: Storm and Flood

Let us start with a comparison of two similar episodes of natural violence: the storm that attacks Aeneas' ships as they are sailing from Sicily towards Italy (*Aen.* 1.81–123), and the flood with which Jupiter punishes a sinful mankind (*Met.* 1.262–312). One is definitely modeled on the other. The abundance and intensity of the movement ease our analysis of fundamental narrative traits like the representation of action, the articulation of a scene, and the joining of scenes to one another.

First the Virgil. Aeolus, king of the winds, who keeps them imprisoned in a mountain, has just acceded to Juno's request that he blast the Trojan fleet, which she hates and fears.

> After saying this, Aeolus turned his spear about and struck the hollow mountain on its side. The winds, as if in fighting formation, rush forth through the gateway that has been offered and blast over the lands. In unison the East and South Winds and the squall-laden African lay upon the sea; they churn it all up from the bottom of its bed and send huge waves rolling towards the shores. Upon this follows the shouting of men, the creaking of ropes. All at once clouds steal the sky and daylight from the eyes of the Trojans; dark night lies upon the sea. The heavens thundered, the upper air flickers oft with bolts of lightning, and all things threaten present death for the men.
> Suddenly, Aeneas' limbs grew slack with fear. He gives a groan and, stretching his palms towards the stars, speaks thus: "O three and four times fortunate, you whose fate it was to meet

death before your father's eyes, beneath the high walls of Troy! O Diomedes, bravest of the Greek race, to think that I could not lose this life to *your* right hand, dying on the plains of Troy, where fierce Hector was laid low by Achilles' spear, where great Sarpedon was also, where the river Simois snatched below its waters and carried down so many shields and helmets of heroes, so many brave bodies!"

As he spoke so, a squall howling from the north strikes the sail square on and lifts the billows towards the stars. The oars are snapped, then the prow comes round, offering the ship's side to the waves. In a mass there follows a sheer mountain of water. Some men hang upon the wavetop; before others the gaping water reveals the ground between the waves, as the surge and sand boil. Three ships, torn away from the rest, the South Wind hurls onto hidden rocks (these rocks in the midst of waters, a huge spine on the surface of the sea, the Italians call the Altars); three others the East Wind pushes from the deep into shallow waters and sandbanks, a pitiful sight, then dashes them upon the shoals and surrounds them in a mound of sand. One, which was carrying the Lycians and trusty Orontes, before Aeneas' very eyes is struck on its stern by a huge, towering sea: the helmsman is knocked from his station and sent tumbling head over heels; while the wave, driving the ship, twirls it about three times in place, and the rapid whirlpool swallows it into the sea. On the vast surge scattered swimmers appear amidst the waves, and arms of men and planks and Trojan treasure. Now the storm has overcome the sturdy ship of Ilioneus, now of brave Achates and the one in which sailed Abas and aged Aletes. All the ships, the seams of their hulls loosened, gape open and take in the hateful water through the chinks. (1.81–123)

The Ovidian passage, like Virgil's, occurs a short way into the first book of the poem. Angered at the criminality of mankind, the decisive example of which has been provided by Lycaon, Jupiter has resolved to punish the whole race. He settles on drowning them in a flood.

Straightaway Jupiter shuts within Aeolus' cave the North Wind and all those that rout the gathered clouds, and he sends out the South Wind. The South Wind flies forth on wet wings, its fearful face hidden in pitch-black darkness. Its beard is thick with storm clouds, water flows from its white hair, mists sit upon its forehead, the feathers of its breast are drenched. Thunder crashes, then dense clouds pour down from the upper air.

Iris, Juno's messenger, dressed in varied hues, catches the waters and brings them as nourishment for the clouds. The crops
are laid low. The farmer's prayers, given up for lost, lie upon the
ground. The toil of a long year has perished, good for naught.

Jove's anger was not contained in his heaven, but his sea-blue
brother came to his aid. The latter summoned his streams. After
they had entered the house of their sovereign, he said: "No
need now for a long speech of exhortation. Pour forth your
strength: that's what's necessary! Open your dwellings, away
with the dams, give your rivers free rein!" He had commanded:
they return and give the streams their head, and in unbridled
course they roll down to the sea. Their leader smote the earth
with his trident: she trembled and with this movement opened
the paths of her waters. Running out of their course, the rivers
rush across the open fields, carrying away trees and crops,
flocks and men, houses and shrines with their sacred objects.
Any house that remained, that could resist so much evil and not
be overthrown, was overtopped nonetheless by water that rose
above its roof; towers sank and were hidden beneath the swirl-
ing water.

And now there was no distinction between sea and land: everything was sea, the sea even lacked shores. This man occupies
a hill; that one, sitting in a hook-beaked skiff, rows where just
recently he was plowing. One man sails over croplands or the
roof of a sunken house; another catches a fish in the top of an
elm tree. An anchor is caught in a green meadow perhaps, or
curving hulls rub against the vineyards beneath. Where but a
moment ago the slender she-goats cropped the grass, there now
the unsightly seals lay their bodies. Beneath the water the sea
nymphs marvel at groves, cities, houses. Dolphins take over
the forests; they bump into the high branches and strike against
the agitated oak trees. The wolf swims amidst the sheep. The
wave carries off tawny lions; the wave carries off tigers. Of no
avail to the boar his lightning-like strength, nor his swift legs to
the stag when he is carried away. After long searching for a
place to land, the wandering bird, its wings wearied, falls into
the sea. The measureless freedom of the sea had overwhelmed
burial mounds, and unfamiliar waves were lapping mountain
tops; those the water has spared are overcome at length by lack
of food and starvation. (1.262–312)

The latter passage, among Ovid's most vivid and picturesque, is
typical of his narrative style. In its use of imagery, in its descriptions,

tone, articulation, construction, and movement, it represents the poem fairly. At the same time that it is typically Ovidian it is also reminiscent of Virgil. It recalls the storm scene at the beginning of the *Aeneid*. That Ovid in composing this passage was influenced by Virgil is suggested not merely by the general similarity in subject and the placement (near the beginning of their respective epics) of the two passages, but even more by a close resemblance in imagery and by several distinct verbal echoes. Ovid nearly invites us to compare him with Virgil. Of the first two lines in Ovid,

> *protinus Aeoliis Aquilonem claudit in antris*
> *et quaecumque fugant inductas flamina nubes,*   (1.262–63)

> Straightaway Jupiter shuts within Aeolus' cave the North Wind and all those that rout the gathered clouds,

the former echoes the Virgilian passage with every word (cf. *Aen.* 1.52, 56, 102), and the latter is modeled on *collectasque fugat nubes* (*Aen.* 1.142, "and routs the collected clouds"). A close look at the echoes reveals that Ovid is neatly turning Virgil inside out: he has Jupiter shut in Aquilo and the cloud-routing winds, just those forces which, when unleashed, had brought about the storm in the *Aeneid*. While imitating his predecessor, he seems to be marking his difference from him; the imitation may even serve as a foil to the difference. A contemporary testifies that Ovid was conscious of this. Gallio, we are informed by the elder Seneca (*Suas.* 3.7), used to say of a certain Virgilian phrase "that his friend Ovid had liked it very much and had done with it what he had done with many other verses of Virgil, not intending to filch it from him but rather to borrow it openly, precisely in order for his borrowing to be recognized." His reworking the phrases about the winds is emblematic of his relationship to Virgil. In any event, the similarity, both overall and in detail, justifies an extensive comparison.

IMAGERY

We may begin with the imagery. Throughout the passage from the *Aeneid*, the storm itself as well as the surrounding episodes, run two strong, marked lines of imagery: horses and politics. Virgil metaphorically represents the winds as horses. This is his first mention of them:

> *hic vasto rex Aeolus antro*
> *luctantis ventos tempestatesque sonoras*

imperio premit ac vinclis et carcere frenat.
illi indignantes magno cum murmure montis
circum claustra fremunt.   (*Aen.* 1.52–56)

Here in a vast cavern king Aeolus checks with his power the
struggling winds and roaring storms; he reins them in with
chains and imprisonment. About their pens they snort in protest and cause a great roar in the mountain.

Besides the words found here—*carcer* ("starting-gate" as well as "imprisonment"), *frenare* ("rein in"), *claustra* (probably = *carceres*; cf.
Manil. 5.76), and *fremere* ("snort")—the passage also includes *habenae*
(63, "reins") and *arrectis auribus* (152, "with ears pricked up"; see
Servius). All these words fit together to make up a picture of the
winds as horses. Virgil also portrays the relationship between the
winds and Aeolus in terms of politics. The indicative words are *patria*
(51, "homeland"), *rex* (54, 137, "king"), *regnum* (78, "kingdom"),
sceptrum (57, 78, "scepter"), *aula* (140, "royal palace"), *imperium* (54,
138, "power of command"), *foedus* (62, "compact"), and *capessere* (77,
a term variously used for public life; see *Thesaurus Linguae Latinae*
3.310–11).

A similar pair of images runs through Ovid's description of the
flood. He takes over from Virgil the horse imagery, applying it to
Neptune's waters, which are the source of the action there: *immittere
habenas* (280, "give free rein"), *ora relaxare* (281, "give them their
head"), *defrenatus cursus* (282, "unbridled course"; *defrenatus* only
here in Latin), and *exspatiatus* (285, "running outside the bounds of
the race-course"; found here for the first time; cf. 2.202, 15.454).
Ovid's second image is not political, but military, yet it too derives
from Virgil. Taking his cue from *venti velut agmine facto* (*Aen.* 1.81,
"the winds, as if in fighting formation"), he describes the waters in
language which suggests that they are soldiers: *auxiliares undae* (275,
"auxiliary waves"), *hortamen* (277, a general's speech of exhortation
before battle), *signo dato* (334–35, "upon a signal's being given"),
bucina (335, "curved military trumpet"), and *receptus* (340, "retreat").

What are we to make of this parallelism of imagery? It is, we have
already observed, a clue that Ovid is imitating Virgil. That Ovid resorts to phrases (*immittere habenas*) or neologisms (*defrenatus*) in sus-
taining an image, whereas Virgil relies on familiar single words, is a
sign of the greater ostentation and self-consciousness with which
Ovid employs imagery. More important, the *use* of imagery within
the poems points to one of the large differences between them. The
imagery of Virgil's storm is carefully connected to other parts of the

poem and so bears on the understanding of the whole. The winds-as-horses belong to a chain of horse imagery that links all those violent, destructive forces which oppose Aeneas and obstruct the founding of the Roman nation, such as the Greeks, Carthage, and Turnus.[1] By creating a pattern in the story of Aeneas, the imagery gives the whole as well as each episode greater coherence and meaning: it gives each episode meaning precisely by fitting it into a "whole." The political imagery of Virgil's storm does not touch other parts of the poem as much as impose a particular way in which the story is to be understood. The accumulation of terms drawn from government gives a political cast to the whole storm scene. The very first conflict in the poem is made to seem more than an isolated event in the story of Aeneas. It looks beyond Aeneas' present trials to their outcome, which is a political and historical one, the establishment of order over violence in the state. The imagery compels the reader to adopt a political interpretation of what happens to Aeneas, and, if he is a Roman, it compels him to relate that to a contemporary situation. By anticipating the outcome in the beginning, it makes Roman history into an intelligible and aesthetically satisfying unity.

Ovid's parallel imageries of horses and soldiers do not serve such purposes; they establish no structures, create no directions. Instead, apart from alluding to Virgil, they have, like the metaphors in the *Aeneid* or any other poem, a local function, to make the action of the rivers vivid for the reader. This, as it seems to me, they do not do especially well. Virgil had fitted the imagery to the action. In his scene the swiftness, strength, and violence of the winds/horses are constantly in evidence, urging the narrative onwards. In Ovid the imagery of warfare and horses hardly squares with the action of the scene, which is sparse and weak. Of the fifty-one verses, only six are given over to the effects of the rushing waters (285–90). Because action is absent from Ovid's narrative for the most part, the images have almost nothing to fasten on to. They remain but loosely connected to the story. Instead of helping to visualize the scene, they exist almost apart from it as decorative elements. The imagery of the *Metamorphoses* tends neither to form part of any larger schemes or patterns in the work, nor to accompany and enhance action. If anything, it takes the place of action.

The imagery points to another feature as well. In depicting the waters as horses and soldiers Ovid is personifying them. We have seen before that personification occurs regularly throughout the poem. Of this phenomenon we find a wide range of examples in our passage. To note them is worthwhile, because they illustrate the constant bent of Ovid's imagination towards the human and the visible. At one extreme is personification simply through metaphor. A fuller, more straightforward example is the description of Iris:

> nuntia Iunonis varios induta colores
> concipit Iris aquas alimentaque nubibus adfert.   (270–71)

> Iris, Juno's messenger, dressed in varied hues, catches the waters and brings them as nourishment for the clouds.

That Iris is the rainbow and that, because she seems to move between heaven and earth, she is also the messenger of the gods, were old notions which show personification at an early stage of Greek mythology. But to represent the rainbow as "dressed in varied hues" and, with reliance on an ancient meteorological conception, as "bringing nourishment for the clouds"—this is typical of Ovid's delight in portraying things as people, in humanizing the inhuman.[2]

As the details become more elaborate, the thing personified approaches what is usually called an allegorical figure. Of this too there is a fine example in our passage:

> madidis Notus evolat alis,
> terribilem picea tectus caligine vultum;
> barba gravis nimbis, canis fluit unda capillis,
> fronte sedent nebulae, rorant pennaeque sinusque.   (264–67)

> The South Wind flies forth on wet wings, its fearsome face hidden in pitch-black darkness. Its beard is thick with storm clouds, water flows from its white hair, mists sit upon its forehead, the feathers of its breast are drenched.

Though the stormy wind in its ensemble resembles nothing precisely human—it seems half man, half bird—each part of it expresses some quality in quasi-human features: swiftness, wetness, darkness, terror. The poet has given to the wind recognizable, external characteristics which represent its essence.

DICTION AND METER

With large passages in hand it is possible to compare Ovid's diction with Virgil's. The difference is so evident and so widely recognized that it needs only brief illustration. Virgil's diction is lofty, highly unusual, remote from ordinary speech. Ovid's by contrast tends to be familiar and prosaic. Archaic words and forms, like Virgil's *extemplo* ("suddenly"), *ast* ("yet"), *quis* (for *quibus*, dative plural), and *virum* (for *virorum*, genitive plural); rare or special words, like *grandaevus* ("grandsire") and *gaza* ("treasure"); novelties, like *brevia* (for *vada*, "shallow waters") and the intransitive use of *avertit* ("turns aside"); startling collocations, like *furit aestus harenis* ("the surge maddens with the sands")—these scarcely correspond to anything in Ovid. One might point to *deplorata*, given an active sense by Ovid ("wept over"), or *vota* ("prayers" ordinarily, but of which the meaning here is "objects of his prayers," i.e., the crops), or point to the apparently new coinages *defrenatus* ("unbridled") and *exspatiatus* ("running out of the course"). Still Virgil's language is far more striking and charged.

In meter too the later poet rarely achieves the expressive effects of the earlier. Virgil's dactylic runs, noticeable because not common, imitate the swift movement of the winds in 83–85, or of the water in 117: *ast illam ter fluctus ibidem / torquet agens circum et rapidus vorat aequore vertex* (116–17, "but the wave, driving the ship, twirls it about three times in place, and the rapid whirlpool swallows it into the sea"). Or the monosyllabic ending of a verse jars the reader as the sea did the sailors: *insequitur cumulo praeruptus aquae mons* (105, "in a mass there follows of water a sheer mound"). This sort of expressiveness, though not absent, is foreign to Ovid, whose hexameters glide by smoothly, even monotonously. The flatness of his diction and meter and the general modernity of his language appear deliberately sought. They differ so widely from the norms of Virgilian style that they represent a turning away from what that style implies: a convention of poetic decorum according to which the loftiness of style matches the importance of the subject and the dignity of the author. Virgil's language and meter convey his engagement with the material. Ovid, by contrast, is nonchalant. His very way of writing is a challenge to his predecessor. He refuses to claim a privileged place for himself or his poem.

TONE

We may learn something further about Ovid's stance towards his story by considering the tone of the narrative. The chief fact is that it is not a steady tone, but wavers. Never solemn or excessively dignified, it is apt to become light and playful even at crucial moments, as it does several times in this passage of universal catastrophe.[3] The personification of Iris and of the rivers perhaps adds a humorous touch. Later, when the waters have risen and covered all the ground, it is not enough for Ovid to say that men had to seek refuge in boats:

he adds (296) that they went fishing and now hooked their prey in the tops of elm trees! Also amusing are the Nereids looking with wonder at the strange sight of underwater cities, and the dolphins swimming among unfamiliar oaks and bumping into the branches (301–3). This wavering tone holds us at some distance.[4] It tends to prevent us from being engaged with the story. Offered both light and serious views of the flood, uncertain how the poet stands towards it, we do not know how we should take it. As described by Ovid, it raises no goose-bumps.[5] The tone, occasionally moving into playfulness, undermines the gravity of the passage and therefore obstructs attempts to attach a particular meaning to it. This effect is reinforced by a certain displacement of interest. Though the flood is Jupiter's punishment of mankind, Ovid seems more interested in the fate of the animals.[6] They are the source of some of the humor; but they are also the ones whose death is most moving:

quaesitisque diu terris, ubi sistere possit,
in mare lassatis volucris vaga decidit alis.   (307–8)

After long searching for a place to land, the wandering bird, its wings wearied, falls into the sea.

We are entitled to wonder what this episode means to the poet, what it is supposed to mean to his readers: are the birds the center of interest (what did they do to deserve punishment?), or are the men? Differing views of the flood—it is Jupiter's rightful punishment of mankind, it is an occasion for mirth, men find themselves in novel situations, the animals suffer—are simply juxtaposed; Ovid makes no effort to harmonize them.

CONSTRUCTION OF EPISODE

The more general question of how the poets structure a whole episode, that is, how they relate its different parts to one another, leads us to a fundamental distinction between their styles. In overall arrangement the two passages are fairly close: each is articulated into parts which nevertheless flow easily into one another (I have made them separate paragraphs in the translations supplied above). Still, it is worth attending to the transitions. Virgil crisply divides the passage into three sections and manages smooth transitions between them. In the first section, verses 81–91, he portrays the coming of the storm, which for the moment is threatening rather than harmful. He summarizes this in a final line that directs attention to the victims:

praesentemque viris intentant omnia mortem (91, "all things threaten present death for the men"). He immediately follows this general observation with the example of Aeneas: *extemplo Aeneae solvuntur frigore membra* (92, "suddenly Aeneas' limbs grew slack with fear"). This begins the second section, verses 92–101, the subject of which is Aeneas' reaction to the storm, expressed chiefly through a short speech. Then after the last words of the speech the poet resumes: *talia iactanti . . . procella / velum . . . ferit* (102–3, "as he spoke so, a squall struck the sail"), which ushers in the third section, verses 102–23, on the effect of the storm upon the fleet. The feebleness of the syntactic connection between the participle *iactanti*, which must be a dative of reference, and the rest of the sentence shows Virgil's evident effort to bind the sections together.

The articulation of the Ovidian passage is less neat, the transitions more blurred and artificial. The first section, verses 262–73, deals with the rain sent from heaven by Jupiter. To pass to the second section, 274–90, about the rising of the earth's waters, which are Neptune's province, Ovid relies on the personification of forces: *nec caelo contenta suo est Iovis ira, sed illum / caeruleus frater iuvat* (274–75, "Jove's anger was not contained in [or content with] his heaven, but his sea-blue brother came to his aid"). The basic idea is "not only did it rain from heaven, but the earth's waters also rose." The two parts are not linked as cause and effect; they do not even stand in any clear temporal relation to one another. Instead they are more or less parallel scenes, joined through the mythological notion that Jupiter, god of the sky, and Neptune, god of water, were brothers and supportive of one another. Then, after the rising waters have covered even the tallest buildings, when the flooding can make no perceptible progress, Ovid in his third section, verses 291–312, turns to describing the effect of the flood on men and animals. The dividing point between the second and third sections is not altogether clearly marked: it may be after verse 290, as I believe, or after 292.[7] In overall arrangement, then, Ovid's narrative is less distinctly articulated into parts than Virgil's; yet at the same time it has a weaker sense of forward movement.

These in turn are strictly connected to several other features which reveal the central principle, the heart, so to speak, of Ovid's narrative style. By comparing his portrayal of action with Virgil's, we are led to recognize a fundamental quality of his writing: its strong tendency towards static pictures. Since these features are closely bound up with one another, let us for the moment abandon our point-by-point comparison of the two poets and instead analyze each one separately.

ACTION IN VIRGIL

In Virgil the clear formal articulation of the passage goes hand in hand with an unwavering narrative focus. The whole of the first section concerns the storm itself; the one reference to Aeneas and his men, *insequitur clamorque virum stridorque rudentum* (87, "upon this follows the shouting of men, the creaking of ropes"), is rather impersonal and firmly tied to the narrative of the storm: the verbal prefix *in-* suggests, besides the hostility of the storm, the closeness of events. Then the entire second section concerns Aeneas; the entire third, the storm acting upon his fleet. Virgil therefore defines each section not only by giving it a distinct overall subject but also by centering the subject on a single person or force. The unity is concrete. It may seem natural that the change of focus serves as an articulation of the Virgilian passage, but we shall see that in Ovid the two matters are loosely connected.

Virgil's narrative, furthermore, is full of action. Except for the speech of Aeneas, the picture is one of continual movement: the winds rush forth and churn up the sea, the heavens thunder, lightning flashes, ships are raised up, cast down, whirled around, and so forth. Here is a sample:

> *talia iactanti stridens Aquilone procella*
> *velum adversa ferit, fluctusque ad sidera tollit.*
> *franguntur remi, tum prora avertit et undis*
> *dat latus, insequitur cumulo praeruptus aquae mons.*
> *hi summo in fluctu pendent; his unda dehiscens*
> *terram inter fluctus aperit, furit aestus harenis.*   (102–7)

As he spoke so, a squall, howling from the north, strikes the sail square on and lifts the billows towards the stars. The oars are snapped, then the prow comes round, offering the ship's side to the waves. In a mass there follows a sheer mountain of water. These men hang upon the wavetop; before these others the gaping water reveals the ground between the waves, as the surge and sand boil.

Moreover, the actions are logically connected. Chronology and cause are carefully observed: one action entails a second, that in turn a third, and so on. This is as true of the three parts as of the subsections within each. The narrative thread is very strong in Virgil, and the reader is propelled forward through the story.

Yet this dramatic narrative at the same time is subject to a strict formal control; its vigorous action is remarkably schematized. Virgil gives the passage an overall symmetry. The three sections form two halves: twenty-one verses about the storm before it has struck (81–101) are balanced by the twenty-two verses of the third section (102–23), in which the storm finally does strike. And within that first half, the eleven lines on the coming of the storm itself (81–91) are matched by the ten that deal with Aeneas' reaction (92–101). Virgil also imposes a scheme on the sequence of actions within the separate sections. In the first, the action moves through the four zones of the world in order: the winds sweep over the lands, churn up the sea, and bring on darkness in the lower air, which is followed by lightning and thunder in the aether.

The formal control is most remarkable in the third section, which is symmetrically divided into four subsections: (1) 102–7, quoted above, six lines, is a general description of the effect on the ships; (2) 108–12, five lines, on the effect on six particular ships, falls into equal halves, one beginning *tris Notus*, the other *tris Eurus*; (3) 113–17, five lines, on the effect on one ship, also falls into two halves, each defined by the completeness of the syntactic unit (these middle subsections are further linked by the word *torquet*, found in the first line of one and repeated in the last of the other); (4) 118–23, six lines, again gives a fairly general description. The numerical symmetry of this part (six lines, five, five, six) is evident. The movement from general to specific to more specific (and more touching) and then back to general is also well marked. The last subsection, which an Ovid would have omitted, is added by Virgil not for the sake of mere symmetry, but for reasons of rhythm and continuity: it provides a falling movement after the climax (the loss of the one ship) and, by surveying the results of the storm, makes a transition to the next scene, in which Neptune reacts to the entire storm, not just some particular event of it.

PICTURES IN OVID

Virgil's narrative, combining powerful action with meticulous structure, stands in strong contrast to Ovid's. The focus shifts continually in the latter. Though the three sections of Ovid's passage are rather clearly delineated from one another, within itself each lacks a single center of interest. The unity of each section, that is to say, remains somewhat abstract; it is not strongly felt, it is not embodied in one character or force, as with Virgil. The first section, for instance, the chief notion of which is that Jupiter sent rain over the earth, moves from Jupiter to the South Wind, then on to Iris, and finally to the ruined crops—all this within twelve lines. The second section, on

Neptune's waters, coheres more. The third section again is made up of many discrete little vignettes; indeed, Ovid's eye wanders so freely over the results of the flood that we cannot be certain what is the intended grammatical subject of verses 311–12: is it the men or the animals? Articulation and focus do not go hand in hand.[8]

But a jumping focus is only the consequence of the most distinctive feature of Ovid's narrative style: the tendency away from relating actions and towards painting static pictures instead.[9] Thus the storm Jupiter unleashes is presented almost wholly through descriptions of the South Wind and Iris; the thunderclaps seem as much a timeless attribute of the South Wind as an event in a storm (268–69). The destroying of the crops is certainly action:

sternuntur segetes et deplorata coloni
vota iacent longique labor perit inritus anni.   (1.272–73)

The crops are laid low. The farmer's prayers, given up for lost,
lie upon the ground. The toil of a long year has perished, good
for naught.

But when the same idea is repeated three times, as here, its dramatic force is diluted. The narrative, instead of marching onward, comes temporarily to a halt and marks time. And attention is further distracted from the sequence of actions through a shift of emphasis: the second and third versions dwell not so much on the destruction of the crops as on the pitiable waste of the farmer's labor. In the second half of the second section, after Neptune's exhortation to the troops, we come to the only truly narrative sequence, lines 281–90. But the third section of the passage, on the results of the flood, reverts to non-narrative description. It is composed of a dozen or so vignettes contrasting the present with the former state of affairs—men now row where they used to plow, for example, and they sail over rooftops—and then Ovid elaborates the paradoxes of the situation:

et, modo qua graciles gramen carpsere capellae,
nunc ibi deformes ponunt sua corpora phocae.
mirantur sub aqua lucos urbesque domosque
Nereides.   (1.299–302)

Where but a moment ago the slender she-goats cropped the
grass, there now the unsightly seals lay their bodies. Beneath
the water the sea nymphs marvel at groves, cities, houses.

These two little scenes are simply juxtaposed. They are vivid, witty, and lightly humorous. They imply no sequence of actions. Reverse

their order, and they will be just as coherent.[10] Contrast this with
Virgil: his scenes are made up of action, and the actions follow one
another in so compelling a sequence that not a line could be shifted
elsewhere. In Ovid the narrative thread disappears behind the collection of vignettes.

The static quality is reinforced through several features of the verbal texture. These too are characteristic of the poem and have the
same effect on the narrative in general as they do on our passage. We
have already noticed how the imagery of horses and soldiers, rather
than enhance the action, tended to substitute for it. Ovid's fondness
for decorative antithesis further slows down the pace of narrative:
examples are the contrasts between the slender she-goats and the
unsightly seals, between the wolf and the sheep, and between the
strength of the boar and the speed of the stag. The observation of
those antitheses, existing out of time, tends to halt the advance of
the story.

Furthermore, Ovid turns to epigram. The following lines read as if
they must come at the very end of the whole passage:

> *iamque mare et tellus nullum discrimen habebant:*
> *omnia pontus erat, deerant quoque litora ponto.*   (1.291–92)

And now there was no distinction between sea and land: everything was sea, the sea even lacked shores.

In fact, however, they appear at the beginning of the third section—
and against all logic they are directly followed by the mention of hills
that are still above water! In reaching for the hyperbole and epigram,
Ovid has downplayed temporal sequence and concerned himself less
than Virgil with the progress of the narrative.

Another way of describing this essential characteristic of Ovid's
style is to say that it shows a feeble sense of time. In noting how the
poet made the transition from the rain-waters of Jupiter to the earth-
waters of Neptune, we have already observed the atemporal relation
between the larger divisions of the passage. The same relation ob-
tains within the sections. The lines just quoted provide an example,
as does the section which they introduce, on the results of the flooding. Although something does take place in the course of the section,
it is obscured by the weakness of the narrator's sense of time. Between the beginning and the end the waters have evidently risen, for
at first some hilltops remain uncovered (293), whereas soon even the
peaks of mountains are lapped by water (310). Yet the steps leading

from one state to the other are implied rather than indicated; one does not feel the rise. Instead of a motion picture, as it were, Ovid gives us scattered snapshots, from which movement tends to be inferred.

Another principle, in addition to the vaguely chronological one (or perhaps in place of it), governs Ovid's arrangement of the vignettes. The sequence of actions is not really linear, but rather affective: the snapshots do not so much tell an unfolding story as evoke a series of feelings. The opening vignettes point up the contrast between the flooded present and the recent past, and they evoke feelings which may seem incompatible: chagrin at the farmers' losses, but mirth at some of the unexpected consequences of the flood. Then the final vignettes all have to do with death: the birds, wearied, fall into the sea, even funeral mounds are covered over by the water—this would have occurred much earlier in a strictly chronological account—and those not drowned perish of hunger. Given this affective scheme of ordering, with the emotional climax reserved for the end, it is not surprising that the entire flood passage is articulated as a tricolon crescendo. Jupiter, who starts things, is given the least space, twelve verses. Neptune, coming to his aid, gets more, seventeen. And, naturally enough, the effects of the flood receive the most space, twenty-two. (We may contrast this with Virgil's essentially symmetrical, two-part structure, which includes a falling movement after the climax of the storm description.) In Ovid, action has yielded to static pictures, and the pictures themselves are arranged in nonlinear ways.

The chief feature of Ovid's narrative is the lack of connected action. Not only have we observed this feature directly, but we have also seen how it is related to description and personification, to focus and articulation, to imagery, antithesis, and epigram, to sense of time, and to rhythm. Because of its centrality it is profoundly revealing of how Ovid looked at the world and what in it he saw as significant. The *Aeneid* deals with a world of historical development, of cause and effect. It traces out two intertwined stories: principally, Aeneas' establishment of the Roman state, and also the formation of the Roman national character, of which Aeneas gives the prototype. The poet is concerned with events which shape the future politically and morally. For Virgil what is real and important therefore is action, narrative, development, history—in short, connected movement through time. And this is reflected, intimately, in his mode of telling the story. Ovid's concerns lie elsewhere.

CONCLUSIONS

The world of the *Metamorphoses* marks its difference from that of the *Aeneid* so sharply that it amounts to a criticism of it. Many features of Ovid's narrative seem to call into question the premises of Virgil's. The connected imagery of the horses which patterns the story of Aeneas implies that history has a wholeness and a unity. The political imagery imposes a political meaning on events. But through the way he constructs his own narrative, Ovid in effect raises objections. Are human events connected to form significant units? Is their significance chiefly political? Do not such views disregard the individual person and the uniqueness of events, in which lies perhaps the possibility of manifold meanings? Virgil's diction strives for loftiness. Agrippa's famous judgment upon it, that Virgil was "the originator of a new affectation in style" (Donat. *Vita Verg.* 44), refers chiefly to its excessive deviation from the proprieties of Latin idiom. Ovid's judgment cuts more deeply. He hints that such diction advances a special claim on behalf of the poet and his material. The unswerving tone of the *Aeneid* is spotlighted by the ever-varying tone in the *Metamorphoses*. This too carries an implicit criticism. It is human after all to have conflicting views of something or to change one's views from one time to another. To assume a single view implies an impossible fixity in both the observed and the observer. We may admire such firmness but we are also right, with Ovid, to be suspicious of it. He liberates us from the tyranny of an "authoritative" viewpoint.

The sense of time, of narrative movement, is very strong in Virgil and may seem to be an aesthetic desideratum, if not an indispensable requirement, in any literary work telling a story. Ovid reminds us that such expectations from a story, which we perhaps all entertain, carry with them certain assumptions—and certain limitations. Fitting an event into a sequence is not the only, or even a privileged, way of understanding it. A point of view which subordinates the multiplicity of events to a general forward movement does not do justice to the abundance of events experienced singly, the particularity of each, the many layers and separate causes, nor to that which is random and unpredictable, the nondirectedness of events. Ovid, we may feel, resists Virgil's way of looking at things and also what it is linked to, a certain stance towards Augustus and the contemporary political-historical situation. Raising a cry of protest against Virgilian schemes, he invites us to see the world otherwise.

The world of the *Metamorphoses* does include action, of course. The individual actions, however, far from adding up to a single significant movement, constitute an unceasing, directionless flux, without order or large coherence. One event follows the other, but Ovid makes no effort to have us feel that the one was caused by the other. The central act of the poem is metamorphosis, whereby in the space of a moment, unpredictably, people become wolves, birds, trees, spiders, springs. Over time nothing general changes, nothing grows, nothing develops; human natures remain the same. In this sense the world of the poem is static. All the stories, and all their parts almost, might be taking place in a single moment, an eternal present. Among the Romans, that history-besotted people, Ovid stands out for his indifference to historical achievement. This timelessness not only is reflected in his anachronistic handling of mythology and his pictorial narrative style but also provides the background against which metamorphosis reveals its significance. In a universe which is perceived as blind, incomprehensible flux, what becomes important is the arrested moment, the unchanging picture, those figures or characteristics of human life which are raised out of the flux and saved against the accidents of time and process. This is achieved principally through the act of metamorphosis. Metamorphosis preserves, we shall see, particular qualities, attitudes, and relations of the individual. By his narrative style Ovid deflects attention away from Virgilian concerns to these, which are his own.

Narratives Compared: Firing the Ships

We may check and amplify these observations by turning to a fresh, somewhat different pair of passages. Both Virgil (*Aen.* 9.1–122) and Ovid (14.527–65) recount how Aeneas' ships, when set afire by Turnus and nearly burned, were changed into sea nymphs. A comparison of the two versions confirms the conclusions just drawn: the narrative is conducted in the same way, and the small differences that appear, when analyzed, bring some useful qualifications. The comparison, moreover, permits us to extend the observations in another direction, towards a fuller understanding of the narrator's place within his creation.

Virgil's version is about three times longer. Juno sends Iris to Turnus, bidding him, in the absence of Aeneas, to attack the Trojans. Turnus obediently collects his troops and marches out against the Trojans' camp. Frustrated in his direct assault, he attempts to burn their ships. Cybele, the mother of the gods, from whose grove the ships' timbers were taken, enters the scene at this point. Remembering a promise which she had won from Jupiter years before, she now saves the ships by changing them into sea nymphs. Ovid's version compresses these several scenes into a single one: when as a result of Turnus' attack the ships are aflame, Cybele comes, rescues them from the fire, and converts them.

CONTRAST

We may begin with familiar matters, of transition, focus, tone, and the portrayal of action. The later version, because it is much abridged, naturally does not correspond at every point to the earlier; much of the material is lacking. Before considering the passages which Ovid cuts out, let us first consider those which lend themselves to direct comparison: the firing of the ships and the arrival of Cybele. Virgil's version is not only longer but also more complex, in that it includes an inserted flashback. Between the fire and the arrival he introduces an entire scene set in heaven, a conversation that had taken place between Cybele and Jupiter at the time Aeneas was building his fleet. She requests that the ships originating on her mountain be spared from destruction; he, after remonstrating with her for wanting to avert fate, solemnly agrees to transform them into nymphs (9.77–106). In moving from the battle on earth to heaven and then back to the battle Virgil maintains a steady focus and smooth transitions. Through the sequence of scenes that make up the first part Turnus has been the center of the action; it all revolved about him. He spoke with Iris, he led the Rutulians into battle, to him the Trojans reacted, he directed the attack on the camp and then the attempt at burning the ships. Now, however, when Virgil needs to leave him and switch attention to Cybele, he ties what precedes to what follows by briefly invoking the Muses: *quis deus, o Musae, tam saeva incendia Teucris / avertit?* (9.77–78, "which god, o Muses, beat aside from the Trojans fires so savage?"). The word *incendia* ("fires") refers to what has just been happening; *tam saeva* ("so savage") indicates the gravity of the situation; the mention of a divinity shows where help is to be found. This is, to be sure, somewhat artificial, but it is a solution nonetheless to the problem of making the narrative appear to run smoothly. From heaven Virgil then returns to terrestrial events with equal care: *ergo aderat promissa dies* (9.107, "accordingly, the promised day was at hand"). *Ergo* ("accordingly") emphasizes the logical connection.

Ovid, by contrast, with little transition, or only a very abrupt one, plunges the reader unexpectedly into new scenes.[11] In the following

passage, for example, he moves very rapidly from the general conflict to the Rutulian attack on the ships:

> multumque ab utraque cruoris
> parte datur; fert, ecce, avidas in pinea Turnus
> texta faces. (14.529–31)

And much blood is spilt on each side; lo! Turnus is bringing eager torches against the pine ships.

There is no transition here: *ecce* ("lo!") might almost mark the reader's surprise, as well as the narrator's, at the start of a new scene. The
shift of focus can be amazing, as the continuation of the above verses
shows: "Turnus brings torches against the ships, and the ones which
have been spared by the water now fear the fire, and Vulcan was
already burning the pitch . . ." (14.530–32). The poet has redirected
attention from Turnus to the ships to the fire, three subjects in as
many lines. Moreover, Cybele herself now appears out of nowhere:
"the ships were already ablaze when the mother of the gods arrived." The chief character thus enters the scene quite unannounced.
With such apparent casualness does Ovid alter the focus of his
narrative.

In comparing the individual parts of the passages we find again in
Ovid the same tendency towards static pictures. The descriptions of
the fires given by the two poets contrast with one another.

> diripuere focos: piceum fert fumida lumen
> taeda et commixtam Volcanus ad astra favillam. (*Aen.* 9.74–75)

The Rutulians snatched away hearth-fires; the smoky torch
gives off a pitchy light, and Vulcan brings the commingled ash
up to the stars.

Thus Virgil. Ovid is slightly fuller here:

> iamque picem et ceras alimentaque cetera flammae
> Mulciber urebat perque altum ad carbasa malum
> ibat, et incurvae fumabant transtra carinae. (*Met.* 14.532–34)

And already Mulciber [Vulcan] was burning the pitch, wax, and
other things fire feeds on, and was running along the tall mast
up to the sails, and the thwarts of the curving hull were
smoking.

We do not have in these verses the same contrast as before, between
action and description; Virgil is no less pictorial here than Ovid. Still,

differences subsist. Unlike Ovid, who is quite direct, Virgil seems
curiously allusive. It is true that his language is often extremely
dense and suggestive, compressing several ideas into one phrase.
Here a full translation of *diripuere focos* might run something like this:
"they tore apart hearth-fires, snatched up the brands, and carried
them away." The fire itself is not mentioned. The words imply the
fire, to be sure, but in fact dwell on the light, smoke, and ashes
which accompany it. Two things, however, ought to be noticed in
this piece of indirect narrative. First, Virgil's description is atmo-
spheric. By referring to the fire thus he envelops the scene in a dark,
unsteady light. And this sense, which is characteristically Virgilian,
suggests perhaps a murkiness, an uncertainty about the outcome of
this dangerous situation. Then the mention of the stars at the end
does impart some slight narrative movement; it directs our gaze upward to the quarter from which Cybele is soon to appear.

Ovid does not indulge in atmospherics: the smoke which appears
in his last verse is not evocative like Virgil's. Instead he seems to
narrate plainly and directly the actions of the fire. By employing the
imperfect tense to recount details of the fire's progress along the
ships he builds up a momentary suspense that is absent from Virgil.
The suspense in turn creates the opportunity for both a reversal of
fortune and a climax: Cybele, we are made to feel, arrives just in the
nick of time to extinguish the threatening fire. As a result the emphasis of the scene lies on the rescue itself, not, as in Virgil, on the
significance of the event. Even here we notice Ovid's tendency towards static pictures. The three details of the fire are not arranged in
evident sequence, for it would have been more realistic (as well as
rhetorically more effective) to save the fire climbing the masts for last
place: presumably the thwarts would have burnt first.

Ovid's fondness for description is more apparent in the subsequent lines about Cybele. Though the whole of the narrative is extremely short, he devotes three verses to the goddess's oft-pictured
entourage:

sancta deum genetrix tinnitibus aera pulsi
aeris et inflati complevit murmure buxi
perque leves domitis invecta leonibus auras.   (14.536–38)

The holy mother of the gods filled the air with the jingling of
struck bronze and the tootling of blown boxwood, and in her
chariot drawn by tame lions she coasted upon the gentle
breezes.

However charming, the description of Cybele's train halts the narrative and even throws it off, like the description of Iris in the flood. And the static, decorative quality is increased by the presence of four "golden" lines in the passage, that is, lines in which a verb placed in the middle divides two nouns at the end from two adjectives which modify them: *inrita sacrilega iactas incendia dextra* (539; see also 538, 543, 556). Virgil practices a different economy of narrative. Rather than interrupt the story, he merely alludes to Cybele's entourage. He speaks of "a cloud and the Idaean bands" (the Corybantes) crossing the sky; the word translated "bands" (*chori*, 112) connotes singing, dancing, revelry. Ovid's lines on Cybele affect the tone of the whole as well as the pace of narration. Virgil created an atmosphere of the supernatural and rendered divinity less sensible, more distant and awesome, in that he did not have Cybele appear to men directly, but only through a "dread voice." Ovid's goddess is all too present, even earthly: with her gay, noisy entourage she disrupts any solemnity the scene might have had, resembling perhaps nothing so much as the leader of one of those raucous street parades which must have been familiar to the citizens of Rome.[12] It is in line with this that by contrast with Virgil's ethereal cloud Ovid's clouds are real and very substantial: *saliente graves . . . grandine nimbi* (14.543, "clouds heavy with dancing hail").[13]

OVID'S OMISSIONS

Passages from the original which Ovid has eliminated are equally valuable, because they suggest which things he was *not* concerned with. The two large excisions he makes in Virgil's account show his indifference on the one hand to fate and divinity, on the other to full portrayal of the human characters in the story. Ovid first cuts out the conversation between Jupiter and Cybele, which had formed an entire scene in the *Aeneid*. He replaces it with a single phrase: *memor has pinus Idaeo vertice caesas* (14.535, "remembering that these pines had been felled on the summit of Mount Ida"). Prosaic, allusive to the point of obscurity—not until several lines later do we learn why this fact prompts the rescue of the ships[14]—the phrase dispenses with Jupiter altogether. Ovid thus eliminates from the episode any divine sanction, any connection of the events with fate.

He also cuts out the series of scenes through which Virgil led up to the firing of the ships. Virgil used these scenes, among other purposes, to build up the characterization of the opposing leaders. Each action tells. Turnus obeys Iris and the accompanying omen (9.16–24): therefore, he is pious. He flies forth at the head of the army (47–48): he is bold, eager. His horse and armor are splendid (49–50): he is proud of his warcraft. In the middle of a challenge to his men, he breaks off and hurls a spear at the Trojans:

> *"ecquis erit mecum, iuvenes, qui primus in hostem—?*
> *en" ait et iaculum attorquens emittit in auras.*   (9.51–52)

"Which of you, men, with me will first against the enemy—?
Here!" he said, and whirling his spear shot it into the air.

We conclude that he is also impetuous. The same preparatory scenes also characterize Aeneas, who had ordered the Trojans not to leave the camp during his absence or fight in the plain. Virgil calls him *optimus armis* (40, "most able in arms")—no mere epithet, since the soundness of his advice is borne out by events.

Ovid is not interested in such indications of character. This feature of his poem deserves some discussion. Narrative or dramatic fiction regularly has one or more chief figures, who shape or participate in the main events, whose fates concern us, and the portrayal of whom is round and full enough for us to comprehend them. Achilles, Odysseus, Oedipus, Medea, and Aeneas are all focal points of the works in which they appear; through understanding them we learn about the poems in which they figure. This is not possible for the *Metamorphoses*. The form of narrative chosen does not allow any of the characters to engage our interest for long; and most of them present but one side even for the short time they are before us. That single side, not any fullness of personality, is preserved in metamorphosis. So Ovid is concerned to characterize neither Aeneas nor Turnus. If any figure in the poem is a center of interest, it is the author himself.

THE NARRATOR

The sense of the narrator's centrality in the poem is reinforced by several other stylistic features. The present passage offers good examples of three which we have not come across before: a pair of smaller features (periphrastic naming and rhetorical antithesis) and one general one (amplitude of the narrative).

In identifying the characters who appeared in their stories poets had always been allowed a certain freedom. They could either simply name someone, of course, or refer to him or her in a variety of indirect ways: through genealogy, place of origin, or some other as-sociation. In the latter case recognition depended on the reader's familiarity with mythology. Within this poetic tradition Ovid's usage, though not unprecedented, is remarkable. In identifying the deities who participate in the story Virgil is more straightforward. Neither poet in fact names the goddess Cybele, but Virgil's *deum . . . genetrix Berecyntia* (9.82, "Berecyntian mother of the gods") is not only a more precise phrase[15] than Ovid's *sancta deum genetrix* (14.536, "holy moth-er of the gods") but also one that is relevant in its context, since in her speech she will appeal to Jupiter as her son. Elsewhere Virgil employs an ancient and familiar poetic device when he uses the name *Volcanus*, the god of fire, for the fire itself (9.76). But Ovid goes a step beyond in calling the fire by a much rarer name of Vulcan's, *Mulciber* (14.533). The equation *Vulcanus = ignis* is lengthened to *Mulciber = Vulcanus = ignis*, the unusual name requiring special knowledge and extra effort on the part of the reader.[16] And whereas when Jupiter ratifies his oath to Cybele *Stygii per flumina fratris* (9.104, "by the streams of his Stygian brother") the reference to Pluto is unmistakable, Ovid's use of *Astraei . . . fratres* (14.545, "the As-traean brothers") for the winds—who are, according to Hesiod (*Theog.* 378), the sons of Astraeus and Eos—is bound to be more obscure.[17] These allusive identifications, characteristic of Ovid, go beyond the traditional usage, and instead of a mere poetic periphrasis become almost a game between him and the reader, as he teases the latter's knowledge and demands his participation in the poem.[18]

A feature akin to this one is the use of rhetorical antithesis, which not only distracts the attention away from the story but directs it towards the narrator himself. Discussion here also bears on the gen-eral question of rhetoric in the *Metamorphoses*. Rather than address the familiar claim that Ovid is more "rhetorical" than Virgil, the truth of which depends on what sense we give that slippery term, let us confine ourselves to the case of rhetorical antithesis and inquire not who uses it more, but rather what purpose it serves in the two au-thors. Examples from our pair of comparison passages give us a clue. In Virgil Jupiter remonstrates thus with Cybele on her request:

mortaline manu factae immortale carinae
fas habeant? certusque incerta pericula lustret
Aeneas?   (9.95–97)

Are ships made by mortal hand to have the right of immor-tality? And is Aeneas to pass surely through unsure dangers?

Formally the antithesis may resemble those in Ovid's passage:

> *ignesque timent, quibus unda pepercit.*   (14.531)

The ships which had been spared by the water now feared the fire.

> *quasque ante timebant,*
> *illas virgineis exercent lusibus undas*
> *Naides aequoreae; durisque in montibus ortae*
> *molle fretum celebrant.*   (14.555–58)

The sea nymphs now girlishly play with the waves they had feared; and though born in the hard mountains they now inhabit the soft sea.

Nevertheless, the difference is striking. In the Virgilian passage the opposition of immortal to mortal is central, since the metamorphosis represents a miraculous change from one to the other, all the more miraculous because the boundary between human and divine is otherwise carefully maintained in the *Aeneid*. This opposition is then repeated in the next verses, recast in terms of "sure" and "unsure": Aeneas as a mortal is bound to be uncertain of what awaits him; only the gods know for a certainty. In Ovid, however, the antitheses water–fire, play–fear, hard–soft are decorative; they give the verse a handsome look. Similar to the antitheses in our Virgilian passage is *mortalin decuit violare vulnere divum?* (*Aen.* 12.797, "was it right to violate divinity with mortal wound?"), where the poet frames the verse with the contrasting words. Ornamental antithesis is extremely rare in Virgil. At one point Anchises recognizes that he himself *novo veterum deceptum errore locorum* (*Aen.* 3.181, "had been deceived by a new error about old places"); R. D. Williams, who is intimately familiar with Virgil's style, remarks on this verse that "the verbal antithesis between *novo* and *veterum* achieves less in the essential meaning of the sentence than is usual in Virgilian rhetoric." For Ovid such an antithesis is not at all unusual. In the opening lines of the poem he announces that his "spirit" (*animus*) is moved to sing of "bodies" (*corpora*). Later he says of the River Peneus: *deiectuque gravi tenues agitantia fumos / nubila conducit* (1.571–72, "by its weighty fall it creates mists of light vapors"). Hundreds more are found. Such antitheses do not arise out of the story itself, and they have no inner connection with it.[19] They are present for their own sake. They amuse the reader, perhaps even distract him from the story. Lacking any point of reference within the story, they (like epigrams) call to mind the narrator.

What these two features, allusive naming and ornamental antithesis, have in common is that they tend to establish between narrator and reader a relationship which exists apart from the story. When Ovid teases the reader's knowledge of Astraeus' offspring or his grasp of the equation *Mulciber = ignis*, he is not simply being obscure: he is playing a kind of game with the reader,[20] and the game does not inform the story of how Aeneas' ships were saved. Similarly, as Ovid studs his narrative with rhetorical antitheses, which may arrest and delight the reader, he is not drawing him into the story, but leading him away from it to a contemplation of his own virtuosity. The relation which thereby becomes prominent is the one between author and reader.

We have observed what might have motivated Ovid to omit the conversation between Cybele and Jupiter and the series of scenes preparing the way for Turnus' attack on the ships. The removal of these scenes also corresponds to a general difference between the narrative styles of the two poets. Virgil's narrative has an amplitude, an epic breadth. The absence of this in Ovid points back to the subjectivity of the narration. Let us look at what Virgil includes in his account. Before his Turnus sets the ships on fire, Iris must come and suggest that he attack the Trojans, the Rutulians must march out and the Trojans react to the sight of them, and Turnus be frustrated in his attack on the camp. This fullness of narrative, moreover, is found in the parts as well as the entire episode. The first scene, in which Iris urges on Turnus, may be taken as an instance. Virgil does not merely announce her arrival, as he might have. He tells us that Iris was sent by Juno and found Turnus in a grove. Nor is he so hurried as not to remind us who the fathers are of Juno and Iris or that the grove is in a sacred wood or even that Iris has a rosy mouth. After this the divine messenger addresses Turnus at length. Her departure is described minutely. Turnus addresses her in turn, purifies himself, and finally prays to the gods. Virgil's narrative tends to be detailed and, since detailed in all its parts, rather evenly paced. In these tendencies lies its amplitude.

Whereas Virgil gives us a wealth of details *within* a scene and builds up these full scenes into episodes, Ovid substitutes details *in place of* a full scene and has single scenes stand for episodes. It is sufficient to recall the passage we looked at before, in which Ovid rapidly moved from the returned legates to the general warfare, to Turnus' attack, to the ships, on to the fire, and then finally to Cybele (14.527–35, nine verses!). We may see this manner of story-telling as a further consequence of the basic distinction drawn before, between Virgil's describing actions and Ovid's presenting vignettes: a style which tends towards discrete little pictures is prone to containing elliptic details and abrupt transitions. Yet at the same time the two poets, telling their stories with greater or lesser amplitude, established different relations between themselves and their narrative. Virgil, whose eye moves more slowly, more steadily, more impassively over the subject, conveys a vision of the world which appears more comprehensive and more objective. It inspires confidence and commands belief. Ovid, by contrast, jumping from scene to scene and noticing only discrete features of each, seems to see the world more selectively. This patent selectiveness is a form of subjectivity. He tells the story in such a way as reminds us of him, who is its organizer and shaper, the prism through whom alone it can be seen.

The Story of Aeneas

From the previous chapter emerged a portrait of Ovid as a critic of traditional mythology, a debunker and exploder and humorist. In recounting the tales of gods and heroes he rendered them contemporary, showed them to be subject to manipulation, and called into question their usefulness for conveying large moral truths. The same holds good even for a myth which Ovid's readers are likely to have considered very important, almost sacred: the story of Aeneas, the cornerstone of Roman historical mythology. Whatever place it might have occupied before, the story of Aeneas had come to stand at the center of national mythology upon the publication of Virgil's *Aeneid* a generation before. Because of that poem's closeness, significance, and success, Ovid's version of it offers the best opportunity to study his treatment of mythology.

The principal conclusion is that Ovid cuts down and reshapes the meaning of the *Aeneid*. Again and again he frustrates attempts to attach Virgilian meanings to the story Virgil had told; he transforms it from a national into a personal history, that is, into a subjective rendering of the history of individuals. He achieves this for the most part through the way he tells the story. Besides coming upon several new features of his narrative style, we also have here the chance to look at the narrative on a still larger scale, to consider how Ovid fits together groups of stories and what this implies. The comparison has two parts. First let us analyze the form of Aeneas' story in the *Metamorphoses*. Then, to examine its content, we may go through its sections, contrasting them with the *Aeneid* book by book. The two parts overlap, naturally.

FORM

In form Ovid's version is far shorter. From the taking of Troy to the fall of Turnus (13.399–14.580), it occupies approximately 1,150 verses. This is hardly surprising. Ovid not only abridges the *Aeneid*, however, but also avoids making it central to his poem. In his hands it often becomes a frame into which other stories are fitted. This is apparent even in the distribution of space. Of the 1,150 verses only one quarter are actually given over to Aeneas and his adventures; the remainder comprises other stories which have but little relation to Aeneas'.

To begin with, the fall of Troy, which in Virgil had been the essential starting point for Aeneas' wanderings and his subsequent foundation of Rome, is subtracted altogether from the hero's story in Ovid's account. Ovid does tell of the city's capture and destruction; and even in the four verses to which he shortens it, he does allude to several of the famous scenes found in Book Two of the *Aeneid*:

> *Ilion ardebat, neque adhuc consederat ignis,*
> *exiguumque senis Priami Iovis ara cruorem*
> *conbiberat, tractata comis antistita Phoebi*
> *non profecturas tendebat ad aethera palmas:*
> *Dardanidas matres . . .*
> *invidiosa trahunt victores praemia Grai.*   (13.408–14)

Ilium was ablaze, and the flames had not yet settled, the altar of Jove had drunk down aged Priam's trickling blood, Phoebus' priestess [Cassandra], dragged by her hair, in vain was stretching out her hands to heaven: the victorious Greeks drag off the Dardanian mothers, their enviable prizes.

And Ovid does introduce Aeneas as the man who, having survived the city's fall, represents its continued existence. His first mention of Aeneas, as departing from Troy, he prefaces with these words:

> *non tamen eversam Troiae cum moenibus esse*
> *spem quoque fata sinunt.*   (13.623–24)

Nevertheless, the fates do not allow the hope of Troy to be overthrown also, along with its walls.[21]

Nonetheless, the destruction of the city has scarcely any relation to Aeneas. In the first passage quoted the imperfect and pluperfect tenses represent the fall of Troy as a background to some other event. What follows immediately, however, is not Aeneas' setting forth, but rather an account of Hecuba and her children instead. More than two hundred verses go by before Ovid begins with Aeneas. The fall of the city, itself very briefly told, becomes the frame for a long series of stories which are unrelated to Aeneas. Thus Ovid severs all except the slenderest connection between the man and his loss of his homeland, which Virgil had made so significant an event in the hero's life.

Just as Ovid detaches from Aeneas' story an episode which had formed a necessary part of it, so he attaches to it other episodes which are not in any way part of it. As Aeneas' story proceeds, the poet interrupts it repeatedly with extraneous material. For instance, the Trojans, while voyaging in search of a homeland, pay a visit to King Anius: the account of the visit is broken with a dinner-table tale of how Anius' daughters were metamorphosed into doves (13.643–74). Then the Sibyl and Achaemenides and Macareus, as their paths cross Aeneas', also recount their own experiences (14.129–53, 160–440); together they bring his story to a halt for more than three hundred verses. Macareus' interruption, moreover, is not a simple one, for within his own story he includes several others that were told to him by one of Circe's maids—those of Picus, of Picus' companions, and of his wife Canens. These stories within stories, as we have seen, are a recurring feature.

We find a similar complexity in the longest of these passages which interrupt the narrative of Aeneas: the episode of Scylla, which runs from 13.730 to 14.74, more than three hundred lines. In the course of their wanderings Aeneas and his men have put ashore near the Strait of Messina, watched over on one side by Charybdis, on the other by Scylla. Scylla, Ovid then remarks, was not always a monster: she was once a girl. Shunning all suitors, she had fled to the sea nymphs. And one of the nymphs, while combing Scylla's hair, tells how the Cyclops had once fallen in love with her, Galatea. This leads in turn to the story of Acis and next of Glaucus, which is followed at last by Scylla's transformation into a monster and then a rock. Now, after this long digression, Ovid brings us back to Aeneas and his men on the shore. Like Macareus, Scylla herself has been the frame for several other stories which are unrelated. (We might also observe that each one introduces a second narrator: Circe's maid, Galatea.) And just as the inner stories interrupt the ones which frame them, so do the whole episodes of Macareus and Scylla interrupt the story of Aeneas.

Scylla's is a good example, furthermore, of how inserted stories interfere with the main ones not only by their disproportionate length and complexity but also by their lack of thematic relevance. How irrelevant Scylla is to Aeneas can be detected at the point of transition from the one back to the other. Ovid had first introduced her with emphasis on her monstrous nature: *illa feris atram canibus suc-cingitur alvum* (13.732, "her black belly is girt with ferocious dogs"). And he had noted at the end of the story that she is dangerous even when transformed into a rock: *scopulum quoque navita vitat* (14.74, "the rock too is avoided by sailors"). We might therefore have expected him to dwell on the threat which she posed to Aeneas and the success of his mission. Thus Virgil had emphasized how dangerous Scylla was and so explained why, to avoid her, the Trojans sailed all around Sicily (*Aen.* 3.420–32). Ovid says nothing of the sort, however. In a remarkable anticlimax he has the Trojans sail past Scylla without any hardship whatsoever: *hunc ubi Troianae remis avidamque Charybdin / evicere rates . . .* (14.75–76, "when the Trojan fleet had rowed around this rock and the thirsty Charybdis . . .").[22] Nothing therefore in Ovid's story of Aeneas motivates or justifies this long digression, which, to be sure, stands well on its own. On the contrary, the Scylla episode, with others inserted within it, interrupts the story of Rome's creation; and by its interruption and its over-whelming of the frame-narrative through size and thematic irrele-vance, it undermines the importance of that narrative.

For a contrasting instance of one story set into another which it enhances or enriches, or with which it maintains at least an important relationship, we may turn to Virgil. In Book Eight of the *Aeneid* the hero, upon reaching the site of Rome, hears from Evander an account of how once upon a time Hercules destroyed there the monster Cacus (8.185–275). The inset and the frame are held together by a narrative link: Aeneas arrives in the midst of a ceremony celebrating the event and is given an explanation of it. And the story gives an aetiology of the Ara Maxima erected to Hercules. But at the same time it is thematically related to the main narrative. Hercules victorious over Cacus is the emblem of reason, light, and civilization victorious over barbarous darkness and cruelty. As such he is a paradigm for Aeneas, who has some notion of what his founding of the Roman nation will represent in the history of the world.[23] The two parts, one clearly subordinated to the other, illuminate one another. Virgil's inset story adds to the whole.

To understand more clearly the related phenomena of structure in the *Metamorphoses*, let us step back for a moment and consider them more abstractly. The question is not the structure of the individual episode or of the entire poem, but rather the structure of a series of episodes which appear to belong together in some way, like the story of Aeneas. Since the episodes which cohere are mixed in with a number of others, the question becomes one of rank: how can we tell which story is the principal one, which the subordinate? There are at least two ways in which the author signals this. Ovid sometimes indicates rank through clear, formal marks of subordination. The capture and destruction of Troy, for example, are marked as subordinate to the story of Hecuba because they are told in imperfect and pluperfect tenses (13.408–14). These tenses, which describe contemporary states and prior actions, set the scene for the chief event. They constitute signs that the first complex of events, because it is introduced as preparation for the second, is less important.[24] More often, however, Ovid indicates hierarchy through sheer size. Lacking any other mark, or even despite one, we tend to feel that what is narrated at greater length is principal; we naturally employ proportion to judge rank. Within the account of Aeneas' descent to the Underworld, in which four verses report what he saw there whereas thirty-four report the story which the Sibyl told about herself on the way back (14.116–53), how can we not feel that the latter is more important to Ovid than the former?

The question of size and relative weighting recurs in literary judgments. In Plato's *Republic* Socrates introduces into a discussion of justice and the individual soul an analysis of the state, on the grounds that justice is more easily studied on a large scale and the results of such a study can then be applied to the individual soul. The analysis of the state occupies approximately four-fifths of the dialogue. Is the *Republic* concerned more with justice in the human soul or with portraying the ideal state? More apt might be a comparison with Catullus' sixty-fourth poem, on the marriage of Peleus and Thetis. In telling of that event the poet describes a coverlet lying on the marriage bed, in which is woven the story of Ariadne and Theseus. The description of the coverlet takes up fully half the poem. Several scholars consequently consider it to be the main part. A more sensible view is that the ecphrasis somehow reflects on the surrounding narrative, providing a perspective or parallel or contrast or modification to it. In his discussion of the problem Klingner, who himself takes such a view of the inset, well distinguishes between two historical precedents: on the one hand, the Homeric poems, in which the inserted stories bear directly on the main narrative, offering examples for the heroes in the *Iliad* or opening the bounded world of the *Odyssey* to broader horizons; on the other, Callimachus, who with the stories inserted in his *Hecale* wholly displaces the cen-

ter of interest and prefers to narrate mythological tales from some
novel point of view.[25] In the *Metamorphoses* the latter technique is
also found, yet it is true too that many inserted stories are related to
their context in neither way. They simply jostle one another and bid
for attention by their size rather than anything else.

On the basis of the notions of formal or proportional subordination we can try to describe the structure which Ovid imparts to a
complex sequence of episodes and stories. Two facts stand out. First,
Ovid establishes unusual hierarchies; his choice of what to emphasize, what to make primary, is strikingly different from Virgil's at
least. By turning the fall of Troy into a background for the metamorphosis of Hecuba, he places private suffering above national catastrophe. Nor is it reasonable to claim that Hecuba's experience, like
the death of Priam in the *Aeneid*, in any way stands for the larger
tragedy: the account of Priam's end clearly suggests more general
ruin and loss (*Aen.* 2.506–58, esp. 554–58), whereas Hecuba's does
not (13.481–575). Similarly, when the visit of Aeneas to the Underworld becomes an occasion for the Sibyl to tell her own story, Ovid is
suppressing that which bears on national history and favoring instead the private and personal. Structure is an index of significance.

The second point about Ovid's hierarchies is that they are not sta-
ble but constantly shift. What is background at one moment may
become foreground the next. Thus Aeneas is in the wings for a
while, but then moves to stage center (14.75–157, with two inserts,
however), only to exit again until verse 441. In the meantime Achaemenides, Picus, Canens, and others have occupied our attention,
while Aeneas himself was put quite out of mind. This feature of
Ovid's narrative may be considered another instance, on a larger
scale, of the poem's tendency to shift focus.

A discussion of rank does not exhaust the possible relationships
among episodes. Often in Ovid no hierarchy at all can be perceived
between adjacent stories: the one story is simply inserted into the
other without any thematic connection. To illustrate this we may
recall some of the stories which Ovid inserts into his account of Aeneas, among them Scylla, Anius' daughters, Macareus, Achaemenides. Let us keep in mind two facts about these inserts. To begin with,
they are often compounded, with a second insert set within the first.
In our passage the stories of both Scylla and Macareus contain other
tales, as unconnected to them as they themselves are to the frame
story of Aeneas. The poem has many more examples.[26] Then too the
inserts do seem irrelevant. They always have some narrative link to
the outer story—"Circe's maid told me about Picus," says Macareus,

for example—but their content has no bearing on the outer story. Again this comes out best in a comparison with Virgil. In both the *Aeneid* and the *Metamorphoses* the wandering Trojans come across Achaemenides, a member of Ulysses' crew abandoned to his fate on the perilous island of the Cyclops; in both poems he tells his story and is rescued by the Trojans. What is the relation of his story to the principal one? In the *Aeneid* (3.612–54) Achaemenides, apart from motivating the Trojans' avoidance of the Cyclops, becomes the object of Trojan magnanimity and generosity; the episode is an instance of the fine Trojan character, which will pass to the Romans. The echo here of the Trojans' earlier reception of Sinon only deepens our sense of their goodness;[27] and the emphasis on the gory, bestial nature of the Cyclops evinces by contrast their humanity and civilization. In the *Metamorphoses* (14.167–222), to be sure, Achaemenides warmly praises his rescuer. He begins his account with lengthy, almost fulsome expressions of his gratitude towards Aeneas, whom he reveres more than his own father (14.167–76): one wonders what kind of piety this would have seemed to the Romans. Yet, unlike Virgil, Ovid makes the goodness a quality of an individual, not a nation. Moreover, this quality finds no resonance anywhere else in Ovid's story of Aeneas; the theme is confined to this one episode. Thus in its content the story of Achaemenides, like many of the other inserts, has no particular relevance to its setting.

What is the result of Ovid's restructuring of the *Aeneid* within his own poem? What does he convey by his subtraction of relevant material, by his imposition of odd and ever-changing rankings upon what he retains, by his adding unrelated material? He keeps the reader constantly off balance, unsure of what will happen next and uncertain where the emphasis lies. In this state, when the narrative itself offers few clues, the reader perhaps senses more keenly his dependence on the author. Ovid reminds him in any case that there is no canonic version of Aeneas' story, that the version fixed by Virgil, however excellent, is not specially privileged but only one among many possible. "Vergil's epic is like all the stories in the *Metamorphoses*—not reality but a creation of reality dependent on the imagination of a single story-teller. Vergil tries to convince us that the primary story for his culture was the destiny of Rome and of the virtues required to realize that destiny, while Ovid makes the story one of a series of stories, many of which contradict the Vergilian virtues."[28] The form which Ovid gives to the *Aeneid* implies an extreme relativity; it teaches us to be suspicious of a neatly unified story and of an ordering narrator.

Although he alters the form of Virgil's *Aeneid*, Ovid nevertheless touches upon much of its content. However shortened, interrupted, and subordinated to other material, nearly all the books of the *Aeneid* do appear in the *Metamorphoses*. Here then is the ground for a final comparison. How, we may ask, does Ovid treat those pieces of Aeneas' story which he retains? He converts them to the record of scattered personal experiences lacking lofty motivation and significance and illustrating instead the private nature of human existence, which is shaped not by the gods or fate or history or nationality or virtue, but rather by ordinary motives and psychology, by circumstance and chance. The epic world is completely revalued.

Aeneas' story begins at the fall of Troy. Among the few details introduced into the episode one sounds an odd note: "the altar of Jupiter had drunk down aged Priam's trickling blood" (13.409–10). The small quantity of blood, which is a sign of Priam's advanced years (cf. 7.315), hardly helps to evoke the picture of a bloodthirsty Neoptolemus butchering the ruler of Troy, and the incongruity is reinforced by the intensive verb *combibere*, which means "to drink thoroughly." Almost comical, the phrase obstructs any move towards Virgilian pathos. In Ovid's version, as we saw, the episode of the city's fall is presented as the background to other stories, unrelated to Aeneas. We have no sense that it means what it did in Virgil, the destruction of Aeneas' country or the hard necessity which that imposed of going out to seek a new and unknown one. Ovid does not omit, however, the picture of Aeneas carrying his father out of Troy, but he gives it some unfamiliar twists:

> sacra et, sacra altera, patrem
> fert umeris, venerabile onus, Cythereius heros.
> de tantis opibus praedam pius eligit illam
> Ascaniumque suum.   (13.624–27)

On his shoulders the Cytherean hero bears a venerable burden: the sacred objects and, another sacred object, his father. From amidst such great treasure the pious man chooses that booty, also his son Ascanius.

Ovid portrays the hero as pious and terms him pious, to be sure, yet the business of Aeneas' choosing of his father and son must strike the reader of Virgil as odd. Ovid alludes to an earlier version of the story, in which Aeneas, allowed by the Greeks to take with him whatever he considered dear, selected his father and his gods rather than gold and silver.[29] The exemplary nature of the episode is diminished, however, by the language in which it is told. To speak of choosing Anchises and Ascanius "from amidst such great treasure" is to place Aeneas' father and son on a level with material goods.[30] And there is as much playfulness as there is respectfulness in the phrase "the sacred objects and, another sacred object, his father."[31] Furthermore, the word *praeda* ("booty") strangely suggests that Aeneas was a victor of the Trojan War. Though contradicted by the text and plainly wrong, the suggestion misleads for a moment and does so on a crucial matter, almost as if Ovid were indifferent to whether Aeneas was in fact victorious or vanquished.[32]

Now begin Aeneas' wanderings, which occupy a far larger place in Ovid than in Virgil, their episodic nature better fitting the poem's unstructured view of the world. After stops at Antander and Thrace Aeneas reaches Delos, seat of Apollo's oracle, where he is received by Anius. In Virgil a brief description of his reception sets the stage for his consulting of the oracle: the Trojans are bidden to seek their ancient homeland, which Anchises understands to be Crete (*Aen.* 3.80–120). Ovid too follows a brief preparatory scene with a longer one, but there the similarity ends. He adds a homely detail: after Anius receives Aeneas,

> *urbemque ostendit delubraque nota duasque*
> *Latona quondam stirpes pariente retentas.*   (13.634–35)

He shows him the city, the famous shrines, and the two trees which once upon a time Latona had held on to while she was giving birth.

This alters the sense of the episode. Instead of a seeker after oracles Aeneas is depicted practically as a tourist, visiting all the well-known sites and, we may imagine, hearing the traditional tour guides' stories. The ritual sacrifice which comes next, complete with incense, wine, and the burning of animal parts (636–37), is not the preliminary to consulting Apollo, as we might expect, but rather the prelude to a splendid banquet at Anius'.[33] And the longer passage that follows, far from being an oracle regarding the Trojans' destiny, arises out of the conversation at table: asked by Anchises whether he didn't have children formerly, Anius tells of their metamorphosis into doves. The story, though touching, remains unconnected to Aeneas' mission. When Aeneas does consult the oracle on the next day, it is anticlimactic. Ovid recounts it in the briefest and flattest manner:

>   *adeuntque oracula Phoebi,*
> *qui petere antiquam matrem cognataque iussit*
> *litora.*   (13.677–79)

And they approach the oracle of Phoebus, who bade them seek out their ancient mother and the shores which were their relatives.

The weight which this episode had in Virgil is shifted. A solemn seeking of divine guidance by the Romans-to-be has become a private sight-seeing tour, a domestic sacrifice, and a personal story.

From Delos the Trojans make their way to Crete, which they soon must leave again. In Virgil the cause of their departure is supernatural: a sudden pestilence attacks their animals and crops, the fields become sterile; Aeneas, visited at night by the Trojan penates, learns that this is a sign from Jupiter that not Crete but Italy is their destined home (*Aen.* 3.137–71). Ovid explains it thus: *locique / ferre diu nequiere Iovem* (13.706–7, "they could not bear the climate of the place"). In this version the departure seems a casual affair: one might almost suspect Aeneas of heading south for the winter. By setting the motivation in the sphere of physical comfort Ovid has radically altered the significance of the episode.[34] Aeneas' subsequent wanderings appear to lack motivation altogether. From Crete to Sicily (708–24) Ovid presents us with a list of eleven geographical names, bare but for small decorative tags. Buthrotum, a city in Epirus, is an example of what he omits: *regnataque vati / Buthrotos Phrygio simulataque Troia tenetur* (13.720–21, "they hold their course for Buthrotum, a counterfeit Troy, where reigns a Phrygian seer"). What a contrast this makes to the description given by Virgil (*Aen.* 3.302, 349–51), who in emphasizing that such a re-creation of Troy is not for Aeneas, reminds us that his hero is destined to establish not merely a new but also a different civilization. Ovid notes that Buthrotum is a facsimile of Troy, yet, unelaborated and unsupported by anything in the context, this reflects nothing about Aeneas' mission.

At Buthrotum Aeneas receives from Helenus another prophecy. In the *Aeneid* this marks the climax of Book Three: though indicating the many dangers which lie ahead, it assures Aeneas of his ultimate success and informs him by what signs he will know that he has reached the appointed place in Italy (*Aen.* 3.374–462). Ovid turns this into a very general, perfunctory account:

>   *inde futurorum certi, quae cuncta fideli*
> *Priamides Helenus monitu praedixerat, intrant*
> *Sicaniam.*   (13.722–24)

From there, certain of future events of which they had been
forewarned fully and faithfully by Priam's son Helenus, they
enter Sicily.

Mentioned in a relative clause dependent in turn on an adjectival
phrase, Helenus' words represent what in general the Trojans knew
when they arrived in Sicily; they do not explain or motivate any of
their actions. By breaking the connection between divine guidance
and the movements of the Trojans, Ovid converts them from pio-
neers and founders to wanderers, and converts their destiny from
what had to occur to what happened to occur. Though within Ovid's
story of Aeneas this is all that Helenus' prophecy amounts to, a
much fuller form is given later in the *Metamorphoses*. In Book Fifteen
Pythagoras, as part of his long discourse on change in the world,
lists a number of Greek cities which formerly were great but now no
longer are. He then turns to Rome, a city rising to world power. Its
greatness, Pythagoras says, had been predicted long before, in a
prophecy which Helenus gave to Aeneas at the fall of Troy. He then
quotes eleven verses (439–49). This passage recognizes Aeneas' difficult situation—Helenus is said to address an Aeneas "weeping and
uncertain of his safety" (438)—and, like the *Aeneid*, it looks to coming Roman greatness. Its giving of retrospective meaning to Aeneas'
story has limits, however. In Book Fifteen the prophecy has a different bearing: Helenus climaxes it by referring to Augustus' apotheosis (446–49). The setting of the passage is ambiguous too: following
upon an account of the great cities overthrown by time, the description of Rome's future sounds hollow. Most important of all, this
longer version of Helenus' prophecy which Pythagoras reports is
entirely separated from Aeneas' story. Only when that story has run
its course is the prophecy introduced, and then in a secondhand
telling.

After leaving Buthrotum and sailing through the Strait of Messina,
where Scylla occasions a long digression, Aeneas is carried away
from Italy to the shores of Libya, the kingdom of Dido. Book Four of
the *Aeneid* turns out like this in Ovid:

excipit Aenean illic animoque domoque
non bene discidium Phrygii latura mariti
Sidonis, inque pyra sacri sub imagine facta
incubuit ferro deceptaque decipit omnes.   (14.78–81)

There Aeneas was received both in her heart and in her home
by the Sidonian woman, who was not going to take well the de-

parture of her Phrygian husband. Atop a pyre made under the guise of a sacred rite she fell upon a sword, and, herself deceived, she deceived everyone else.

The phrase *excipit . . . animoque domoque* ("received both in heart and in home") is an instance of zeugma. The sense of *excipere* varies with each ablative: literally, with *domo*, it refers to Dido's hospitality; figuratively, with *animo*, to her falling in love. The figure proposes that the inner event and the outer are on the same level, an equation which undermines the meaning of Virgil's version. (Note also that Dido is not named.) Then in the next line Ovid speaks of Aeneas as Dido's husband. By designating him so, he both raises and sidesteps a problem that came up in the *Aeneid*. Dido there considered herself married to Aeneas, though in fact she was not. Virgil, while strongly censuring her for this—*coniugium vocat, hoc praetexit nomine culpam* (*Aen.* 4.172, "she calls it marriage, with this name she conceals her failing")—nevertheless shows the tragic consequences. Ovid sidesteps the matter: his Dido and Aeneas experience no anguished choosing between public responsibilities and private satisfactions.

Next, having moved quickly from Aeneas' arrival to his departure, he dwells on Dido's suicide. The detail that her funeral pyre was "made under the guise of a sacred rite" is picked up by the closing phrase: "herself deceived, she deceived everyone else." The repeated verb makes the phrase epigrammatic, but the play of words remains on the surface: any connection between the two deceptions has to be imagined, and in any event we expect an explanation of why Dido killed herself, not why she chose this manner of doing it. The epigram at the end redirects the understanding of the episode. It lacks the abundant significance which it had in the *Aeneid*. What has happened to Aeneas' cruel and characteristic dilemma, whether he should follow his own human longings and remain with Dido or carry out the historical mission entrusted to him, which dictates that he leave? Why do we hear nothing of Dido's love for Aeneas, nothing of the hate that comes to take its place, as in that ringing curse in which she foreshadows the grim wars between Carthage and Rome? To introduce these elements would be to invest the story with wide moral and historical significance.

The fifth book of the *Aeneid* is passed over rapidly, the chief events merely touched upon. The funeral games for Anchises are not directly referred to: *sacrificat tumulumque sui genitoris honorat* (14.84, "he sacrifices, and shows honor to the funeral mound of his sire"). In Virgil the games were in effect moral tales: each victory showed the power of some virtue—piety, prudence, generosity, discipline. Of this no trace shows in Ovid, who is not prone to finding moral meanings in events. The games are followed in the *Aeneid* by the episode in which the Trojan women, stirred up by Iris on orders from Juno, set fire to their ships. The ease with which they are aroused indicates how much they long to cease wandering and to settle somewhere. And, even though most of the ships are saved, the whole affair places Aeneas once again in the predicament of deciding whether or not to go on (*Aen.* 5.700–703, 719–20). Thus Virgil illustrates the human difficulty inherent in the carrying out of a historical plan. This too fails to draw the attention of Ovid, in whose account the near burning of the ships is but a preliminary to sailing onward and is syntactically subordinated to it: *quasque rates Iris Iunonia paene cremarat, / solvit* (14.85–86, "he loosed the ships which Junonian Iris had nearly burned"). After brief mention of several more places which Aeneas sails past, Ovid brings him to Cumae and the Sibyl.

In all the *Aeneid* few books are as loaded with importance as the sixth, in which the hero, descending to the Underworld with the Sibyl, both reviews his past and has a vision of the future Romans whom he is to establish as a nation. Again Ovid's version is reductive. It is not surprising that in the *Metamorphoses* all trace has been removed of those details which in the *Aeneid* had imparted solemnity, mystery, and awe to the scenes that pave the way for Aeneas' descent: the description of the grove of Trivia, of the Cumaean temple, and of the priestess's cavern, the terror the Trojans feel at her words, and the funeral of Misenus.[35] This is what we would expect from Ovid, who pays no heed to the divine and supernatural. Still, it is surprising how he diminishes the awesomeness of the oracular seat when he calls Cumae *loca feta palustribus undis* (14.103, "a place teeming with swampy water").

Such is the pedestrian setting for Aeneas' descent to the Underworld. The proportions of its parts give a measure of where Ovid's interests lie: thirteen verses describe the preliminaries (14.103–16), three and one-half the visit itself (116–19). The heart of Book Six of the *Aeneid* Ovid rewrites thus:

> *formidabilis Orci*
> *vidit opes atavosque suos umbramque senilem*
> *magnanimi Anchisae; didicit quoque iura locorum,*
> *quaeque novis essent adeunda pericula bellis.*   (116–19)

He saw the wealth of dread Orcus and his ancestors and the aged shade of great-hearted Anchises. He also learned the laws of the place and the perils to be met in new wars.

Two plays with words may distract us from Aeneas' journey. In the phrase *Orci . . . opes* ("the wealth of Orcus") Ovid is perhaps alluding to another name for the god of the Underworld, Dis, which was connected etymologically with *dives* ("wealthy").[36] And *magnanimus* ("great-hearted") is transferred from Aeneas, who in Virgil regularly bears this epithet, to Anchises, who never does; in a similar reversal Anchises was earlier called *pius* (13.640). In any event, this summary dispenses with all the heavy baggage of significance that Aeneas had toted. In Virgil the climax of his visit to the Underworld is the panorama of future Romans, his descendants, awaiting the moment of their birth. Here is unrolled for Aeneas the pageant of all Roman history, which he is to initiate. Inspired by this, he at last has some sense of what his mission is and what its fulfillment will be, and from this point on his determination is unwavering. Ovid's version skips over this episode altogether. Neither does Aeneas know what task he is about nor does the reader. Ovid has little interest in Aeneas' mission and its alleged importance for world history, and no interest at all, of course, in Virgil's metaphysical speculations about the punishment, purgation, and rebirth of souls. The meaning of the episode is confirmed later in the poem, when Aeneas' mother, Venus, far from considering it a turning point in his career, looks upon it as just another hardship he endured. She complains to Jupiter that she has seen her son

> *longis erroribus actum*
> *iactarique freto sedesque intrare silentum*
> *bellaque cum Turno gerere.*   (15.771–73)

driven on long wanderings, buffeted by the sea, entering the abode of the dead, waging war with Turnus.

The visit to the Underworld is placed in parallel with trials like wandering and warfare.[37]

As Nestor's campfire tales substitute for the fighting of the *Iliad* and the story of Anius' daughters for the oracular consultation, so a casual conversation that Aeneas strikes up with the Sibyl substitutes for the visit to the Underworld; action becomes narration. Transforming the heroic and the supernatural into the everyday, Ovid, with unimpeachable logic, describes the way back to the upper world as uphill—and therefore tiring, of course:

> *inde ferens lassos adverso tramite passus*
> *cum duce Cumaea mollit sermone laborem.*   (14.120–21)

Aeneas, bearing thence his wearied steps along the uphill track, softens the toil through conversation with his Cumaean guide.

The Sibyl then recounts her own story: Apollo had offered her immortality in exchange for her love and, when refused, had given her instead a long life without benefit of eternal youth; so that she looks ahead to a distant time when she will disappear and exist only as a bodiless voice. Taking the place, as it were, of Book Six of the *Aeneid*, what a contrast this story makes! It is a wholly personal tale, without larger significance, and the Sibyl's resigned prophesying of her own disintegration seems intended as the very opposite of Virgil's confident prediction that Aeneas' descendants will one day rule the world. By cutting Virgil's version and altering its proportions through the Sibyl's story, Ovid remakes it as an account of private hardship.

The second half of the *Aeneid* is recounted more summarily than the first and extends over less space. After the long inserted stories of Achaemenides and Macareus (14.158–441), which are bracketed by references to Aeneas' nurse, Caieta (14.157, 441–44)—this arrangement is purely formal—the hero at last reaches the mouth of the Tiber. In Virgil this became a magnificent and memorable moment. The dawn rises over the sea, and the winds are stilled; the grove is impressive for its size, the river for its rapid eddies and quantity of yellow sand. The poet makes the scene inviting: the stream is "pleasant"; the birds flying overhead "charm the air with their song"; and Aeneas is "happy" as he sails upstream (*Aen.* 7.25–36). To mark further the importance of this occasion Virgil pauses now and for the second time in the poem invokes the Muse (36–45). The corresponding passage in Ovid consists of one clause, which does not stand out among the three others to which it is joined in parallel: the rope is untied, they leave Circe behind, they head for the mouth of the Tiber, and Aeneas wins Latinus' daughter and his kingdom (14.445–49). In this flat narrative, matters ordinarily judged of very different importance are given equal weight, the loosing of a rope and the gaining of a territory; we might call this a syntactic zeugma. The arrival is described thus:

> *lucosque petunt, ubi nubilus umbra*
> *in mare cum flava prorumpit Thybris harena.*   (14.447–48)

And they head for the groves where the Tiber, misted in shade, bursts forth into the sea with its tawny sand.

Ovid's Aeneas does not arrive at a promised land.

The end of the *Aeneid* comprises the war waged between the Italians, under their prince Turnus, and the newly arrived Trojans. In the words *neque Aeneas Euandri ad moenia frustra* / . . . / *venerat* (14.456–

58, "not in vain had Aeneas come to Evander's walls") Ovid recounts
Book Eight of the *Aeneid*. The pluperfect tense represents the action
as subordinate, a preliminary to something greater. The negative,
allusive way of expressing the fact that Evander has given Aeneas
troops is typical. Ovid omits not only the prodigy of the white sow
with thirty young, by which Aeneas is assured he has reached the
promised land, but also the visit to the site of future Rome, which is
so evocative a passage. As Aeneas in Virgil's Book Six had moved
through time to see his descendants, so here he comes to the actual
place which will be their seat; and carved on the shield which he
receives at the end are scenes from the Roman future. In no other
ancient poem is the distant outcome of the action more crucial than
in the *Aeneid*. The Ovidian versions of Books Six and Eight break the
strong links which Virgil forged between Aeneas' present and his
past and future. No divine guidance leads his Aeneas from Troy on a
quest which is destined to reach its fulfillment not so much within
his own lifetime as in his progeny of distant ages. This denies to the
story the special meaning which Virgil had given it.

The next episode in which Ovid confronts the *Aeneid* is the embassy to Diomedes. Ovid here, and Virgil at a somewhat later point
in his poem (Book Eleven), both recount how the Latins send an
embassy to Diomedes, a Greek hero now settled in Italy, asking him
for aid against the Trojans, and how the request is denied. Diomedes' speech of reply to the ambassadors forms the center of both
versions. It is natural that the metamorphosis of his companions into
birds, which is mentioned almost in passing by Virgil's Diomedes,
occupies the larger part of his speech in Ovid. But the *motive* for
recounting it is different, as is, accordingly, the function of the entire
episode. Diomedes' speech in Virgil demonstrates the moral superiority of the Trojans to the Greeks. He openly accepts the guilt of the
Greeks, including himself. "We have violated the Trojan fields with
our sword," he says, and as a result "are paying the full penalty of
our crimes" (*Aen.* 11.255, 258). Cape Caphereus, on which the returning Greek fleet was wrecked, is called "the avenger" (11.260).
The fate of his own men he introduces as further proof of Greek
wickedness:

> *et socii amissi petierunt aethera pinnis*
> *fluminibusque vagantur aves (heu dira meorum*
> *supplicia!) et scopulos lacrimosis vocibus implent.*   (11.272–74)

My companions, lost, have climbed the sky on wings, and now
as birds wander over the streams and fill the rocks with their
tearful cries—dire punishment, alas! of my men!

He recognizes, moreover, the insanity of his having wounded Venus: *ferro caelestia corpora demens / appetii* (11.276–77, "in my madness I attacked a divine body with my sword"). Diomedes then praises both Aeneas' courage and his piety. He ends his speech with the suggestion that the Latins make peace with the Trojans (11.282–93). By fixing all blame on the Greeks and emphasizing the sterling qualities of the Trojans' leader—and what could be stronger than praise from one's foe?—Diomedes shows that the Trojans are superior to the Greeks. This is the chief bearing of the episode. As in Book Two, where the generosity and trust of the Trojans are exampled in their treatment of Sinon, so here Virgil is at pains to show the virtue of the Trojans, the Romans-to-be.

Despite similarities, Ovid's version is fundamentally different. Diomedes also describes at length the sufferings of the Greeks on the voyage home. He does not, however, consider them deserved punishment. Caphereus is not an avenger, merely *cumulum . . . cladis* (14.472, "a heap of slaughter"). Ovid's Diomedes in fact explicitly denies the general guilt of the Greeks, assigning it instead solely to Ajax, son of Oileus, who in the sack of Troy had dragged Cassandra away from the temple of Minerva:

> *Naryciusque heros a virgine virgine rapta,*
> *quam meruit poenam solus, digessit in omnes.*   (14.468–69)

> The Narycian hero passed on to all the punishment which he alone deserved, since he had carried off a maiden from a maiden.[38]

He does refer to his own punishment for having wounded Venus, yet he makes it sound more like a personal vendetta than an act of just retribution: *antiquo memores de vulnere poenas / exigit alma Venus* (14.477–78, "nourishing Venus exacts remembering punishment for her wound of long ago"). (What a moment to call Venus "nourishing"!) Furthermore, Diomedes' men are transformed into birds, not because they had impiously violated Troy, but because a few of them, impatient with endless wandering, spoke to Venus defiantly. The paucity of his remaining followers therefore prevents him from aiding the Rutulians. In both Virgil and Ovid the embassy to Diomedes comes to naught. The different reasons which are given for rejecting the request indicate, however, the poets' different purposes in including the episode. Virgil uses it to establish the superior character of the future Romans; to Ovid it is the occasion for another story of metamorphosis.

In regard to the two versions of Turnus' attempt to burn the Trojan ships, here it is sufficient to recall that Ovid undid all connection with fate and divinity and made Cybele appear out of the blue. The remainder of the *Aeneid* Ovid passes over very rapidly now. In fact he establishes an entirely new motivation for the war with the Latins and then at once brings the war to a close.

> nec iam dotalia regna,
> nec sceptrum soceri, nec te, Lavinia virgo,
> sed vicisse petunt deponendique pudore
> bella gerunt.   (14.569–72)

Their object now is no longer the kingdom that will come with the dowry, nor the father-in-law's scepter, nor you, maid Lavinia, but rather victory: they continue to wage war for shame at giving it up.

This is a psychologically sound observation: it sometimes does happen that the means becomes the end, and one fights on for the sake of winning itself, not for any further goal. Yet, as we cannot fail to notice, Ovid explicitly rejects Virgil's account of what motivated the war. This affects in turn the interpretation of Aeneas' victory. For Virgil's combination of moral, divine, and historical causes Ovid substitutes a personal and psychological one.

As if to play down Aeneas' story Ovid elides its end:

> tandemque Venus victricia nati
> arma videt, Turnusque cadit: cadit Ardea, Turno
> sospite dicta potens.   (14.572–74)

And at last Venus sees her son's arms victorious, and Turnus falls: Ardea falls, considered powerful so long as Turnus was alive.

The poet slides over the end of the *Aeneid* and at once moves on to a description of how, like a phoenix, the heron arose from the ashes of the city. The elegiac note in *cadit, cadit* makes this, not Aeneas' victory, the center of attention. Moreover, by showing his victory, such as it is, from Aeneas' mother's point of view, Ovid makes it a personal matter, almost as if to say "Venus was glad to see her boy succeed." As he had begun his "Aeneid," so he ends it, without fanfare. The reader would hardly know from his version that anything momentous has taken place. Not a word suggests that, all obstacles removed, the Roman nation has at last been established.

Criticism of Virgil

The *Metamorphoses* does not criticize the *Aeneid* directly. Such is not to be expected from a narrative, but rather from a personal lyric or epigram, like Catullus' poems against Volusius (36, 95), or from a prose polemic of the sort Carvilius Pictor's *Aeneidomastix* must have been (Donat. *Vita Verg.* 44). Then again if Ovid had wanted to attack the Virgilian view of the world, he could (I suppose) have written a rival account of Aeneas which painted in the blackest tones, without any shadings, the consequences of belief in such notions as nationality, divine providence, and historical mission. Imagine how a novelist of our day might deal with this side of the *Aeneid*. Nor does Ovid parody Virgilian epic. His treatment of the subject can be humorous but it goes on too long to merely mock epic, which is the usual aim of parody. *The Battle of Frogs and Mice* is a mock epic, the *Metamorphoses* is not.

Instead Ovid's poem is the representation of an alternative view, which by the fact of its difference calls the other into question. It is true, of course, that Ovid did not want to repeat what had already been done: no writer does. But the desire to be fresh and show his originality cannot adequately explain the nature of his poem, for he might have varied from Virgil in many ways. He counts on the reader's thorough familiarity with the *Aeneid* precisely in order to have him grasp the differences and realize what is distinctive in the *Metamorphoses*. Twice in his version of Achaemenides' tale Ovid "corrects" Virgil.[39] Virgil's Achaemenides tells the Trojans: "my companions left me behind in the vast cave of the Cyclops" (3.617–18). If we recall the story as found in the *Aeneid* and, behind it, the *Odyssey*, it must seem very improbable that his companions left him *in* the cave and that, in case they did, he managed to escape. So it seems to Ovid at least, whose Achaemenides was "left behind under the cliffs of Aetna" (14.160), that is, on the shore where the Trojans come upon him. Similarly, whereas the Virgilian character saw "two" of his companions (*duo*, 3.623) crushed and eaten by the Cyclops, the Ovidian saw "two at a time" (*bina*, 14.205), which is what Homer says (*Od.* 9.289, 311, 344). These details open an interesting perspective on Ovid's stance towards tradition. They do not aim at reestablishing the authority of Homer or faulting Virgil for inconsistency, but rather they remind the reader that no single version of a story can claim to be canonical. We, who have a Bible, may feel it lies in the nature of classical mythology that versions of stories are always liable to variation. Ovid more likely felt it lay in the nature of story-telling, which is to say, of story-tellers. Every narrator is a separate person, with his own desires and interests and fears. Truths are multiple, not single. Ovid objects to literature which assumes an exclusive point of view.

More narrowly, the *Metamorphoses* challenges the possibility of epic.[40] In its formal properties and conventions and diction the epic genre shades off into all others; it is not large enough to contain the varieties of experience or the expression of them. An impersonal narrator cannot exist. Divinity, heroes, purposeful action—the stuff of epic—are all impossible. Ovid's stories, the manner of their narration, and their relation to one another conspire to deny that epic can be written.

A convenient way to sketch Ovid's alternate vision is to describe his Aeneas. Like the other figures in the poem, Aeneas has no character, that is, no set of personal qualities which give him an identity and distinguish him from others. He resembles the others in what shapes his existence and what does not—this is the *homo Ovidianus*. His homeland is never said or shown to be of any importance. In the words "the fates did not allow the hope of Troy to be overthrown along with her walls" (13.623–24) the poet makes the only link between Aeneas and his country, and even that merely lies implicit in the negative statement. Nowhere else is the hero identified with Troy. To cut him off from his country is to deny it any influence. More surprisingly, Aeneas is nowhere at all represented as founding the Roman nation. Nationality is not a defining trait—a very un-Roman thought. As all lands are the same to Ovid, so are all ages. His Aeneas is not fixed in time. His story, it is true, is both preceded and followed by others, so he can be located, however hazily, somewhere along the line of world history, and the parts of his story stand in some sequence. He cannot be fixed in time, though, in the sense that no necessity determines the sequence of events; no cause appears to tie events to one another. For Aeneas the present is not a sum of past events. Just as he has no past (that is, no operative past), he has no future. On the poet's showing, his actions do not lead to anything outside his own life. Absent is a notion of quest or mission, of destiny, of a promised land: only if Ovid had held such a notion could he have celebrated Aeneas' arrival in Italy. With gods and fate removed and ordinary human causality much attenuated, a man's deeds do not extend beyond a small sphere. Aeneas is not a specially important figure; he is not central either in Ovid's narrative or in the history of the world. He is not conspicuous for any virtue, or for any vice either. He does not evince in his behavior any moral quality, and the one time he is called "pious" is at his introduction into the narrative (13.625), where the poet avoids naming him yet signals his identity to the reader not only in the words "Cytherean hero" and "exile" but in that adjective which is strictly an epithet of his.

In Ovid's world personal experience is recognized, and nothing larger. We hear about Hecuba's sufferings rather than the fall of Troy, about what happened to the Sibyl rather than what lay in store for the Roman nation, about Aeneas' and Turnus' eagerness to win victory for its own sake rather than for the possession of the Latin territory. Ovid has his own yardstick of what is important: a person is reckoned an individual, not the member of a collectivity. *Homo Ovidianus* finds himself alone in the world, not tied to any group or setting and not granted any perception of a framework, historical or cosmic, which might make sense of his experience. By contrast with his Virgilian counterpart, he stands free from a host of tyrannies. He is unburdened of nationality, liberated from the past, unoppressed by the future, delivered from responsibility and morality. Much can and ought to be criticized in such a vision of man: its indifference to time and cause seems particularly culpable. And yet, when we compare it with the constricting and in some ways terrifying vision of the *Aeneid*, where man is caught in immense webs of his own and the gods' making, how open it is, how full of freshness and potential and spirit! Ovid's Aeneas is moved not by some universal design or elaborately sanctioned code of behavior, but by familiar desires like eagerness for a good meal or the avoidance of unpleasant weather or the desire to see new sites and hear unfamiliar stories.

Nor does his apotheosis make him appear otherwise. Metamorphosis, by preserving, often marks some strong quality of a character, such as the hardheartedness of Anaxarete or the conjugal love of Ceyx and Alcyone. The only explanations for Aeneas' becoming a god are the two arguments which his mother Venus presents to Jupiter: Aeneas through her makes Jupiter a grandfather—as if he lacked offspring!—and he has already seen the Underworld once (14.588–91). And once made a god, he is not said to benefit the world but only to receive worship under the title *Indiges* (14.608, "native"). Even his deification, then, does not really remove him from the familiar everyday world. It does not betoken any virtue in him. The Ovidian man is not shaped by personal, historical, or other circumstances, nor by striving for any ideal. He simply is what he is, a recognizable, unheroic figure set in a world where only the representation and the perception of the self are important.

CHAPTER FIVE

METAMORPHOSIS

In contrast to Virgil's *Aeneid*, Ovid's version is told in such a way as to deprive it of large meaning. Ovid offers no reason to consider the story of Aeneas particularly important; he draws from it no code of behavior which is endorsed. In short, he knows no morality, to use the term in a wide sense. This is true generally for the world of the poem, which lacks sense and meaning, discrimination of better from worse, or any single standard of judgment, and which refuses to authorize, much less prescribe, any course of human conduct. At the heart of the poem stands no morality at all, but rather the phenomenon of metamorphosis. Metamorphosis is the opposite of morality. Being a process through which the characteristics of men are only rendered visible and manifest, metamorphosis precludes the judgments on them that morality would make. We can understand the place occupied by metamorphosis more clearly by noting the absence of its opposite.

Narrative without Morality

Many features of the poem have suggested that the stories, singly and collectively, lack meaning. The poem displays a certain skepticism in regard to narrative. Despite the various hints of comprehensive structure, the fifteen books ultimately, and self-consciously, defy analysis. The apparent thematic links between stories prove to be false leads, since experiences are too varied to be readily comparable. Within a single story the switches in tone are abrupt and jarring, since no single perspective is adequate to experience. Reality is too varied, too changeable, to be caught in narrative. The poet sees little possibility for deriving sense from the flux of human experience.

The difficulty in attaching meaning to the stories is deepened by the existence of the narrator. His omnipresence provides a constant reminder that the stories have no privileged origin, but are the subjective products of a very human narrator. Freely invented, casually joined to one another, often openly queried or criticized by the poet himself, what can they mean? The more we are made aware of the teller, the less importance the tale itself has. This is not true universally, but it seems to be true here, where the mediation of the narrator tends toward interruption and undercutting.

This is congruent with how the poet handles his material. His representation of gods and men and of the settings and substance of what they did has the effect of "flattening" the stories, reducing them to mere stories, removing whatever meaning they might have had. He goes so far in this direction that he becomes a critic of mythology. Mythology, which provided nearly the entire subject matter of ancient literature and was always a vehicle of moral truths, is transformed by Ovid into an empty, and even misleading, form of discourse.

An important qualification must be added here. Many of the stories in the poem concern one form or another of love. This is to be expected, given that love is the most personal and most subjective human experience and that the poem takes the part of the personal and subjective against what is grand or universal or thought by others to be objective. Among the love stories several appear which celebrate conjugal love—Ceyx and Alcyone, Baucis and Philemon, and a few minor ones. Noting the tenderness, the fidelity, and the pathos, I for one cannot help feeling that in these Ovid created images that were special for him. Only in them do I sense some virtue or quality to which he might give his allegiance.

ANIUS' DAUGHTERS

The general conclusion, that the poem lacks a morality, may be reinforced by considering several other stories in addition to that of Aeneas. We might begin with a story about which it can be shown not only that, despite some clues to the contrary, it has no moral, but also that those misleading clues were probably added by the author. Inset into the story of Aeneas is an account of Anius' children, narrated by the father himself (13.644–74). His four daughters had the power to turn everything they touched into food; sought for this reason by Agamemnon, who wanted to use them to feed his troops before Troy, they fled, two of them to Andros, where their brother was king; as the brother, threatened by Agamemnon, was about to hand them over to him, they were rescued by Bacchus, who transformed them into doves. Several other versions of this story are known to us from antiquity: Servius Danielis provides one (ad *Aen.* 3.80), Lycophron another (*Alex.* 570–83), and the scholia on the latter, drawing upon Pherecydes and Callimachus, give still other notices. Servius is the only one of these who mentions the brother, but merely as a member of the family, in no way figuring in the tale of his gifted sisters. A comparison of Ovid's version with the mythological vulgate suggests therefore that he has introduced the brother into the story. He has done this in order to create the brother's dilemma, which he dwells on at some length (662–66): should he surrender his sisters to Agamemnon or not? By his construction of the story the poet brings the question of piety into the foreground.[1]

Now Anius is telling this story to none other than Anchises and Aeneas. To prevent us from losing sight of this fact Ovid has Anius make reference to his Trojan audience three times in thirty verses (656–57, 665–66, 673–74). Does this story, nominally concerned with piety and told to a hero distinguished in Latin literature for this virtue, therefore have any moral significance? Evidently not. Ovid's Aeneas is never called pious, although in this passage, as if to poke us in the ribs, his father is (640). Moreover, the story itself hardly inculcates the virtue; instead *victa metu pietas* (663, "piety was overcome by fear"), as Anius says, asking forgiveness for his son. The son's action is humanly understandable and familiar enough in daily life. It is not a conflict between similar kinds of motivation. Fear is an emotion, and its victory acknowledges that people respond to fear. The victory of piety would have endorsed a code of behavior. Ovid, who introduces the theme of piety, pays it no heed in the end.

ERYSICHTHON

The inset about Anius' children, creating the expectation of a moral which is never realized, resembles the tale of Erysichthon in Book Eight. For cutting down a tree sacred to Ceres, Erysichthon is tormented to death with insatiable hunger. Otis terms this story a "theodicy," and Büchner believes Ovid's imagination, as exampled in it, to be directed towards "the moral world in the broadest sense."[2] It is hard to accept such claims. If we examine the manner of the narration—the diction, the tone, the invention, the emphases, the literary echoes—we see that it obstructs any moral interpretation. Such an examination is made easier because we can compare Ovid's account with that of Callimachus, who had made the story the centerpiece of his *Hymn to Demeter*.[3]

At the beginning Achelous, the narrator Ovid has chosen for the tale, portrays Erysichthon as a blasphemer, a violator of divinity. The picture is built up in many ways. The moral terms applied to Erysichthon are remarkably strong and frequent for this poem. He is called *sceleratus* (8.754, 792, "criminal"; cf. 774), *impius* (761, "impious"), *sacrilegus* (792, 817, "sacrilegious"), and *profanus* (840, "profane"); his deed is *nefas* (766, "abomination"). This distinguishing trait is reinforced by several Virgilian echoes which hint that Erysichthon is another Mezentius, in the *Aeneid* the very type of the god-spurning mortal.[4]

The early scenes of the tale heighten the crime. Callimachus' Erysichthon declared that he was cutting down the grove in order to build a banquet hall for himself and his companions (*Dem.* 54–55); though impious, this motivation was at least given a social setting and made comprehensible. Ovid's Erysichthon, by contrast, offers no reason, and so seems to act more from pure evil. Callimachus dwelt on the density of the trees and simply stated that Ceres loved the place (25–30). The Roman poet, changing the grove to a single tree, emphasizes not only its immense size—*una nemus* (744, "it, alone, is a grove")—but also its sacred character: fillets, garlands, and commemorative tablets testify to its numinous power, and wood nymphs were accustomed to dance beneath it (743–50). The narrator then depicts the man's wickedness winning out over the holiness of the tree when, after indicating the latter, he continues: "Nevertheless, he did not, on that account, restrain the iron axe" (751–52). The prosaic collocation of particles, concessive and logical (751, *tamen idcirco,* "nevertheless, on that account"), makes plain the obstacle overcome.

The narrative builds up to the criminal act itself with an impressive climax. In Callimachus there were only two stages. Demeter appeared to Erysichthon first in the guise of her own priestess, warning him not to cut down the grove, and then in her own person, prophesying his punishment (41–64). Ovid's version is more elaborate (751–73). Erysichthon, when he sees his servants hesitate, grabs an axe himself, declaring that the tree will fall even if it be a goddess. Then, as he sets to, the tree groans, turns pale, and begins to bleed. Horrified at this, one of the servants tries to stop the man, who then turns the axe upon him instead. Finally the tree speaks, predicting Erysichthon's punishment for this outrage. By delaying the fateful destruction of the tree with a number of prodigies and attempts at prevention, the teller enhances the audience's sense of how momentous the deed is.

After it has magnified our sense of Erysichthon as a wrongdoer, the narrative, nonetheless, even as it continues to its conclusion, drops and then loses the notion of justice done, of Erysichthon punished for his crime. The teller does not follow through on the moral theme. He shifts the center of interest from the father to the daughter. Erysichthon sells her for food money but, by virtue of a power granted her by Neptune, she is able to transform herself at will and so in varying guises escapes from the masters who have purchased her. This shift is appropriate to the setting, for Achelous recounts the story as an instance of multiple metamorphosis. But it also undoes the meaning that the story presented at its start. The shift of subject is accompanied by an altered tone and diction. The principal scene in this section is the dialogue between Erysichthon's daughter and the man who has bought her. Changed now into a man, she is fishing by the shore when her master comes along. With his address to her, lofty diction falls into burlesque; a fisherman is hailed in language appropriate to epic: *o qui pendentia parvo / aera cibo celas, moderator harundinis* (855–56, "O thou who concealest the dangling bronze in a bit of food, wielder of the reed pole"). Her reply to his inquiry about her own whereabouts is ingenious, if not ingenuous:

> *sic has deus aequoris artes*
> *adiuvet, ut nemo iamdudum litore in isto,*
> *me tamen excepto, nec femina constitit ulla.*   (866–68)

As I hope the god of the sea may aid these arts, it is true that
no man except me has stopped on this shore for some while,
and no one who is a woman either.

Besides the quibble, we should note (with Hollis) the *double entendre* in *has . . . artes*, which refers simultaneously to the arts of fishing and of metamorphosis, both in the power of Neptune. Büchner aptly compares this scene to a satyr-play. The displacement of subject and shift in tone tend to drive out the theme of impiety avenged.

We do not altogether lose sight of Erysichthon at the end. His sufferings are represented, their grotesqueness well brought out through paradox and epigram. His insatiable appetite is described thus: *cibus omnis in illo / causa cibi est* (841–42, "in him all food is the cause of food"), and he is driven finally to eat himself: *minuendo corpus alebat* (878, "he nourished his body by diminishing it"). Calli-

machus set his Erysichthon within a family and a society and depicted his hunger in terms of relations with these: his embarrassed
parents, for instance, invent pretexts for their son's not accepting
invitations to dine out; and he himself ends up begging for crusts
and garbage at a crossroads—a disgraceful fate for the son of a king.
And Callimachus stated the moral outright at the end: he who out-
rages Demeter is repugnant to men. In Ovid, by contrast, Erysichthon's hunger seems a supernatural event; at the end nothing reminds the audience that it is a punishment. The moral language of
the beginning has evaporated, or been channeled in a new direction.
Thus the phrase *vis mali* (875, "the power of the evil"), used in regard
to Erysichthon, refers only to his hunger, not the sacrilege that led to
it. And there is a subtle paradox in the reward that the daughter
gave: *praebebatque avido non iusta alimenta parenti* (874, "she offered to
her greedy parent nourishment that was not just"). The girl was
doing her filial duty; yet the food was "unjust," since it was obtained
through trickery. Despite its beginning, then, the story of Erysichthon hardly inculcates a moral. Ovid doubtless could have composed
it so that any sense of Erysichthon's guilt was much diminished from
the start or was never even aroused. Instead he chose to create the
expectation of a moral and then to disappoint it. He thus forces the
reader to enact a certain pattern of response to mythological story-
telling—to look for something in it but find nothing.

THE SPEECH OF PYTHAGORAS

Our final example is a large one, often considered significant in relation to the entire poem: the speech of Pythagoras, which occupies
the first half of Book Fifteen (15.75–478). The meanings attached to
this passage have ranged up through the ambitious to the grandiose,
and the number of critics holding some such view is large and impressive.[5] Haupt and Ehwald are almost restrained in saying that the
speech gives the poem a deeper meaning and is connected with its
central concerns. Alfonsi has written:

> At the beginning and end it is precisely philosophy which uni-
> fies the immense mass of poetic material and always justifies it.
> Ovid felt the need to interpret, on the basis of the great specu-
> lative principles, the reality which was symbolized for him in
> transformation. The myth accepted in its own right was not
> enough: for him metaphysical principle was necessary. Thus by
> means of philosophy the poet has fashioned from the "changed
> forms" the history of the cosmos in both its present-day and its

eternal reality; he has explained its law and its destiny. He has treated not only physical but also human reality, drawing from it moral commitments for men of all times as well as favorable omens for the Roman empire.[6]

The motives for such a critical response are easy to identify. The chief one is obviously the content of Pythagoras' speech: from beginning to end, under the most varied aspects, it is concerned with change. The philosopher begins by describing how the soul changes its abode. Warming to his theme, he proclaims that time itself changes: the parts of the day are different from one another; the sun and moon, by which we measure time's passage, present ever-varied faces; the seasons of the year yield to one another in constant succession. Similarly our bodies undergo steady alteration between the womb and the grave. Nor do the elements themselves stand still: earth is rarified into water, fire condenses into air, and so forth. Then follows a long section on changes in the earth's geographical features. Pythagoras reels off examples of rivers which have altered their courses, peninsulas which were formerly islands and islands which were peninsulas, cities now under water, and plains become hills; he enumerates springs that have strange powers of transformation and discusses the most violent phenomenon of natural change, the volcano. He speaks next about generation and how creatures undergo remarkable changes just before or after birth. Finally he draws attention to the rise and fall of great cities. Pythagoras even provides us with the tags by which to recall the theme of his lecture: *omnia mutantur* (15.165, "everything changes"), he says, and *cuncta fluunt* (178, "all things are in flux"). All of this constitutes a cordial invitation to relate the speech to the themes of the poem.

Moreover, the size and setting of Pythagoras' discourse urge the acceptance of the invitation. In length the passage is unsurpassed, its more than four hundred verses being approached only by the story of Phaethon (1.750–2.328) and the debate over Achilles' arms conducted by Ajax and Ulysses (13.1–383). It is placed, moreover, at the beginning of the poem's last book. The importance of the position is underlined by echoes of the first book.[7] The very length of the speech implies a substantial significance; and, because it comes near the end and by echoing the beginning appears to mark the end, it suggests a retrospective view of the whole poem. It is hardly surprising therefore that many a critic has seen in Pythagoras' discourse one of the keys to the poem's concerns.

Nevertheless, a more attentive reading, such as the passage has received from several critics, shows that it is far from being a grand statement or a climax of the poem; instead, it is a kind of red herring drawn across our path. The speech is entertaining, it is true, especially on account of Pythagoras' passion and ingenuity. Within it the prophecy of future Roman greatness which Helenus gives to Aeneas prepares the way for the episodes at the end of the book which will bear it out—Cipus, Aesculapius, the apotheosis of Caesar, the praise of Augustus. Moreover, it includes a detailed account of the Phoenix' metamorphosis (391–407). But it neither holds any special significance in itself nor lends any to the poem as a whole.

First of all, the Pythagoreanism which the *auctor ipse* professes here does not inspire unqualified regard. This is not the place to enter upon the much-discussed (and, in my view, mostly irrelevant) question of precisely what is Pythagorean and from where Ovid derives the rest. We can be reasonably certain, however, that in at least one major point the doctrine is faulty. Ovid's Pythagoras, though he describes the migration of the immortal soul from one body to another, in no way suggests a divine origin or divine essence for the soul, and yet we know from other testimony that the historical Pythagoras believed in this.[8] Furthermore, whatever the details of Pythagorean belief, the sect itself was not highly regarded. Despite the teaching of Sotion, whom Ovid may have heard and who had so great an effect on Seneca,[9] Pythagoreanism at Rome was generally held in ridicule, because of its notions of metempsychosis and vegetarianism.[10] Ovid himself may hint at the status of Pythagoras' teaching when he introduces it thus: *talibus ora / docta quidem solvit, sed non et credita, verbis* (73–74, "with words like these he opened his mouth, which was learned, to be sure, but was not also believed"). If we accept the speech then as a straightforward philosophical presentation, we are obliged to take account of the conspicuous omission and of the aura of foolishness surrounding the school. Both work against any profound understanding of the speech.[11]

In fact, however, regarded as a whole, it is hardly a philosophical discourse at all, and to consider it such is misleading. The framework renders nearly trivial what philosophizing there is. That framework is vegetarianism, which Ovid makes the alpha and omega of Pythagoreanism. Exhortation to avoid meat and eat vegetables instead is the chief (nominal) aim of the speech. Not only does it both open and close with harangues to this effect (75–110, 453–78), but it includes several other mentions as well along the way (138–42, 173–75). It is in these passages, moreover, that Pythagoras waxes most passionate and most eloquent, for instance:

heu! quantum scelus est in viscera viscera condi
congestoque avidum pinguescere corpore corpus
alteriusque animans animantis vivere leto![12]   (88–90)

Alas and alack! what a crime it is that organs be stored in organs, that hungry flesh be fattened on flesh eaten, that one creature live by the death of another!

The philosopher-poet even finds suitable mythological images for that which he abhors. He calls the eating of meat "custom of the Cyclopes" (93), and elsewhere he talks with horror of "heaping flesh on Thyestean tables" (462). He too knows that mythology is what you want to make of it.

Through repetition and other devices of rhetoric he makes plain the bearing of the speech. The whole business is but a brief for vegetarianism. Hundreds of hexameters about universal change serve to reinforce the conclusion that, in order to avoid cannibalism, we must eat vegetables, not meat (see particularly 454–62).[13] In this way Ovid stands Pythagoreanism on its head. Elevated concepts like metempsychosis and the immortality of the soul, instead of giving rise to vegetarianism as a logically entailed consequence, are subordinated to it; they are introduced merely to lend it some support. Ovid reduces Pythagoras' teaching to the most material terms.

The inversion of concepts at the heart of the speech is reflected variously. Vegetarianism, once made the highest principle, provokes some startling redefinitions. Pythagoras says:

ergo, ne pietas sit victa cupidine ventris,
parcite, vaticinor, cognatas caede nefanda
exturbare animas.   (173–75)

Therefore—and I who warn you am divinely inspired—lest piety be overcome by the belly's lust, do not disturb kindred souls with impious murder.

Who, reading these verses out of context, could guess what they refer to? The killing of animals for food is called "impious murder." *Pietas*, to be sure, is a broader term than the English "piety"; still, here (and also at 109) its meaning is remarkably stretched to include vegetarianism. Man is portrayed as torn between steak and string beans, as if this were the central conflict of the moral life.

Elsewhere Pythagoras gives a novel interpretation to the Golden Age. In his view the Golden Age was characterized by its abstention from meat:

at vetus illa aetas, cui fecimus aurea nomen,
fetibus arboreis et, quas humus educat, herbis
fortunata fuit, nec polluit ora cruore.   (96–98)

That long-ago age, to which we have given the name "golden,"
was blessed because of the produce from trees and the herbs
which grow from the ground, and it did not pollute its mouth
with gore.

Correspondingly, mankind declined from the Golden Age because it
desired meat (103–10).[14] This desire becomes, as it were, the original
sin.[15] The proposed redefinitions of piety and of the Golden Age,
two notions especially important in Roman literature, are instances
of how, by reducing Pythagoreanism to vegetarianism, Ovid has
trivialized it.

Certain special qualities of the language also help persuade us that
Ovid is far from composing a grand philosophical epilogue to the
poem. Pythagoras' speech tends towards a kind of playful exaggeration which undercuts solemn interpretation. This is particularly noticeable at the beginning and end, where vegetarianism is being
urged on the audience. Thus, excoriating those who kill cattle, the
philosopher exclaims:

immemor est demum nec frugum munere dignus,
qui potuit curvi dempto modo pondere aratri
ruricolam mactare suam, qui trita labore
illa, quibus totiens durum renovaverat arvum,
tot dederat messes, percussit colla securi.   (122–26)

Altogether unmindful and unworthy of the gift of grain is the
man who, right after removing the weighty, curving plow, can
slay his fellow country-dweller, who strikes with the axe that
toil-worn neck by which he has so many times renewed the
soil, produced so many harvests.

Both the rhetoric of the sentence—the gnomic perfects, the asyndeta
of the relative clauses and of the two verbs in the *quibus* clause,
which are instead linked through anaphoras—and the pathos—the
ox called *ruricola*, his peripeteia—seem hyperbolic.[16] In the perora-
tion high-flown language reappears, again out of line with the subject: *horriferum contra Borean ovis arma ministret! / . . . / nec celate cibis
uncos fallacibus hamos!* (471, 476, "Let the sheep provide arms against
the chill north wind! . . . Do not hide curving hooks under treacherous food!"). What a way of saying "let sheep be used for wool, not
meat" and "do not fish"![17]

Finally, we may notice a certain inversion of language. Pythagoras often speaks in phrases that call to mind Lucretius, who in his hexameters had expounded the philosophy of Epicureanism.[18] Pythagoras indeed not only resorts to Lucretian language but also declares that his goal is that of the Epicureans, namely to free men from the fear of death (153–55). Nonetheless, his doctrine is precisely the contrary of the Epicureans'; for whereas they teach that the soul, being material, dissolves at death, he explains that the soul is immortal and upon the death of one body moves to inhabit another. Lucretian language is used to express the very opposite of Lucretian thought. This might stand as an emblem of Pythagoras' entire discourse, which, while purporting to espouse a serious philosophy of change in the universe, turns it upside down and makes it into an extended joke.

Something even more important than its doctrine, framework, or language obstructs our taking the speech as a commentary on the subject of the poem: the subject of the speech is not really metamorphosis at all, but rather mere change. Pythagoras' discourse, it is true, harmonizes with the poem's strong sense that the world is variable, complex, chaotic, incomprehensible; it is the most forceful statement of that sense. And yet this is only the background against which the poem's central phenomenon is to be seen. The theme of the poem is not mutability, but metamorphosis, which is very different. Ovid's Pythagoras gives no moral explanation of why the soul migrates from one body to another, as Segal observes: change is not upward, nor in any sense for the better.[19] Moreover (I would add), it is not downward nor for the worse either. Change is directionless. This is shown most clearly when Pythagoras presents antithetical sets of examples, for instance, earth turning into water, then back to earth (239–51), or islands which have become peninsulas and peninsulas which have become islands (287–92).

The reversibility of change, which proves its lack of direction, is also strikingly illustrated when Pythagoras comes to speak of Rome (431–52). This well-known passage works in a curious way. When we have finished reading it, we feel quite certain that the sage, both speaking on his own and quoting a prophecy of Helenus, has been predicting the future greatness of the city. And this sense is reinforced by echoes of verses from the *Aeneid* in which Virgil had referred to Rome's power and distinction.[20] The beginning, however, suggests something else. Pythagoras has at that point just been listing great cities which have now sunk to mere names—Sparta, Mycenae, Thebes, and Athens. He continues thus: *nunc quoque Dardaniam fama est consurgere Romam* (431, "They say that now Dardanian Rome also is rising"). The word *quoque* ("also") is important. It leads us to believe that Rome is introduced as another example in the series of famous cities now fallen—that though its peak of greatness still lies ahead, it too is destined to sink. This light suggestion is not borne out in what follows, where Pythagoras speaks only of rising. Still, what a jarring suggestion it is! and all the more remarkable in that around this time, in Ovid's day and Augustus', the concept of *Roma aeterna* was taking shape![21] The passage offers a double perspective on Roman history: seen from the point of view of Pythagoras, at its commencement, it is the story of rise to greatness; seen from Ovid's contemporary point of view—and the anachronism of referring to Thebes and Athens as already declined urges adopting this perspective—the city has reached its peak and will certainly decline, like the others.

The treatment of Rome is the most forceful evidence that within Pythagoras' discourse change is both unending and without direction—which is to say that its subject is not metamorphosis. In the poem metamorphosis is permanent and, although it moves neither upward nor downward, nevertheless it constitutes an important positive element in the world.

Metamorphosis without Morality

In finding not only no evidence of morality in Ovid's stories but even some attempts to deny them morality, we have been considering for the most part the style in which they were narrated, on the grounds that this throws up the chief roadblocks to assignation of meaning. But what about the other thing common to all the stories, the act of metamorphosis? Does the poem's central phenomenon itself represent a judgment?

NEITHER REWARD NOR PUNISHMENT

One way of tackling this is to investigate whether metamorphosis is good or bad. Critics often speak about it as if it were a reward or a punishment for the person transformed. The assumption is usually casual. It cannot be denied that metamorphosis sometimes does appear to represent a punishment (as of Lycaon, for instance) or, much more rarely, a reward (as of Baucis and Philemon). Nevertheless, this impression is misleading. Such readings of a story rest upon statement in the text or upon an inference drawn from the sequence of events. Under examination neither form of argument proves to be strong.

As to direct statements that metamorphosis is a reward, there are none; that it is a punishment, very few (fifteen). An example is found early in the poem when Jupiter says of Lycaon: *poenas . . . solvit* (1.209, "he has paid the penalty"). It is revealing that all except four of these fifteen statements are uttered not by Ovid himself, but by characters in the poem.[22] Thus it is Jupiter who labels Lycaon's transformation, and Dryope who proclaims of herself, *patior. . . poenam* (9.372, "I suffer punishment"). Ovid's characters (like his readers) may be quick to declare that a particular metamorphosis is punishment, but not so the narrator. His perspective is different, less judgmental. In any event the number of direct statements is low—fifteen, among some two hundred fifty tales of metamorphosis. If Ovid held transformation to be an act of judgment, he certainly did not go out of his way to emphasize it.

More often such an impression is created by the sequence of events in a story, from which the reader may merely infer that metamorphosis is a punishment. Lycian peasants prevent a thirsting Leto from drinking the water of a pool; she waxes wroth at them; they become frogs (6.331–81)—who would not feel that they are punished thereby? And even if the god himself did not tell us so, would we not assume anyway that when Lycaon, after attempting to murder Jupiter, is changed into a wolf (1.209–39), he is paying the penalty for his crime? The inference certainly lies close to hand.

Nevertheless, it is tenuous, and two considerations urge against making it. First, the agent of metamorphosis is almost never specified. Neither Leto nor Jupiter, for instance, is said to cause the punishment. Minerva's turning Arachne into a spider (6.131–38) is an exception nearly unique in the poem.[23] If the agent were specified, we would draw the inference more assuredly. Being able to assign the responsibility to some figure (ordinarily a god) would strengthen the sense that metamorphosis represents a judgment, because it would forge within the story a link of causation between deed and retribution. But the narrator carefully refrains from identifying an agent, who remains regularly unknown. Second, a better formulation of what metamorphosis is can be made, one that fits more exactly what we are told in individual stories and that embraces all the instances of metamorphosis, including those of Lycaon, the Lycian peasants, and Arachne.

DELIBERATE AMBIGUITY

Metamorphosis, then, is neither reward nor punishment. Not only can no general relationship be traced between metamorphosis and any such category of judgment, but several stories even underscore the uncertainty of what transformation means in a particular case. These stories induce puzzlement in the reader: some feature in each compels him to wonder how he is to understand the metamorphosis which is its end.

In Book Thirteen Anius is telling how his daughters, fleeing from Agamemnon, prayed for help to Bacchus, who had given them the gift for which they were being pursued:

> "*Bacche pater, fer opem!*" *dixere, tulitque*
> *muneris auctor opem, si miro perdere more*
> *ferre vocatur opem.*   (13.669–71)

They said, "Father Bacchus, bring us your aid," and the author of their gift brought them aid—if you call a miraculous destruction the bringing of aid.

The girls are changed into doves. Anius' remark is provocative: the transformation can be viewed as timely and welcome assistance, or as annihilation. Anius expresses no preference between these incompatible views; he merely offers both of them as possible. He thus makes it evident that this metamorphosis is an ambiguous act.

A comment made about Actaeon is similar. Actaeon, while hunting, had inadvertently seen Diana naked; he is turned into a stag and devoured by his own hounds. The narrator then adds:

> *rumor in ambiguo est: aliis violentior aequo*
> *visa dea est, alii laudant dignamque severa*
> *virginitate vocant: pars invenit utraque causas.*   (3.253–55)

Popular accounts vary. To some the goddess appears more violent than is fair, whereas others praise her and say that her virginity deserves strict guarding: each side finds good reasons.

Here the poet creates two groups of anonymous commentators, through whom he conveys the notion that either Actaeon merited his fate or he did not.

Another, stronger instance comes from a very early story, nearly the first in the collection: Daphne and Apollo. A pair of complex similes in this case invites us to view the girl's metamorphosis in two opposing lights. Her change into the laurel tree is motivated by Apollo's love for her: his amorous pursuit provokes her to beg for the change. Before the pursuit begins, the narrator indicates the nature of the god's love in a simile: *utque leves stipulae demptis adolentur aristis, / . . . / sic deus in flammas abiit* (1.492–95, "as the light stalks are burnt once the ears of grain have been removed, so did the god burst into flame"). The simile suggests the extent and rapidity of the conflagration in Apollo's heart, and also, together with the short simile following, the terrible power of that love, which can consume whole fields.[24] And yet at the same time, as we learn from a passage of Virgil's, the language of which is echoed here (*Geor.* 1.84–93), burning the stubble after the harvest was a means of renewing the soil's fertility. Is Apollo's love for Daphne ruinous or fruitful then? This simile suggests both views.

The climactic pursuit of the mortal by the god is embellished with another simile, this one full and familiar:

> *ut canis in vacuo leporem cum Gallicus arvo*
> *vidit, et hic praedam pedibus petit, ille salutem*
> *(alter inhaesuro similis iam iamque tenere*
> *sperat et extento stringit vestigia rostro,*
> *alter in ambiguo est, an sit comprensus, et ipsis*
> *morsibus eripitur tangentiaque ora relinquit):*
> *sic deus et virgo: est hic spe celer, illa timore.*   (1.533–39)

As when a Gallic hound spots a hare in an empty field, and
with their feet the one seeks its prey, the other its own safety
(the one, appearing on the verge of fastening upon the other,
hopes at every moment to grasp it and with its muzzle thrust
forward grazes its footsteps; the other is uncertain whether it
has been seized and snatches itself away from the very bites of
the hound and leaves behind its touching jaws): so with the
god and the maiden; he is swift because of hope, she because
of fear.

The simile has epic ancestors. It closely resembles a simile from the end of the *Aeneid* (12.749–57, esp. 754–55), in which Aeneas pursuing Turnus is compared to a hound pursuing a stag. The parent of this in turn is a passage from the *Iliad*. Of Achilles chasing Hector around the walls of Troy Homer says: "He pursued him swiftly, since they strove not for a sacrificial animal nor an ox-hide, which are the prizes of men in footraces, but they were running for the life of Hector" (22.159–61). Ovid has picked up from Homer the contrast between "prizes" and "life," rendering it in his simile as a contrast between "prey" and "safety," but he puts it to a different use. In Homer it distinguishes this running from others, whereas in Ovid it distinguishes one point of view from another: for Apollo this is a kind of sport, for Daphne a matter of life and death. The epic simile bears down unevenly on the two figures: applied to the amorous god, it is hyperbolic and ironically inappropriate and makes him appear almost silly; applied to Daphne, who believes her existence is at stake, it makes a moving and tragic figure.

This simile too therefore invites contrasting views on what Daphne's metamorphosis means: if Apollo's pursuit was playfully amorous, then the metamorphosis continues his feelings with no harm done; if the pursuit was leading to Daphne's destruction, the metamorphosis rescues her. The uncertainty is never resolved. On the contrary, it is spelled out and underscored in the passage which forms a bridge between this and the next story. After Daphne's change into the laurel tree, at the cave of the girl's father, Peneus, his fellow river gods assemble, and the narrator describes them as *nescia, gratentur consolenturne parentem* (578, "not knowing whether they ought to congratulate or console the father"). The river gods, we may feel, are almost stand-ins, expressing the reader's own puzzlement too over whether Daphne's metamorphosis is for the better or the worse. The reader may be similarly puzzled about many other metamorphoses; what is distinctive in this one, set early in the poem, is that Ovid has in several ways raised the question.

METAMORPHOSIS AS COMPROMISE

Not only does Ovid suggest that metamorphosis has nothing to do with moral judgments, but he demonstrates occasionally how it may even remove the necessity of making such judgments. Metamorphosis sometimes represents a compromise, an intermediate path avoiding the judgment that would be attached to either of the others. These seem to me extreme, and therefore especially illustrative, instances of the mutual exclusivity that exists between metamorphosis and morality.

In Book Seven Cephalus tells of a hunting dog he had which Diana, on presenting it to him, had promised would surpass all animals in speed of foot. The hound is sent in pursuit of a ravaging fox which is destined never to be overtaken in running.[25] The outcome of the apparently interminable chase Cephalus describes in these words:

lumina deflexi revocataque rursus eodem
rettuleram: medio (mirum!) duo marmora campo

adspicio: fugere hoc, illud captare putares.
scilicet invictos ambo certamine cursus
esse deus voluit, si quis deus adfuit illis.   (7.789–93)

I turned my gaze away and scarcely had turned back again
when (a miracle!) I saw two marble statues in the middle of the
field: you would think one was still fleeing, the other still pursuing. A god evidently wanted both to be undefeated in the
race—if a god had anything to do with them.

In passing we may note that the narrator wonders aloud whether a
divinity was responsible and that the animals are changed into statues, the realism of which is emphasized.[26] For present purposes it is
enough to observe how metamorphosis here is a means of suspend-
ing judgment.

The example of Myrrha is more powerful in that the decision
which metamorphosis precludes is of greater moment. This young
woman, who had fallen in love with her own father and been made
pregnant by him, after much wandering is on the verge of giving
birth:

> *tum nescia voti*
> *atque inter mortisque metus et taedia vitae*
> *est tales complexa preces: "o siqua patetis*
> *numina confessis, merui nec triste recuso*
> *supplicium, sed ne violem vivosque superstes*
> *mortuaque extinctos, ambobus pellite regnis*
> *mutataeque mihi vitamque necemque negate!"*   (10.481–87)

Then, not knowing what to ask for and caught between fear of
death and weariness of living, she summed up her wishes in
prayer: "Whichever divinities you are who are open to confes-
sion, I have deserved my unhappy suffering and do not deny
it; but, so that I not pollute the living by my survival or the
dead by my demise, banish me from both kingdoms, deny me
both life and death—by changing me."

Myrrha restates, or cloaks, her personal dilemma in terms of pollution. Her prayer is granted, and she is transformed into the myrrh
tree. To let her live would end her sufferings and might appear to
vindicate her, or at least imply that her crime had been paid for;
whereas to let her die would impose still further punishment, as
if she had not suffered enough already for what she had done.[27]
Moreover—and this is probably just a sophistic argument of Myr-

rha's own—either course would involve pollution. In this predicament metamorphosis is called for, as a compromise which avoids any taking of a position on what Myrrha has done and what she deserves.[28]

A Definition of Metamorphosis

It may appear presumptuous or futile to attempt a general definition of metamorphosis. Many of the stories, as we have seen, far from climaxing in a metamorphosis, include one casually or tangentially, which could discourage the whole enterprise. And within particular stories metamorphosis represents a wide variety of phenomena: punishment inflicted by a god or reward requested, salvation or consolation for loss, memorial, psychological realization or miraculous surprise. Terms like these describe metamorphosis, appropriately, in relation to the narrative which precedes it; they view it as in some sense an outcome.

Yet it is desirable and possible to define metamorphosis globally. Such a definition would disregard the varying circumstances of the act and attend instead to its intrinsic properties, specifying what is regularly found in the instances of it and what is regularly absent. To seek a definition of this sort is more valuable than to explore the variety of conditions under which metamorphosis takes place. Ovid, it is true, is fascinated by a character's psychological state, a condition he is prone to observing, and this makes up a part of the poem's interest for its readers. He is not, however, much concerned with causality. A cardinal feature of Ovidian metamorphosis is continuity between the person and what he is changed into, but the particular form which the continuity takes is not determined by any prior condition and cannot be predicted. It seems fair, then, to study metamorphosis separately from what comes before it.

What is metamorphosis? It is clarification. It is a process by which characteristics of a person, essential or incidental, are given physical embodiments and so are rendered visible and manifest. Metamorphosis makes plain a person's qualities, yet without passing judgment on them. It is—and this constitutes a central paradox of the poem—a change which preserves, an alteration which maintains identity, a change of form by which content becomes represented in form.

LYCAON, A PARADIGM

A splendid example is furnished early in Book One—indeed by the very first human transformation of the poem. Like Daphne, whose fate gives notice that metamorphosis is of uncertain significance, Lycaon is placed where he is on purpose, his metamorphosis combining the elements so comprehensively and so transparently that it seems programmatic. In order to test whether Jupiter, who has come to his house, is really a god, Lycaon prepares to slay him at night; moreover, he slaughters a man and has him served up to the King of Olympus. Thereupon he is changed into the wolf. Ovid tells us that he headed for the countryside and howled instead of speaking, and then continues thus:

> *ab ipso*
> *colligit os rabiem solitaeque cupidine caedis*
> *vertitur in pecudes et nunc quoque sanguine gaudet.*
> *in villos abeunt vestes, in crura lacerti:*
> *fit lupus et veteris servat vestigia formae;*
> *canities eadem est, eadem violentia vultus,*
> *idem oculi lurent,[29] eadem feritatis imago est.*   (1.233–39)

From himself his mouth acquires ferocity, his accustomed murderousness he directs against the herds, now too he delights in blood. His clothing turns into fur, his arms into legs. He becomes a wolf and keeps traces of his old form: the same grayness, the same violence in his face, the same yellow gleam to his eyes—he is the very same picture of savagery.

Lycaon undergoes a change of form as a result of which he is now evidently and easily seen for what he was all along. To see Lycaon now is to recognize his savagery at once. His chief characteristic is made manifest in his appearance; his essence, externalized and given physical form, becomes clearer. This is what I mean by "clarification": not an explanation, but the bringing of essence out to the surface. Ovid tells us neither what made Lycaon ferocious in the first place nor whether he is good or bad. Metamorphosis has not so much fundamentally altered Lycaon as it has clarified him for the world.

An essential feature of Ovid's concept of metamorphosis is continuity between the former and the metamorphosed states. Some similarity remains after transformation. In the case of Lycaon Ovid makes this abundantly clear. He states it outright in the words "he keeps traces of his old form." And several other phrases confirm it. "From himself (*ab ipso*) his mouth acquires ferocity" suggests that his (new) mouth is somehow a thing distinct from him, though deriving its character from him. "Now too (*nunc quoque*) he delights in blood"—the phrase *nunc quoque* makes a regular refrain in the poem.[30] And in the closing sentence of the passage the word *idem* ("same") repeated four times underscores the continuity between the old and the new Lycaon. Besides his character there is another source of continuity in his name, which is derived from Greek *lykos*, "wolf." This too is common in metamorphosis.

Furthermore, the change in Lycaon is permanent. Having become a wolf, he will remain one through all time; the presence of the wolf in our world memorializes him forever. This is what distinguishes Ovidian metamorphoses from the mere changes catalogued in Pythagoras' speech, which were endless and often reversible. Even the very fixedness of the new form is a kind of clarity. Lycaon not only is but always will be recognizable for what he is. He will undergo no further changes; the unceasing flux and movement which are the rule of the universe and are in part the cause of the general deceptiveness of appearances will now leave him, at least, untouched.

James Joyce in his first novel was concerned among other things with the figure of the godlike artist, the great representative being the Daedalus portrayed in Ovid's *Metamorphoses*: it is enough to recall his hero's name and the epigraph for the book, which is drawn from the story (8.188). In the first draft for *A Portrait of the Artist as a Young Man* he has Stephen Daedalus expound, after his own fashion, Aquinas' aesthetic notions: "*Claritas* is *quidditas*. . . . When the relation of the parts is exquisite, when the parts are adjusted to the special point, we recognize that it is *that* thing which it is. Its soul, its whatness, leaps to us from the vestment of its appearance."[31] For "epiphany" (Stephen's term for such a revelation) substitute "metamorphosis," and he might almost be talking about Lycaon.

CLARIFICATION

In Book Eleven Daedalion is changed into a hawk. His story is recounted by his brother Ceyx, who points to the bird and explains to his curious companions:

> *forsitan hanc volucrem, rapto quae vivit et omnes*
> *terret aves, semper pennas habuisse putetis:*
> *vir fuit et (tanta est animi constantia) iam tum*

acer erat belloque ferox ad vimque paratus,
nomine Daedalion. (11.291–95)

You might perhaps think that this bird, who lives by rapine and
terrifies all the others, always had wings. He once was a man,
Daedalion by name, even then keen, fierce in war, and prone to
violence: such is the persistence of spirit.

After this introduction, which again confirms explicit statement about
persistence with clear indications of it, Ceyx emphasizes Daedalion's
warlike nature by contrast with his own peaceful one, and then tells
the story of his niece Chione. She, the mother of children by both
Mercury and Apollo, became so arrogant as to compare herself favor-
ably with Diana; she was slain by the goddess's arrow. The narrator
describes Daedalion's rushing about in wild grief over her death
thus: *iam tum mihi currere visus / plus homine est, alasque pedes sump-
sisse putares* (336, "then already he seemed to me to be running in a
superhuman manner: you might have thought his feet had acquired
wings"). This foreshadows his metamorphosis, which soon follows.
Retaining his *virtutem antiquam* (343, "former courage"), he is made
a bird:

et nunc accipiter, nulli satis aequus, in omnes
saevit aves, aliisque dolens fit causa dolendi. (344–45)

And now as a hawk, fair to none, he exercises his rage against
all the birds, and, sorrowing himself, becomes a cause of sorrow to others.

Like Lycaon, Daedalion now reveals himself plainly. By his behavior
as a hawk he displays his natural bellicosity, which, joined to angry
grief over the loss of his daughter, results in swift, murderous attacks upon others. Ovid has emphasized each feature during the
course of the story and now combines them in the final transformation. The hawk encapsulates the man.

Ceyx himself, the narrator of this story, becomes the subject of the
one after the next, which shows that metamorphosis can make manifest gentler qualities. He and his wife Alcyone are remarkably devoted to one another. Their mutual affection is illustrated in a sequence of scenes: her reluctance for him to undertake a long voyage,
their farewell when he does depart, his thinking only of her as he
drowns in a storm at sea, her dream of his death, her wandering
along the shore from which he had left, and finally their reunion
when his body is borne back by the waves and the pair are changed

into birds (11.410–748). The love of Ceyx and Alcyone is made manifest and permanent in the behavior of kingfishers, which are noted for their conjugal affection:

> *fatis obnoxius isdem*
> *tunc quoque mansit amor nec coniugiale solutum est*
> *foedus in alitibus.* (742–44)

Subject to the same destiny, their love abided then too, and the conjugal bond was not loosed when they became birds.

Several other features also embody traits of Ceyx and Alcyone. As the birds' mournful cry, observed as early as Homer (*Il.* 9.561–64), continues their lament over the loss of one another (134–35), so the seven days of calm weather in winter, the halcyon days during which the birds make their nests and hatch their young, represent their domestic and parental ties to each other (744–48). Their chief characteristics are realized in physical, perceptible form.

The unhappy tale of Tereus, Procne, and Philomela offers another complex example. Tereus rapes his wife's sister Philomela, cuts out her tongue, and keeps her hidden in the forest. Procne, once she learns of what has happened, in rage slaughters her own son Itys and serves him as dinner to Tereus. When he then pursues the two sisters with a sword, they are all changed into birds, the women into a nightingale and a swallow, the king into a hoopoe (6.424–674).

> *pendebant pennis. quarum petit altera silvas,*
> *altera tecta subit; neque adhuc de pectore caedis*
> *excessere notae, signataque sanguine pluma est.*
> *ille dolore suo poenaeque cupidine velox*
> *vertitur in volucrem, cui stant in vertice cristae,*
> *prominet inmodicum pro longa cuspide rostrum:*
> *nomen epops volucri, facies armata videtur.* (668–74)

They floated on their wings, one heading for the woods, the other staying about the house. Not yet have the signs of the murder left their breasts: their feathers are marked with blood. He, made swift by his grief and eagerness for revenge, is changed into a bird. Crests stand upon his head, in place of the long sword an immense beak thrusts forward: the bird is called the hoopoe, in appearance he looks armed.

The swallow and nightingale still inhabit their earlier abodes, the former remaining near human habitation, the latter preferring the depths of the forest. The chestnut parts of the swallow and reddish-brown coloring of the nightingale represent the blood and stains from the slaughter. Tereus' armor—his sword and the crests of his helmet—are still present in the hoopoe. Through physical attributes all three retain and reveal their character, or some important piece of it, in their metamorphosed state. The nature of what is preserved varies from one to the other. Tereus' lust, the spring of the whole story, is absent from the hoopoe; only his appearance when he went in pursuit, armed and violent, is kept. Similarly, Ovid chose to highlight the bloody vengefulness of the sisters. He refrained from mentioning the nightingale's mournful cry, which would have represented the continuation of the mother's lament over Itys.[32] Moreover, the vengefulness in their character is not innate but is produced by human misdeeds. Ovid is not concerned with such distinctions. He does not insist that the very essence of character always be preserved through metamorphosis, only something. The process includes an element of the arbitrary.

The story of Iphis and Anaxarete is particularly touching and instructive. Iphis is a young man who falls in love with the proud and cruel Anaxarete. Although he tries approaching her through her nurse, although he lies outside her door all night, he has no success in his suit and out of despair finally hangs himself. The metamorphosis of Anaxarete takes place as she witnesses his funeral. Her eyes becomes rigid, the blood leaves her body, she cannot move her foot or turn her face:

> paulatimque occupat artus,
> quod fuit in duro iam pridem pectore, saxum.   (14.757–58)

And little by little the stone which for a long time already had been inside her hard heart takes over her limbs.

Ovid has emphasized the unfeelingness of her conduct throughout the narrative by repeating like a leitmotiv the word *durus* (707, 709, 713, 749, 758; cf. 693). Her transformation thus is perfectly natural and allows her to be seen for what she is. Of course Ovid is also enjoying a kind of literary joke here, in that he actualizes an image familiar from Roman love elegy: the lover often complains that his mistress is as hard as stone.[33]

The third-century Hellenistic poet Hermesianax had told the story in a version which, preserved for us by Antoninus Liberalis (39), makes a useful comparison with Ovid. The general line of the story runs the same, but the differences reveal what is distinctly Ovidian in the conception of metamorphosis. Hermesianax has the young man's suit rejected not by the unfeeling girl, but rather by her father, who, proud of his own noble descent, finds the lad's Phoenician origins disgraceful. The Greek poet also motivates Aphrodite's intervention differently: according to his version, she hates the girl but also is indignant at the parents for mutilating the nurse who had acted as go-between.[34] These details of the narrative weaken the connection between the girl's character and her metamorphosis, and at the end no reason whatever is given for why she becomes a stone. Ovid, by contrast, retells the story in order to bring out precisely this.

It is not always character which is clarified and fixed by metamorphosis, but sometimes an activity or an emotion, a history or a relation—some aspect of character or a contributing element. When Daphne escapes from Apollo by turning into the laurel, the appearance of the tree both contrasts with and continues the former state: *pes modo tam velox pigris radicibus haeret* (1.551, "her foot, so swift but a moment ago, now is held fast in motionless roots"); but *remanet nitor unus in illa* (552, "only the brightness remains in her"), where *nitor* simultaneously suggests the glossiness of the leaves and the glow of that youthful beauty which attracted Apollo. Ovid gives greater weight to representing the tree as still especially dear to the god: he will always crown with laurel himself and the victors in his Pythian games, as well as triumphant Roman generals; the emperor Augustus, a favorite of his, will bedeck his doors with laurel; and as Apollo's hair is ever uncut, so the laurel will always keep its leaves (1.558–65). Neither the wit of the analogy nor the direct reference to the emperor should prevent us from seeing that the laurel is still Daphne, at least in her relation to Apollo. This relation is what is made manifest in metamorphosis.

Callisto and Arcas undergo more than one transformation. Callisto, raped by Jupiter, gives birth to Arcas and is changed into a bear. Later mother and son are metamorphosed into the constellations of the Great and the Little Bear. It is the final stage of their metamorphosis that interests us here. When they are already stars, Juno, angered at the honor shown to Jupiter's paramour and bastard offspring, prevails upon Tethys and the Ocean never to allow the pair to touch their waters (2.508–31). Thus Ovid invites us to view the familiar fact that these constellations never set as perpetuating her hatred of them.[35] Another pair of animals provides a further instance. The tale of Atalanta and Hippomenes is capped by an unusual metamorphosis. The lovers offend Cybele by making love in her temple and are therefore changed into lions. Ovid makes no connection between their former characters and their present appearances, but rather explains a certain relationship: they are now the lions who draw Cybele's chariot.[36]

Occasionally it is a particular activity which is fixed through metamorphosis. In Book Six Leto is wandering about the Lycian countryside with her infant children, Apollo and Diana, seeking water. When she is about to drink from a pool, the peasants nearby prevent her. They talk abusively to her and stir up the mud at the bottom with their hands and feet. Angered, Leto prays that they may live forever in the pool, and they become frogs:

> nunc quoque turpes
> litibus exercent linguas pulsoque pudore,
> quamvis sint sub aqua, sub aqua maledicere temptant.
>
> . . . .
>
> ipsaque dilatant patulos convicia rictus.   (6.374–76, 378)

Now too they ply their foul tongues in quarreling and, losing all shame, although they are under water, under water they try to curse. . . . Their abusive language spreads wide their jaws.

The permanent continuation of the peasants' activity is spelled out clearly. Elsewhere in the same book the poet recounts the story of Arachne, who had boldly challenged Minerva to a weaving contest. The goddess, grieved at the girl's success in the contest, beats her until, unable to bear it, she hangs herself. Arachne is thereupon metamorphosed into the spider, the Greek word for which her name has become (6.132–45). To see the spider weaving her web or hanging in the air is to behold a memorial of Arachne's characteristic activity and her suicide. Though Minerva declares Arachne's change to be a punishment (137), the change consists chiefly of her becoming more clearly what she has been all along.

Like Arachne's hanging herself, other events or histories are given permanent embodiment through metamorphosis. While the women of Thebes celebrate the arrival of Bacchus in their city, the three daughters of Minyas remain at home and refuse to join in the worship. For their despite they are changed into bats, the characteristics of which Ovid contrives to represent as derived from the events of the day. As the women had spent the whole time in their dark, smoky home and been frightened by the supernatural light of the Bacchic apparitions, so the bats still seek the dark rather than daylight and live in homes, not forests; and their high-pitched cry con-

tinues the women's complaints (4.413–15).[37] Elsewhere we are told
the story of Daedalus' unfortunate nephew Perdix. As clever as his
uncle, the boy invented the saw—the backbone of a fish gave him
the idea—and the drawing compass. Arousing only Daedalus' jealousy, he is hurled by him over a cliff but rescued in midair by Minerva, who transforms him into the partridge. In the shape of the
bird he keeps something of his old self:

> *vigor ingenii quondam velocis in alas*
> *inque pedes abiit; nomen, quod et ante, remansit.*
> *non tamen haec alte volucris sua corpora tollit,*
> *nec facit in ramis altoque cacumine nidos;*
> *propter humum volitat ponitque in saepibus ova*
> *antiquique memor metuit sublimia casus.*   (8.254–59)

The vigor of his mind, formerly so quick, passed into his wings
and feet. His name remained what it had been before. Yet this
bird does not rise aloft or make its nest in high branches or
treetops: it flies near the ground and lays its eggs amongst
hedges; it fears heights, mindful of its earlier fall.

Not only Perdix' native quickness receives physical, visible embodiment through metamorphosis, but also the circumstances of his end.
    A remarkable example is the transformation of Turnus' city Ardea,
once it has been destroyed by the sword and fire of the Trojans, into
the heron (Latin *ardea*). Ovid describes this as follows:

> *congerie e media tum primum cognita praepes*
> *subvolat et cineres plausis everberat alis.*
> *et sonus et macies et pallor et omnia, captam*
> *quae deceant urbem, nomen quoque mansit in illa*
> *urbis, et ipsa suis deplangitur Ardea pennis.*   (14.576–80)

Out of the rubble flies forth a bird seen then for the first time.
Beating its wings, it shakes off the ashes. In it there has remained the sound, the thinness, the pallor, and everything appropriate to the captured city, also the name. Ardea is mourned
with its own wings.

To make us hear human wailing in the heron's cry and see the ashes
of a burnt city in the down of its wings, the grief and hunger of the
inhabitants in its being wan and skinny—this has to be reckoned a
great stroke of imagination on Ovid's part. His effort is to encapsulate the city's destruction in the appearance of the heron: history is
manifested as form.
    Often the aspect of character made clear through metamorphosis

is an emotion. Niobe, having boasted of the number of her children, sees all fourteen of them slain by Apollo and Diana, and when for grief she sits there unmoving, she is transformed into a rock, and then becomes a cliff, a face of Mount Sipylus in Lydia. Her tears, now streams running down the cliff, complete the picture of a weeping woman (6.301–12). A careful study of Ovid's sources for this story shows that his fundamental divergence from them is his removing the gods and concentrating attention instead upon Niobe, whose transformation proceeds almost from within.[38] In an extreme but typical way Ovid represents her as in some sense already being that which she becomes. The cliff that was formerly Niobe, let us also note, manifests not her pride, which Ovid stresses in the tale, but rather the maternal grief which the pride led to.

In view of his fine awareness of human psychology, it is not surprising that Ovid fashions various embodiments of a single emotion, depending on how it affects the character. Or perhaps we should rather say that, despite the covering term which identifies it, each state is unique and comes to clarity in its own way. Byblis, consumed with a grief different from Niobe's, dissolves into tears and becomes a fountain (9.655–65). The grief surrounding the death of Apollo's beloved Cyparissus is represented in still another, and more complex, way. Anguished because of having accidentally killed a beloved pet deer, Cyparissus prays that he may mourn eternally; his prayer granted, he becomes the cypress tree (10.134–42). The tree makes the situation clear in several ways: the boy's grief is manifested in the cypress's gloomy, dark-green color (an emotion), Apollo's in the fact that he will weep over it himself (a relation), and it will also be a symbol of death and sorrow to mankind (an association).

Let us take as a final example Clytie, a girl in love with the Sun but spurned by him. Rooted to the spot and looking constantly at her beloved, she becomes the sunflower, who even now turns ever towards the sun (4.264–70). Ovid says at the end: "changed, she preserves her love." The words *mutata servat* might almost serve as a motto for the *Metamorphoses*.

CONTINUITY

Two essential elements in the Ovidian concept of metamorphosis as clarification are continuity and permanence.

The poet on several occasions states explicitly the persistence of characteristics through metamorphosis. Sometimes he draws attention to the ease of the transformation. When explaining how Cyane was changed into a fountain, he says: *brevis in gelidas membris exilibus undas / transitus est* (5.433–34, "the passage of her slender limbs into cool waters was a brief one"). Elsewhere he recounts the fate of Propoetus' daughters, the world's first prostitutes:

> *utque pudor cessit sanguisque induruit oris,*
> *in rigidum parvo silicem discrimine versae.*   (10.241–42)

And as modesty ceased and the blood in their faces grew hard,
they changed into unmoving flint: the difference was slight.

Sometimes he simply proclaims outright that a trait continues. Besides Lycaon and Daedalion, he does this in a number of other cases: the weasel Galanthis, in whom *strenuitas antiqua manet* (9.320, "her ancient vigor remains"); Pierus' daughters, who have become magpies, though *nunc quoque in alitibus facundia prisca remansit* (5.677, "now too their former loquacity has remained in the birds"); and twigs that have grown hard in water: *nunc quoque curaliis eadem natura remansit* (4.750, "now too the same nature has remained to the coral"). In another passage Aeacus describes how the population of Aegina, decimated by a plague, was re-created from a colony of ants:

> *mores, quos ante gerebant,*
> *nunc quoque habent: parcum genus est patiensque laborum*
> *quaesitique tenax, et quod quaesita reservet.*[39]   (7.655–57)

The men now too have the same character as before: they are a
frugal race, enduring of toil, and tenacious in their seeking, and
what they have sought they save.

Though the reverse of the usual transformation, in that animals here turn into men, this again registers the continuity.[40]

It may sometimes appear that the continuity between the before and after states rests on what is nearly a play with language. A word is used once in a literal, once in a figurative sense. Thus in Book Fourteen an Apulian shepherd who mocks and reviles the dancing of the nymphs is metamorphosed into a wild olive. Ovid concludes his account:

> *arbor enim est, sucoque licet cognoscere mores:*
> *quippe notam linguae bacis oleaster amaris*
> *exhibet: asperitas verborum cessit in illas.*   (14.524–26)

He is a tree: you might recognize his character from its juice:
the bitter fruit of the wild olive display the mark of his tongue:
the harshness of his words has passed into them.

By employing "bitter" and "harsh" in two senses, Ovid makes the reader feel that the shepherd's character has been given physical embodiment. This is witty, to be sure. It also renders physical and concrete a familiar process in language history, by which a word extends its meaning from literal to figurative.

Ovid similarly plays with figurative and literal hardness in the case of the Propoetides. Elsewhere the Sun, seeing that his beloved Leucothoe has been buried alive by her father and is beyond his aid, sprinkles her with nectar in order to turn her into frankincense. He says to her consolingly: *tanges tamen aethera* (4.251, "nevertheless, you will touch heaven"). This refers both to the persistence of his feelings for her and to the religious practice by which frankincense was burnt as an offering to the gods. While describing the re-creation of mankind from stones, the poet notes that "what had just now been a vein kept the same name" (1.410). Characteristically, he repeats the joke but runs it the other way: the veins of the girl Aglauros turn into the veins of the rock she becomes (2.824). And the *latus* of Aeneas' ships, which was probably a technical term,[41] is similarly transformed into the *latus*, "side," of the nymphs (14.552). Such passages indicate not only how interested Ovid was in the phenomena of language but also how keen he was on demonstrating that some important quality is preserved through metamorphosis.

Ovid's notion of continuity in metamorphosis is illuminated in an essay by Dörrie, which examines its relation to ancient philosophical thought.[42] Dörrie shows the parallel between our poet and the philosopher Posidonius (ca. 135–50 B.C.), who exercised great influence upon the Roman statesmen and intellectuals of his day. Posidonius held that there were two kinds of substance, one material, the other qualitative; the former changed, the latter did not.[43] This implies that behind the flux of material alteration there exists some essence of a being which persists. The notion resembles Ovid's in that it combines the possibilities of change and continuity. Where and how it sees the manifestations of continuity, whether in this point also it resembles Ovid's, we do not know. Dörrie traces Posidonius' doctrine in turn to Pythagorean teachings about the transmigration of the soul, according to which the soul is reborn into the body to which it has acquired the greatest similarity: a cunning person might be reborn as a fox, for instance. Here Dörrie makes an instructive contrast with Ovid: in the Pythagorean view the vehicle of continuity is the soul, which of course plays no role whatever in the Ovidian notion of metamorphosis. Though Ovid is far from being a philosopher, as Dörrie is careful to emphasize, and though some uncertainty still surrounds Posidonius' thought, the connection remains intriguing.

In several cases, it must be admitted, the poet indicates no continuity between the person and his metamorphosed state. He testifies explicitly to the lack of continuity between Picus the man and Picus the woodpecker: *nec quicquam antiquum Pico nisi nomina restat* (14.396, "nothing of his former self was left to Picus except his name"); the narrative, however, belies this somewhat by suggesting that the reddish body and tawny neck of a woodpecker represent the man's purple riding cloak and golden fibula (393–95, with reference to 345). Another passage, however, is unequivocal. Anius' daughters are changed into doves for no apparent reason; the father, who recounts their story, himself admits: *nec qua ratione figuram / perdiderint, potui scire aut nunc dicere possum* (13.671–72, "I could not know for certain how they lost their shape, nor can I tell you now"). Also transformed without any suggestion of continuity are the Tyrrhenian sailors, now dolphins (3.670–86), and Iphis, a boy instead of a girl (9.786–91).

PERMANENCE

Metamorphosis may take place at any time. No rule governs what leads up to it. Though determined to trace some continuity between the states before and after metamorphosis, Ovid does not bind them by any necessary connection. As the elements which will be preserved are unpredictable, so too is the timing of the process. These contribute to the irrational disorder of the world.

Once metamorphosis does take place, however, it is permanent. Daphne will be the laurel, Anaxarete a rock, the Lycian peasants frogs—all forever. A few exceptions are found. Io and Tiresias are returned to their original forms, having been for a time a cow and a woman, respectively (1.588–746, 3.322–38). Erysichthon's daughter undergoes a series of transformations, none of which lasts (8.848–74). Actaeon is changed only once, into a stag, yet when he is devoured by his own dogs, no trace of him remains (3.193–252). But these hardly alter the general picture. Daphne, Anaxarete, and all the others by virtue of their metamorphosis are protected from vicissitude: the form they have now is eternal.

Ovid's keen consciousness of the transition and its significance is manifested in a certain feature of his style which, despite its frequent occurrence, has gone unremarked. He is particularly drawn to describing in-between states, usually during the process of transformation. Thus Hermaphroditus and the nymph who loves him, while being joined into one, resemble neither:

nec duo sunt sed forma duplex, nec femina dici
nec puer ut possit, neutrumque et utrumque videntur.   (4.378–79)

They are not two, but the form is double, so it can be called neither woman nor man: it looks like both and neither.

The cast of the language points up the situation. The correlatives *nec*
. . . *nec* ("neither . . . nor"), as elsewhere *ut* . . . *sic* ("as . . . so"),
register the two poles of definite, identifiable being between which
the creature exists for the moment. The echo in *neutrumque* . . .
utrumque ("neither . . . either") depicts the simultaneous similarity.
Moreover, the verbs *dici possit* ("can be called") and *videtur* ("is seen,"
"looks like") hint at the presence of an observer—Ovid, the reader,
or someone else whose faculties of discerning and naming would be
taxed by this creature. Caught for a moment before its metamorphosis is complete, it represents that absence of definition, clarity, and
fixity which is the mark of ordinary experience.

While she is on the way to becoming a horse, the girl Ocyroe
utters neither words nor whinnies: *nec verba quidem nec equae sonus ille*
videtur, / sed simulantis equam (2.667–68, "that sound indeed seemed
neither words nor the sound of a mare, but rather of one who imitated a mare"). Actaeon is similarly affected in his ability to speak:
sonumque, / etsi non hominis, quem non tamen edere possit / cervus, habet
(3.237–39, "he made a sound which, though not that of a man, was
yet not such as a stag could utter"). And Diomedes has trouble describing the form of his metamorphosed followers: *ut non cygnorum,*
sic albis proxima cygnis (14.509, "theirs was not, to be sure, the form of
white swans, yet it was close to swans' ").

The most elaborate and most interesting such passage is found
near the beginning of the poem. The stones which Deucalion and
Pyrrha have tossed behind them slowly turn into men:

ut quaedam, sic non manifesta videri
forma potest hominis, sed, uti de marmore coepta,
non exacta satis rudibusque simillima signis.   (1.404–6)

The form of man could be seen. It was, though some kind of
form, yet not very clear. It closely resembled a half-worked
statue of marble, begun but not yet finished.

Again Ovid dwells on an intermediate stage of metamorphosis,
when these things were no longer stones but not yet men. The comparison to statuary is ingenious and apt.

Ovid's fascination with such moments extends beyond metamorphosis. The huntress Atalanta is portrayed thus: *facies quam dicere vere / virgineam in puero, puerilem in virgine possis* (8.322–23, "her appearance was such as you could truly call maidenly in a man, manly in a maiden"). A time of day, the dusk, also lends itself to such treatment:

> *tempusque subibat,*
> *quod tu nec tenebras nec posses dicere lucem,*
> *sed cum luce tamen dubiae confinia noctis.*   (4.399–401)

> The time was at hand which you could have called neither
> shadows nor light, but yet it was the boundary between day-
> light and uncertain night.

The emphatic pronoun *tu* ("you") beckons especially to the reader.[44]

This bent of the imagination is characteristic of Ovid. Not only are there many instances in his poem, but there are hardly any outside of it. The only similar passage I know comes from the *Argonautica*, in which Apollonius describes the creatures into which Circe has changed those who fell into her clutches: "beasts not like savage beasts, yet not similar in body to men either" (4.672–73). The marked interest which Ovid displays for in-between states fits with his general interest in processes, physical ones above all. He is fond of recording in detail the changes which come over his characters: Dryope becoming the lotus (9.350–55) or Aeneas' ships becoming sea nymphs (14.549–55), to take just two instances among many. Ovid makes the point that process itself can be as fascinating as product when he narrates how the nymphs came from far around to watch Arachne weave:

> *nec factas solum vestes, spectare iuvabat*
> *tum quoque cum fierent (tantus decor adfuit arti).*   (6.17–18)

> They enjoyed looking not only at the made garments but also
> when they were being made: such was the glory of her art.

It may not be accidental that the poet represents the spectators as engrossed in the work of an artist.

More particularly, these intermediate phases are intense, vivid examples of the flux from which metamorphosis removes the characters. They are the extreme of indeterminacy and shapelessness, the foil to fixity. By dwelling on moments when a figure is neither one thing nor another, when it temporarily lacks identity, Ovid sharpens our sense of the permanence which metamorphosis will bring.[45]

LOSS

Nevertheless, metamorphosis does not take place without loss. In exchange, so to speak, for what they win in clarity and permanence, the transformed men and women give up something. Through metamorphosis they preserve only one aspect, occasionally a few aspects, of their character. They no longer possess it in its rich, complex entirety. Clarification means simplification. Moreover, their motion or activity or location is much circumscribed. Daphne is rooted to the spot, no longer free to roam the trackless groves. Perdix always flies low. Niobe remains fixed in Asia. Ovid calls attention to this several times, as in the contrast he draws in the case of Daphne: "her foot, so swift but a moment ago, now is held fast in motionless roots" (1.551). The limitation placed upon movement is virtually a symbol of the person's inability to grow, develop, alter. The permanence of the condition means that independence is impossible.

The loss which Ovid dwells on most often is the loss of speech. Sometimes this is an important part of the metamorphosis. The Cercopes, changed into monkeys because they lied, are deprived of the ability to speak (14.98–100). By being made a bear, who can only growl, Callisto is prevented from beseeching Jupiter (2.482–83). Usually, though, this loss is simply a concomitant of metamorphosis, without any special appropriateness. Lycaon as a wolf *frustraque loqui conatur* (1.233, "attempts to speak, in vain"). After becoming a heifer Io is no longer capable of human speech: *conatoque queri mugitus edidit ore* (1.637, "from a mouth attempting to utter complaints there came forth only moos"). When she spots her father, she can identify herself only by scratching her name in the ground with her hoof (1.647–50). Lucky she, to have a name composed of two easy letters!

Nowhere does Ovid highlight the loss of speech more than in the case of Actaeon. As soon as the hunter catches sight of himself, now a stag:

> *"me miserum!" dicturus erat: vox nulla secuta est!*
> *ingemuit: vox illa fuit.*   (3.201–2)

He was going to say "Woe is me!": no voice came forth! He groaned: that was his voice.

Later, as he flees from his own hounds, "he would have liked to shout, 'I am Actaeon: recognize your master': the words did not come" (3.229–31; cf. 237–39). Ovid reinforces the point by means of a contrast between Actaeon, who cannot even speak his own name, and his dogs, of whose names he has just finished giving an epic catalogue (206–25, thirty-six names).[46]

What Ovid says about Dryope suggests a reason why loss of speech held such interest for him. At the moment of her metamorphosis into a tree, he writes, *desierant simul ora loqui, simul esse* (9.392, "her mouth had at the same moment ceased to speak and to exist"). It matters little whether he means that she spoke up to the very last second of her life or that once she ceased speaking, she ceased living. Life, or at least the life of an individual self, is practically coextensive with talk. In Ovid's rhetorical view of life, discourse creates identity, and correspondingly, the failure of speech "exemplifies the fact that the person transformed can no longer create his own identity or his present reality but becomes captured in the materiality of natural force."[47]

That speech, identity, and metamorphosis form a kind of nexus in the poet's imagination is suggested by two groups of figures in whom he has a special interest. He is intrigued by those who have the power to make and remake their own identity. In the charming tale of how Peleus had to hold on to Thetis through all her metamorphoses in order to win her as wife (11.238–63), he is the focus rather than she. Ovid seems to identify strongly with that other pair of self-transformers, Erysichthon's daughter Mnestra (8.852–74) and Vertumnus (14.643–56, 685–86, 765–71), who share certain qualities.[48] Both are witty and attractive; both assume new roles with their new guises; and both employ words in double senses. (Vertumnus, moreover, is a story-teller). Ovid is also fascinated by characters who create their own selves through speech, as do in different ways Echo, Niobe, Medea, Scylla, Byblis, Myrrha, and Ulysses.

Metamorphosis renders statement useless: appearance and action alone tell who a person is. In taking away speech metamorphosis robs him of the power to name himself, to form or change his self, to feign another. It is hardly surprising that for Ovid this should be the severest loss.

ANIMALS AND GODS

Animals are ordinarily ranked lower than men in the scale of animate beings, as gods are ranked higher, the criterion being rationality. This scheme hardly belongs in Ovid's poem, however, and has been a source of confusion in understanding metamorphosis. Changes from man into beast or divinity do not represent movement up or down in quality of being.

Many critics have assumed without hesitation that metamorphosis into an animal—a wolf, a bear, a nightingale, a frog—is a form of degradation.[49] But Ovid refrains from rankings of every sort and gives no warrant for the belief that the animal kingdom (not to mention the vegetable) is inferior. He attaches no moral connotation to the turning of men into animals. An animal is not a degraded but a clarified form of man. It is simply a creature that has no inner life or concealed character, no chance for growth, whose appearance and customs declare everything about it.

An interesting passage from the comic writer Philemon makes a similar point (frag. 89 Kock). He contrasts animals with men. Whereas men's characters are as varied as their bodies, animals of the same species have but one appearance and one character: all lions are brave, all hares cowardly, all foxes cunning. Fränkel amplifies this: "In contrast to the infinite variety of human characters and modes of relationship, each animal has its own fixed and familiar characteristic. . . . Hence animal creation provides guidelines for orienting us in the human world and ready symbols for the quick apprehension of the characters and actions of persons."[50] This comes so close to describing not only the nature of animal metamorphosis but also the role of metamorphosis in our perceptions that one is almost astonished to realize he is not discussing Ovid, but similes in Greek lyric poetry.

As for divine metamorphosis, Ovid includes four apotheoses among his transformations, none of which is a rising to a higher form of existence. Hercules is the first (9.262–70). He loses all similarity to his mortal mother and preserves traces only of Jupiter. Like a snake laying aside his old skin, *parte sui meliore viget* (269, "he flourishes in his better part"). Anderson, pointing out the unadmirable position of the gods within the poem and the ambiguity of the simile here, has shown that this change marks no distinction.[51] It ought to be noted also that divinity is not bestowed on the hero through metamorphosis, it is in him all along and merely comes to predominate. Again with Aeneas (14.600–607), whose mother is a goddess, the emphasis lies on the purging of mortal members rather than the acquisition of a new status.[52] The apotheosis of Romulus follows at a short distance (14.823–28). His divine parent Mars, it is true, in pleading with Jupiter cites the growth of Rome under Romulus and the current dispensability of his leadership, so that he is ready for his reward. Yet Mars stresses Jupiter's earlier promise of immortality more heavily than any grounds for it, and Romulus' shedding of his human parts, jarringly compared to a lead bullet melting as it hurtles through the air, merely makes him handsomer and more worthy of heaven. (The apotheosis of his wife Hersilia is added as a kind of appendix.)

In each case divine ancestry is made clear through metamorphosis. This is true as well for the last apotheosis, Julius Caesar's, to which Ovid gives an unusual twist. Again Venus pleads for her offspring. The poet himself spells out the grounds:

> *Marte togaque*
> *praecipuum non bella magis finita triumphis*
> *resque domi gestae properataque gloria rerum*
> *in sidus vertere novum stellamque comantem*
> *quam sua progenies.*   (15.746–50)

Famed in war and peace, he became a new star, a comet, as much by virtue of his offspring as by his triumphant campaigns, domestic achievements, and early glory.

In a sense, Augustus deifies Caesar. Then with a witty reversal Ovid also has Caesar deify Augustus: *ne foret hic igitur mortali semine cretus, / ille deus faciendus erat* (760–61, "therefore, lest Augustus be sprung from mortal seed, Caesar needed to be made a god"). No less than the flattery, which is extended in Jupiter's prophecy of Augustus' deeds and deification (822–42) and in Ovid's prayer to Augustus (861–70), the sophistry and humor of the passage are obvious. The circularity of the "argument" prevents this metamorphosis from seeming like an elevation in status.

Metamorphosis in Literature

This notion of metamorphosis which I have been describing is not only sovereign in Ovid: it is also distinctive. Though not unique, it nevertheless is neither forceful nor frequent enough in any other writer to be considered significant. This can best be brought out through a series of comparisons between Ovid and other authors.

Many stories similar to Ovid's are preserved in the *Metamorphoses* of Antoninus Liberalis, a compilation from the late second century A.D.[53] This work gives concise prose versions of forty-one stories of metamorphosis. Marginal notes purport to cite the original sources, among whom the principal ones are said to be Nicander and Boios, Hellenistic poets both drawn on by Ovid. Despite Antoninus' brevity and occasional mingling of separate versions, and despite the unreliability of the attributions, he provides much useful material for comparison.

The collection does include a few tales in which the shape assumed after metamorphosis reflects some trait of the original being. The twenty-second, for instance, concerns the shepherd Kerambos, famous for his singing and his invention of the lyre, who because of an insult offered to the nymphs is transformed into an insect whose head and horns resemble a lyre made from a tortoise shell. But also derived from Nicander is Antoninus' account of the Minyads (10), the three sisters who prefer to weave rather than worship Bacchus and who are changed into a bat and two varieties of owl. It tells that all three avoid the light of the sun; it gives no indication of why, however. By contrast Ovid's account stresses continuity, not only in the birds' shunning of the light but also in their living in houses and emitting shrill cries. Similarly, Nicander (29) describes Galinthias' metamorphosis into a weasel and informs us that she bears young through her mouth. Yet we must turn to Ovid (9.281–323) if we want to learn the reason for this: she gives birth in this way because through her lying mouth she had made it possible for Alcmene to bring forth Hercules; as a weasel now she tells all the world her story. And comparing Boios' version of the story of Aedon (11) with Ovid's parallel tale of Procne (6.424–674) shows once more that the Hellenistic account is not concerned with preservation or clarification through metamorphosis.

The instances of metamorphosis found in other works of Hellenistic literature confirm the distinctiveness of Ovid. In his *Argonautica* Apollonius of Rhodes reports the transformation of the Hesperides into trees: "Hespere became a poplar, Eretheios an elm, and Aegle the sacred trunk of a willow. After becoming these trees they were just as they had appeared before" (4.1427–30). Apollonius declares the similarity of the before and after states, but that is all he does. He says nothing about where the similarity lay. Ovid would have stressed this. Coming down further in time we arrive at Parthenius, a Greek writer who, brought to Rome, exerted a great influence upon Virgil and his contemporaries. Among Parthenius' *Love Romances* one (15) recounts the story of Daphne. We may contrast with Ovid's version this one, which ends: "They say she became the laurel, the tree which is named after her." Parthenius gives no hint of why, except for the name, that girl became that tree. He too is not concerned to note continuity through metamorphosis.[54]

To bring out again the distinctive features in Ovid's notion let us turn to a final pair of comparisons, this time with a Roman poet—

Virgil. The difference between the two is apparent in their versions of Cygnus' story. Mourning the fate of his cousin Phaethon, who was struck from the Sun's chariot by the thunderbolt of Jupiter, Cygnus is changed into the swan. Virgil's account is brief:

> *namque ferunt luctu Cycnum Phaethontis amati*
> *populeas inter frondes umbramque sororum*
> *dum canit et maestum Musa solatur amorem,*
> *canentem molli pluma duxisse senectam*
> *linquentem terras et sidera voce sequentem.*   (*Aen.* 10.189–93)

> They say that because of grief over his beloved Phaethon, Cyg-
> nus, while he was singing and with song was consoling his un-
> happy love amidst the leafy poplars, the shade of his sisters,
> put on hoary old age through his soft plumage, and he left the
> earth and followed the stars with his cry.

The interpretation of this passage is not free from uncertainties. Do the words "followed the stars with his cry" refer to Cygnus' becom- ing a constellation, or do they indicate that as he flew upwards he uttered his distinctive cry?[55] Does the phrase about "hoary old age" mean that Cygnus actually grew old, or is it a roundabout way of expressing that he had whitish feathers?[56] If Cygnus does look aged all at once, we might understand that grief is made permanent in the swan's appearance. In each case, however, the second view seems more plausible. The only continuity between the man and the bird is the mournful song. Implied rather than shown, this remains feeble.

Ovid too suggests a connection between Cygnus' lament and the shrill voice of the swan (2.371–73). But to this he adds a couple of other features which make us sense that the existence of the man is continued and made manifest in the bird:

> *nec se caeloque Iovique*
> *credit, ut iniuste missi memor ignis ab illo;*
> *stagna petit patulosque lacus, ignemque perosus*
> *quae colat elegit contraria flumina flammis.*   (2.377–80)

> He does not entrust himself to heaven and Jupiter, since he re-
> calls the fire unjustly hurled by him. He seeks out pools and
> broad lakes: hating fire, he chooses to inhabit streams which
> are its opposite.

Thus Cygnus' feelings for Phaethon persist in the tendencies to fly low and to live by the water.

To be sure, Virgil was not writing about the theme of metamorpho-

sis, and in his epic narrative he was not likely to dwell on the details
of it. It is wrong to expect or search for a doctrine of metamorphosis
in his work. (This is likewise true for Apollonius and Parthenius, and
also for Antoninus in so far as he recounts stories told by others.)
Nonetheless, the casual descriptions which we do find are illuminating. They remind us that there *is* an Ovidian doctrine of metamorphosis, it is neither the only one nor a necessary one, it is not commonplace, and indeed it is something of an oddity.

Finally we may examine a pair of longer passages. Both writers
describe the transformation of Aeneas' ships into sea nymphs. In
each case Cybele, the presiding deity, appears as if by magic. Virgil
continues like this:

> *et sua quaeque*
> *continuo puppes abrumpunt vincula ripis*
> *delphinumque modo demersis aequore rostris*
> *ima petunt. hinc virgineae (mirabile monstrum)*
> *reddunt se totidem facies pontoque feruntur.*   (*Aen.* 9.117–22)

Each of the ships at once bursts its bonds to the shore. Sinking
their beaks like dolphins, they head for the depths of the sea.
Thence do they return—a remarkable prodigy!—the same number of maidenly forms, and they are borne along the sea.

Virgil is at some pains to ease the transition from the ships to the sea
nymphs. He suggests an intermediate stage in which they were *like*
dolphins, and he finds a fit embodiment of it in the word *rostra*,
which at the same time can apply to both the "beaks" of the ships
and the "snouts" of the dolphins. Despite this, the event remains
miraculous, as is emphasized by the narrator's exclamation. At any
rate, the nymphs are not said to bear any resemblance to the ships.
Metamorphosis here is absolute alteration.

Ovid's version, rather longer, is unusually inventive and also a
splendid instance of what metamorphosis means for him.

> *stuppea praerupit Phrygiae retinacula classis*
> *fertque rates pronas medioque sub aequore mergit;*
> *robore mollito lignoque in corpora verso*
> *in capitum faciem puppes mutantur aduncae,*
> *in digitos abeunt et crura natantia remi,*
> *quodque prius fuerat, latus est, mediisque carina*
> *subdita navigiis spinae mutatur in usum,*
> *lina comae molles, antemnae bracchia fiunt,*
> *caerulus, ut fuerat, color est.*   (14.547–55)

[The mother of the gods] bursts the hempen halters of the Phrygian fleet and, carrying the ships face downwards, sinks them under the sea. The solid wood is softened and changed into flesh, the curving bows are changed into the appearance of faces, the oars become toes and legs to swim with. What was formerly the side, still is. The keel beneath each ship is changed to serve as a spine. The rigging becomes soft hair, the yard-arms become arms. The color is sea-blue, just as before.

The passage hardly requires comment. The poet himself twice explic-itly points out the identity of the before and after states. And he exerts his ingenuity to the utmost in order to induce us to see the nymphs as representing a permanent continuation of Aeneas' ships.

That metamorphosis means clarification is therefore a distinctively Ovidian notion, almost without parallel in the ancient world. The notion did not die with him, however, but has recurred in more recent literature. Two later writers widely separated in time and place, extremely different from one another and from Ovid, but both directly and markedly influenced by him, may serve to illustrate its lasting power. In the *Divine Comedy* Dante often represents the fig-ures whom he meets in the next world as changed into new forms that express the essence of their character. Thus in Canto Nineteen of the *Inferno* the simonists, who sold for money the holy offices and sacred functions of the Church, are planted upside down in holes; three popes are found in this position. Dante pictures their sin as the inversion of the Church's proper role in the world. He gives visible, physical embodiment to their nature.[57] Of course, despite this simi-larity, the medieval poet differs sharply from the ancient in that each of his "metamorphoses" represents a moral judgment, and every judgment fits into a comprehensive and carefully graded structure of absolutes. Nothing could be more foreign to Ovid.

The most famous modern story of metamorphosis has perhaps a closer kinship with Ovid. I have in mind, of course, Kafka's short story "Die Verwandlung," where Gregor Samsa's prior existence—instinctive, blind, parasitic yet solitary, hectic yet insignificant, even grotesque and foul—is encapsulated through his metamorphosis into a giant insect. Kafka too might well have commented that "the change was slight."[58]

Allegory

We are now able to survey the principal features in the world of the poem. This world is permeated by a sense of the flux, disorder, and chaos of experience. The hints of order thrown out are numerous, but they all prove unreliable and inadequate. A sequence of events rarely is related as cause and effect. The point of view on what happens is ever shifting. No firm patterns emerge. The emphasis is laid upon the diversity, even the uniqueness, of the individual's experience—indeed sometimes upon the indeterminacy of the individual's self, of his very identity. No meanings or moralities can be read in this universe. The manner of narration is itself an obstacle. The relations between stories and between parts of stories establish no sense of what is important. The mythological tales are presented in versions which tend to deny them significance. And even metamorphosis itself, the central phenomenon in the world of the poem, imparts no meaning.

Instead metamorphosis introduces clarity of perception. It distills and makes manifest human experience. It expresses no judgment. It removes the obscurity created by an inner life or by the possibility of change. It externalizes something about character, history, or a relation. It regularly makes essence visible, plain, clear. The gods, to the extent that they do govern the process of metamorphosis, merely see to it that men's natures are realized.

The poem has a distinct movement, away from the uncertain flux of experience towards the surface clarity given by metamorphosis. This movement is reflected also in another prominent feature of the narrative. We have already observed Ovid's tendencies to represent inanimate things as human (for instance, Mount Tmolus as the umpire of a singing contest) and to find appropriate physical embodiments for the intangible (such as the South Wind). In the same vein are the extended descriptions of so-called allegorical figures which we find in the poem. Ovid's portraits of Envy, Hunger, Sleep, and Rumor are famous and have a long history in literature. Here we are interested in them because they are brilliant examples of the general striving towards clarity.

Let us begin with the description of Hunger. With the aim of punishing the impious Erysichthon, Ceres sends a messenger to summon Hunger from her home in the Caucasus:

quaesitamque Famem lapidoso vidit in agro
unguibus et raras vellentem dentibus herbas.
hirtus erat crinis, cava lumina, pallor in ore,
labra incana situ, scabrae rubigine fauces,
dura cutis, per quam spectari viscera possent;
ossa sub incurvis exstabant arida lumbis,
ventris erat pro ventre locus; pendere putares

pectus et a spinae tantummodo crate teneri.
auxerat articulos macies, genuumque tumebat
orbis, et inmodico prodibant tubere tali.   (8.799–808)

In a stony field she saw the one she was seeking: Hunger, tearing with teeth and nails at the sparse vegetation. Her hair was
shaggy, her orbs hollow, her face pallid. Her lips had become
gray with disuse, her throat flaked with mold. Her skin was so
taut that through it her entrails could be examined. Beneath
crooked hips her dry bones protruded. In place of a belly there
was a space for a belly. Her chest sagged and was held, you
might have thought, only by the lattice of ribs from the spine.
Gauntness had enlarged her joints: the circle of her knees was
swollen, while her ankles stuck out with enormous swelling.

Here Ovid conveys everything about Hunger by describing her appearance, the outer surface of her being. Hunger is the very image of
a hungry person. That she has not tasted or swallowed anything is
evidenced by her gray lips and scabrous throat. The consequences of
not eating can be seen in her pallor, her fleshless body, and a dozen
other details. Furthermore, Ovid gives her an appropriate setting:
she dwells in cold and barren Scythia, where she must grub in the
stony soil for plants. The purely external, visual nature of the description stands out more clearly if we consider what is not found in
it: Hunger has no inner life, no feelings or thoughts; she is considered entirely by herself, not in relation to anyone or anything else;
she is not moralized in any way. Nothing is said about her which the
eye could not take in at once. The figure of Hunger displays the
same clarity as does Lycaon after his metamorphosis. Essence lies on
the surface. Though in one it is the end of a process whereas in the
other it is a given, the result is the same.

By examining three allegorical descriptions from earlier literature
we can see more clearly how distinctive our poet is. The topos begins
with the *Iliad*. In Book Nine, Phoenix, advising Achilles to relent,
accept Agamemnon's offer, and rejoin the battle, tells him of the
Litai, or Prayers:

> For in fact the Prayers are the daughters of great Zeus, lame and
> wrinkled and looking askance with their eyes, who are at pains
> to follow behind Ruin. But Ruin is strong and sound of foot,
> wherefore she races far ahead of all the others and is the first
> to do men harm over the entire earth. But the Prayers make
> amends afterwards. Whoever respects the daughters of Zeus
> when they draw near, they benefit him greatly and they listen to

him when he prays. But whoever spurns them and denies them harshly, they go to Zeus, son of Kronos, and beseech him to send Ruin after that man, so that he may by his suffering make atonement. (*Il.* 9.502–12)

The passage, to be sure, opens with physical description. But unlike the hollowness of Hunger's eyes, the lameness, wrinkles, and sidelong glances of the Prayers do not in themselves immediately convey something to the reader: they require interpretation. On reflection, and after considering the rest of the passage, we might conclude that they are lame because people are slow to repent and to entreat, wrinkled because people are not cheerful in countenance when they do so, and looking askance because in such circumstances people are ashamed to look the entreated one directly in the face.[59] A far larger portion of the portrait is relational: we understand who the Prayers are through their conduct towards others (the entreating, the entreated, Ruin, and Zeus) rather than through their own physical appearance. And Phoenix tells all this in order to point a moral. We are far from Ovid.

Closer perhaps is a passage from the pseudo-Hesiodic *Shield of Heracles*. Among the horrors of war carved on the shield the author depicts *Achlus*:

Beside them stood *Achlus*, gloomy and dread, pale, dried and crouching with hunger, swollen in the knees. Long nails lay at the tips of her fingers. From her nose ran mucus, from her cheeks blood dripped onto the ground. She stood there grinning unapproachably. Dust, thick and soaked with tears, covered her shoulders. (264–70)

The passage consists wholly of physical description. Yet, though the figure is vividly portrayed, it is by no means clear what it represents. Several important words, including *Achlus* itself (which usually means "mist," especially "the mist of death"), are too obscure now to help us in identifying it. The chief difficulty is that the details—the long fingernails, the mucus, the blood, etc.—do not coalesce to form a single distinct picture. If the figure is rendered visible and vivid to us, this is the result of the poet's describing her as an image carved on a shield: the narrator conceives of her vaguely but nevertheless, as almost a requirement of his situation, in visual terms.

The next examples of such extended allegories are found in the *Aeneid*. In Book Seven Virgil depicts the Fury Allecto, whom Juno employs to rouse Turnus, Amata, and the Italians against the Trojan newcomers. The poet executes her portrait in various ways. He characterizes Allecto by declaring her parentage (Pluto and Night, 7.327, 331), by recounting her effect on others (even her father and sisters hate her, 327–28), and by listing the things that are dear to her (war, wrath, treachery, wrongdoing, 325–26). He also searches for some physical embodiment, much of which is not specific but general and interpretive: Allecto is said to have "violent looks" (329), "a savage face" (415), and "a frenzied mouth" (451). What is specific is grotesque and inhuman: a Fury, she has snakes for hair (329, 346–47, and elsewhere). And, as is typical of Virgil, this allegorical description is strongly moralized. Besides the adjectives just mentioned, which convey obvious judgments, Virgil calls her "grief-producing" (324), one of the "the dread goddesses" (324), a true "monster" (328).[60]

Practically none of these qualities of the Virgilian allegory are to be found in Ovid, whose descriptions are specific, visible, human, immediately understood, and free from moralizing. The most brilliant of his allegories is *Invidia*, or Envy. Here Ovid outdoes himself in refinement of composition and ingenuity of language. The passage repays careful study.

> *protinus Invidiae nigro squalentia tabo*
> *tecta petit: domus est imis in vallibus huius*
> *abdita, sole carens, non ulli pervia vento,*
> *tristis et ignavi plenissima frigoris, et quae*
> *igne vacet semper, caligine semper abundet.*
> *huc ubi pervenit belli metuenda virago,*
> *constitit ante domum (neque enim succedere tectis*
> *fas habet) et postes extrema cuspide pulsat;*
> *concussae patuere fores: videt intus edentem*
> *vipereas carnes, vitiorum alimenta suorum,*
> *Invidiam visaque oculos avertit; at illa*
> *surgit humo pigre semesarumque relinquit*
> *corpora serpentum passuque incedit inerti,*
> *utque deam vidit formaque armisque decoram,*
> *ingemuit vultuque deae suspiria duxit.*[61]
> *pallor in ore sedet, macies in corpore toto,*
> *nusquam recta acies, livent rubigine dentes,*
> *pectora felle virent, lingua est suffusa veneno;*
> *risus abest, nisi quem visi movere dolores,*
> *nec fruitur somno, vigilantibus excita curis,*
> *sed videt ingratos intabescitque videndo*

successus hominum carpitque et carpitur una
suppliciumque suum est.   (2.760–82)

Minerva headed at once for Envy's abode, which is foul with
filthy gore. The house is hidden away at the bottom of a valley,
untouched by the sun, open to no breeze. It is gloomy and
filled with a torpid chill. Always it lacks a fire, always it is
shrouded in mist. The virago terrifying in war, when she had
arrived and stood before the house—she thought it forbidden
to enter—knocked with the tip of her spear. The doors flew
open; within she saw Envy feasting on vipers' flesh, the nourishment of her own vices, and having seen her she averted her
eyes. Envy now sluggishly arose from the ground, left off the
half-devoured snakes, and came forward with a slothful step.
Upon seeing the goddess's beauty and bright armor, she
groaned; over the goddess's lovely face she heaved a sigh. Pallor is settled over Envy's countenance, emaciation over her
whole body. Her glance is all asquint; her teeth are black with
mold, her breast is green with spite; her tongue is steeped in
poison. Kept awake by anxious cares, she does not sleep. Instead she sees, without pleasure, human successes and is dev-
astated by the sight. At the same time Envy gnaws and is
gnawed: she is her own torment.

Ovid has elaborated the abstraction Envy as fully as possible. Not
only her appearance but her abode, gestures, and even diet convey
to the reader her nature and effect. One scholar has culled from
ancient literature instances of the association of envy with such ills as
disease, darkness, secrecy, and cold.[62] Welcome as this confirming
evidence is, the reader hardly needs it to understand the description,
which speaks for itself.

Several things are special here. Ovid has animated the description
by imparting movement to it: he makes the parts follow a narrative
line. One can readily visualize it as a movie, filmed by a single camera without cutting. The scene opens with a view of first the setting
of Envy's house, then (as the camera moves in, so to speak) the
house itself, as they appeared to Minerva. Next Minerva arrives and
knocks on the door, which flies open. Through the door she then
catches sight of Envy, and Envy in turn sees her. Finally Ovid describes Envy's actions as she approaches Minerva and then her appearance. Though this last marks the climax of the scene, everything
that has preceded is turned to good effect: not one detail fails to
impart something about Envy. After the end of the description Ovid

moves away from the present scene towards general statements: for instance, that Envy does not smile or sleep. So far does he go in the direction of abstraction that he can soon say that "at the same time Envy gnaws and is gnawed" and then, as an epigrammatic curtain line, the logical consequence of this: "she is her own torment." The wit derives from representing Envy simultaneously as a feeling affecting a person and the person affected.[63] Except for the end the passage conveys only what can be seen of the figure.

Another special feature of the passage is the use of words which have both physical-real and abstract-figurative applications. In the successive phrases *livent rubigine dentes, / pectora felle virent* (776–77), we note the chiasmus and the contrast of colors. More remarkable is the double sense of each verb. *Livent* means both "be livid, discolored" and "be envious." *Virent* means both "be green" and "be blooming with, full of." The language is perfectly apt for the portrait of an abstraction given physical reality.

Ovid builds up his portraits almost solely through descriptions of appearance, that is to say, of surfaces. To understand Envy we need only to look at her. She simply is what she seems to be. In no ordinary sense of the word then can we call her and similar figures "allegories," for there is no "other" that they refer to, no meaning or significance that does not lie on the surface. The poet, in his reliance on surfaces alone as means of representation, is not unlike a painter.

CHAPTER SIX

ART

Metamorphosis as Art

One more step remains towards our understanding of metamorphosis. We have established that metamorphosis is clarification, but the purpose that it serves is still unexplored. The best way of getting at that purpose is to notice that metamorphosis is a kind of art and that therefore the poem is about art. By calling it "a kind of art" I mean that metamorphosis results in a form—a bird, a tree, a stone—which shares the essential properties of a work of art. After the similarity (or identity) between metamorphosis and art has been indicated, the investigation of art's relation to nature, the place of the artist, and the function of art in the world will all shed light on the poem's central phenomenon. Ovid's employment of several terms, principally *imago*, yields some of the most valuable evidence on these questions.[1] The conclusion which emerges is that art/metamorphosis is necessary for perception.

INDICATIONS

The poem invites us to draw the parallel between metamorphosis and art in a number of ways, for instance, through a simile found near the beginning. Mankind, all but wiped out in the flood, is restored through the stones which Deucalion and Pyrrha are ordered to toss behind them. Ovid describes the stones as they appeared at the midpoint of their transformation:

> *ut quaedam, sic non manifesta, videri*
> *forma potest hominis, sed, uti de marmore coepta,*
> *non exacta satis rudibusque simillima signis.*　　　　(1.404–6)

The form of man could be seen. It was some kind of form,
though not a very clear one. It closely resembled a half-worked
statue of marble, begun but not yet finished.

The simile suggests that the processes of metamorphosis and artistic
creation are alike: while turning into people the stones are on the
way to becoming statues. The language reinforces this, echoing famous passages in which two poets had referred to art. The word
exacta ("finished") may recall Horace's verses on his own artistic creation: *exegi monumentum aere perennius* (*Carm.* 3.30.1, "I have com-
pleted a monument more enduring than bronze"). A phrase applied
to the stones a few lines earlier, *ducere formam* (402, "mold their
shape"), is especially suitable to sculpture: the Virgilian *vivos ducent
de marmore vultus* (*Aen.* 6.848, "they will mold lifelike faces from marble") may be compared. And earlier Deucalion, observing that they
two were the only mortals left, had said to his wife, *hominumque
exempla manemus* (366, "we remain the *exempla* of mankind"). Whether
exempla means "(sole) copies," with regard to the other, lost originals,
or "(artist's) models," with regard to the people whom they are to
create afresh, this word too belongs to the realm of art.

The implication of the simile and its context is borne out by the
language Ovid often chooses for metamorphosis, through which he
represents the results of it directly as a work of art, either a painting
or a sculpture. Many characters are changed into stones, and some
of these are said to be statues, Aglauros for one. Refusing because of
jealousy to allow Mercury to enter the bedroom of her sister, she
slowly loses all movement and turns into a rock: *signumque exsangue
sedebat* (2.831, "she sat stock still, a bloodless statue"). Anaxarete,
who treated her suitor so harshly, also becomes a rock, and *dominae
sub imagine signum / servat adhuc Salamis* (14.759–60, "the city of Salamis still preserves her statue in the likeness of its mistress"). Similarly we hear in passing about "the statue of a long dragon made of
rock" (7.358); the word here is *simulacrum*. Metamorphosis into stone
would have been adequate, because it would have preserved eternally Aglauros' standing fast and Anaxarete's lack of feeling. In each
case, though, Ovid did not stop with that but took the further step of
identifying the transformed figure as a statue.

By far the most prolific creator of statuary is the head of Medusa.
Perseus relates how on his way to do battle with her he had seen the
effects of her glance upon the neighborhood:

> *passimque per agros*
> *perque vias vidisse hominum simulacra ferarumque*
> *in silicem ex ipsis visa conversa Medusa.*   (4.779–81)

Throughout the fields and roadways he had seen statues of
men and animals, changed from their own selves into stone because of having looked at Medusa.

Cutting off the head and taking it for his own use, he moves on to
his next adventure, with Andromeda. At the marriage feast, finding
himself outnumbered in battle by Phineus, to whom Andromeda
had first been betrothed, and Phineus' henchmen, Perseus resorts to
the ultimate weapon. Thescelus, preparing to cast at him, is his first
victim: *in hoc haesit signum de marmore gestu* (5.183, "he remained
fixed in this gesture—a marble statue"). He, like the others, it should
be noted, is changed into marble, not merely stone (cf. 206, 214,
234). Soon all but the leader are turned into statues (*simulacra*, 211), a
two-hundred-piece sculpture gallery created with the twinkle of an
eye. Before doing in Phineus, Perseus taunts him with the thought
that his statue will remain in their house; he speaks of it as a *monumentum*[2] and an *imago* (227, 229).[3] That the statues are not intrinsic
in the story of Medusa but special to this version we may confirm by
comparison: Apollodorus nowhere refers to or hints at statuary in his
handbook summary of the story (2.42–43), neither do Hyginus (*Fab.*
64) or the First Vatican Mythographer (74), nor does Claudian in an
otherwise strikingly Ovidian account of how Minerva wielded the
petrifying visage (*Gigant.* 91–113).

A key term in the coinciding vocabularies of art and metamorphosis is *imago*, "image" or "representation." The frequency with which
it is used of the results of metamorphosis indicates how strongly
Ovid felt them to be like works of art. In its general sense *imago* can
be applied to statues. Thus the poet says of one of Perseus' victims,
immotusque silex armataque mansit imago (5.199, "he remained stone
unmoving, an armed image").[4] *Imago* can also have the more specific
sense of "picture," which suggests the art of painting. Ovid summarizes his portrait of Lycaon thus: *eadem feritatis imago est* (1.239, "he is
the very same picture of savagery"). For aid in battle Jason avails
himself of special means, and each warrior produced by transformation from the dragon's teeth is called *imago hominis* (7.128–29, "an
image of a man"). An identical phrase is used for both Procne and
Hecuba as each, possessed by thirst for revenge, begins her metamorphosis: *poenaeque in imagine tota est* (6.586 and 13.545, "her entire
being is in the image of punishment").

The sense of metamorphosis as a form of art runs so strong in
Ovid that he employs terms from the latter sphere where they hardly
seem to fit; the strain upon the language indicates the bent of his
imagination. The dead Adonis is addressed thus by Venus:

> *luctus monumenta manebunt*
> *semper, Adoni, mei, repetitaque mortis imago*
> *annua plangoris peraget simulamina nostri.*   (10.725–27)

The monuments of my grief will remain eternally, Adonis, and the repeated image of your death will perform the annual simulations of my lament.

The words *monumenta, imago,* and *simulamina* (here translated quite literally) are all regularly used for works of art.[5] And yet here they refer not to any physical object, but rather to the Adonia, an annual ritual evocation of Adonis' death celebrated widely through eastern Mediterranean lands. *Simulamina* perhaps suggested "reenactments," which of necessity cannot be the real, original thing, and this notion may have been picked up by the peculiar *imago*; perhaps too Ovid was influenced by the earlier lines 515–17 (on which see below). However that may be, the poet's tendency towards employing the vocabulary of art for metamorphosis is evident.

CONTENT

The content of the parallelism thus indicated is also evident. Art shares the qualities of metamorphosis which we have recognized in the poem, and our sense of them is reinforced by special turns of phrase. The word *imago,* for instance, is several times used in such a way as to assert the connection between art and clarity. When Ovid says of the transformed Lycaon *eadem feritatis imago est* (1.239), his choice of language refers both to Lycaon's similarity to a work of art and, as such, to his ready recognition. Now an image, the wolf is easily grasped. The English idiom, "the very picture," conveys the multiple sense of *imago* here. Closely akin is the use of the word in a verse from the opening of the poem: *modo quae fuerat rudis et sine imagine tellus* (1.87, "the earth which just now had been rough and without *imago*"), where *imago* means something like "recognizable appearance." *Simulacrum* has the same meaning at least once. Aesculapius promises he will transfer his abode to Rome but will receive worship there in the form of a snake, no longer a man: *veniam simulacraque nostra relinquam* (15.658, "I shall come, leaving behind my familiar appearance"). The phrase repeated for Procne and Hecuba also points to the likeness between metamorphosis and the clarity won by art, as does another with which Ovid describes Hecuba: *Asiae florentis imago* (13.484, "the very picture [or embodiment] of a prospering Asia"). Such passages invite us to view all the transformed figures as *imagines*, "clear pictures," of their former characters, relations, or activities.

Naturally, the many who are changed into rocks must remain motionless. Ovid shows keen awareness of the (obvious) fact that immobility is a property of statues. When Perseus catches sight of the chained Andromeda, the narrator remarks parenthetically:

> *nisi quod levis aura capillos*
> *moverat et tepido manabant lumina fletu,*
> *marmoreum ratus esset opus.*   (4.673–75)

Except that a light breeze had moved her hair and warm tears were flowing from her eyes, he would have thought her a marble statue.[6]

The proposition is restated elsewhere through its corollary, that motion is the sign of a living being, not a statue: the sculpture Pygmalion made, we are told, was so lifelike that you would think it wanted to move (10.250–51). This is the other feature of works of art, their fixity and permanence. We may take the immobility of statues as representing the inability of all metamorphosed creatures ever to change again. Once changed, they will remain what they are now. A price is paid, however, in obtaining the results of metamorphosis. Though perhaps able to move about, the creature is "dead" in that it has lost its personal existence. Of Niobe, stiff with grief and in the process of becoming a statue, Ovid says, *nihil est in imagine vivum* (6.305), which may equally well mean "there is no life in her appearance" or—such is the ambiguity in a language lacking the article— "there is no life in an artistic representation."[7] Plucking something from the random flux of the universe, fixing it, establishing it as a clear point of reference for the rest of us, metamorphosis acts like the eye and hand of an artist.[8]

Nature as Art

We may widen our understanding of metamorphosis therefore by considering the place of art within the world of the poem. Ovid's interest in this is obvious, for he adverts to it often, directly as well as obliquely. It arises chiefly as the question of how art stands in relation to nature.

NATURE OVER ART

Much of the evidence goes to suggest the view, familiar in antiquity and still today, that art is an imitation of nature, and that though art is better in proportion as it succeeds in imitating nature, yet it always remains a secondary order of reality, ever striving to match nature but unable to do so completely. Such a view Ovid expresses most clearly when he emphasizes the realism of works of art, the extent to which they seem actually to be what they represent. One of Phineus' comrades is caught by the Medusa's glance, and the poet says, *adapertaque velle / ora loqui credas* (5.193–94, "you would believe his opened mouth wished to speak"). Cephalus, after relating how both his hound and the fox it had been pursuing were changed into marble statues, adds, *fugere hoc, illud captare putares* (7.791, "you would have thought the one was fleeing, the other still pursuing"). An important example is the sculpture which Pygmalion makes:

virginis est verae facies, quam vivere credas
et, si non obstet reverentia, velle moveri. (10.250–51)

The appearance is that of a real maiden: you would believe she was alive and, if not prevented by modesty, eager to move.

And in the realm of what might be called painting, though the medium is colored, woven thread, we are told about Arachne's representation of the rape of Europa that *verum taurum, freta vera putares* (6.104, "you would have thought the bull real, the seas real too"). All four passages invite attention to the work of art's lifelike quality. It is noteworthy, moreover, and not coincidental, that in each one the realism is reported by an indirect statement depending on a second-person potential subjunctive. The form of the verb momentarily establishes a point of view outside the story and secures the audience's special interest,[9] breaking the frame slightly in order to insist on fiction's close proximity to what is real.

This view is also implicit in a certain distinctively Ovidian semantic usage. With remarkable latitude Ovid often employs the word *imago* in the sense of "deceptive appearance." This connotation repeatedly given to a word which is a standard term for art suggests that art is unreal, in that it merely represents a thing: the gap between thing and representation justifies the notion of deception and in effect asserts the priority of nature over art. The breadth of the uses to which Ovid extends the word gives a measure of his fascination with it. Here is a survey. *Imago* = "disguise": *Liber falsi sub imagine cervi* (7.360, "Bacchus under the guise of a false stag"); *inque pyra sacri sub imagine facti* (14.80, "atop a pyre made under the guise of a sacred rite"); also 1.213, 2.804, 3.1, 3.250, and elsewhere. More abstractly, without reference to actual appearance, *imago* = "illusion": *amicitiae mendacis imagine* (7.301, "through the illusion of feigned friendship"); *genitoris imagine falsi* (1.754, "the delusion of a false father"); also 2.37. *Imago* = "reflection": *me . . . in imagine vidi / . . . aquae*, says the Cyclops (13.840–41, "I saw myself in the reflection of the water"); also 4.349, 15.566. By extension from the visual to the auditory, *imago* = "echo": *deceptus imagine vocis* (3.385, "deceived by the echo of her voice"). *Imago* used for the figure in a dream-vision: *deceptus imagine somni* (13.216, "deceived by an image of sleep"); also 7.649, 8.824, 9.474, 11.587, and elsewhere. Collectively these uses of *imago*, reinforced by the words found in the neighborhood, hint at the strictly imitative, secondary nature of art.[10] In a pair of other passages Ovid plays on two senses of the word: *Maeonis elusam designat imagine tauri / Europam* (6.103–4, "Maeonian Arachne outlines Europa, deceived by the image of the bull"). Here, as also at line 110, *imago* refers at the same time both to the god's disguise and to the artistic representation of it by the weaver-artist. The points of view of Europa and of the spectators, of actor and audience, coincide in a deception.

The doctrine that art is an imitation of nature is, of course, hardly special to Ovid. On the contrary, it was extremely common, perhaps nearly universal, in classical antiquity. A few examples serve as reminders. The doctrine recurs incessantly in the pages of Pliny the Elder which deal with the history of art, Books Thirty-Four through Thirty-Six of his *Natural History*: it is nearly as strong a theme there as it was to be centuries later in Vasari. Beside the figure of the practical encyclopedist we may set that of the greatest of philosophers. Plato views the relation of art to nature in the same way; indeed, in Book Ten of the *Republic* he ranks the reality of art third, the bed painted by the artist being an inferior copy of the object itself, which in turn is less real than the "idea," or "form," of the bed. Phrases that fall from poets' lips betray the same notion. In a passage very similar to several from Ovid, Apollonius of Rhodes emphasizes the lifelike quality of the figures on a mantle Jason wears. "In it was Phrixus the Minyan as though he were really listening to the ram, while it looked as if it were speaking. You would fall silent at the sight of them, and you would deceive your heart with the hope of hearing from them some shrewd utterance, and with that hope you would continue to gaze for a long time" (*Argon.* 1.763–67). And in that famous passage from Book Six of the *Aeneid* where Anchises expounds the distinctive skills of the Greeks and the Romans, he foretells to his son:

excudent alii spirantia mollius aera
(credo equidem), vivos ducent de marmore vultus.   (*Aen.* 6.847–48)

Others will forge more softly breathing bronze statues (so I believe), they will shape living countenances from marble.

That is, the sculpture of the Greeks will be superior by virtue of its
approximation to life. Again, nature is the norm. This is the traditional notion which we find echoed in the *Metamorphoses*.

ART OVER NATURE

And yet at the same time the poem embraces the very reverse, a
doctrine that is astonishing for its utter novelty and unexpected-
ness—namely, that nature imitates art. In this view art becomes the
norm, the prime creator or definer of reality. This runs completely
counter to the commonsense view of how art is made and what role
it plays in the world. No one before Ovid, so far as I know, ever
conceived this; since him, however, it has reappeared occasionally.[11]
The poet's bold originality in turning a conventional notion upside
down commands our attention. Though it coexists in the poem with
its opposite, it does not seem equal in importance; rather, on account
of its startling nature and not infrequent expression, it outweighs the
other. The doctrine that art follows nature is a kind of foil: in the
doctrine that nature follows art we have a valuable clue for understanding metamorphosis.

Again, the best evidence for this view lies in Ovid's comparisons
between the two realms. He several times compares the beauty of a
person to that of a work of art, implying the superiority of the latter. The bull into which Jupiter transforms himself in order to rape
Europa is depicted as tame and lovely: *cornua parva quidem, sed quae
contendere possis / facta manu* (2.855–56, "his horns were small, to be
sure, but such as you would assert had been made by hand"). Emphasized by *quidem . . . sed*, the contrast here between size and artificiality—a bull's horns are esteemed for size and splendor[12]—shows
that the resemblance to human craftsmanship constitutes praise for
the horns. Ovid's account follows that of Moschus, and at this point
the Greek poet had also introduced a simile: "the matched horns
rose from his head opposite one another in a half-orb like the half-
circle of the horned moon" (2.87–88).[13] Ovid has refashioned and
refocused this simile so as to make prominent the idea of art.

Elsewhere, in the description of the centaur Cyllaron, we are told
how extraordinarily beautiful his human parts are: *cervix umerique*

manusque / pectoraque artificum laudatis proxima signis (12.397–98, "his
neck and shoulders, hands and breast were most like the renowned
statues made by artists").[14] Art also sets the standard by which to
judge the looks of Adonis:

> *qualia namque*
> *corpora nudorum tabula pinguntur Amorum,*
> *talis erat, sed, ne faciat discrimina cultus,*
> *aut huic adde leves aut illi deme pharetras!*   (10.515–18)

Like the bodies of naked Cupids painted on canvas, such was
he; but, so that adornment not make a distinction between
them, either give a lightweight quiver to the one or take it away
from the other!

The remarkable editorial comment, in which the narrator adjusts his
own simile, is no less distinctive of the poem than is the simile itself.[15] Other comparisons of people to works of art carry the same
implication, that the beauty of art is superior. The effect of Hermaphroditus swimming in the waters of the pond Salmacis is "as if
someone should cover an ivory statue with clear glass" (4.354–55).[16]
And with similar connotation the poet likens both Andromeda
(4.675) and Narcissus (3.418–19) to marble statuary, and Pygmalion
carves his ideal woman in ivory (10.245–69), though in the former
the point is also immobility,[17] in the latter chastity.

The superiority of art over nature is not confined to beauty, but is
more general, and indeed Ovid makes his strongest statements of
this in regard to something neither beautiful nor ugly. He is setting
the scene for Peleus' meeting with Thetis, on the coast of Thessaly;
sea and sand are present, and also the myrtle tree,

> *est specus in medio, natura factus an arte,*
> *ambiguum, magis arte tamen.*   (11.235–36)

and in the middle was a grotto: it was uncertain whether made
by nature or art, yet more by art.

Here the terms are stated directly. After a moment's hesitation the
poet decides that the grotto is more artifice than phenomenon of
nature,[18] despite the fact that all the other surroundings appear
natural. More remarkable is the description of another grotto, where
Diana is bathing when she is seen by Actaeon:

> *cuius in extremo est antrum nemorale recessu*
> *arte laboratum nulla: simulaverat artem*

ingenio natura suo; nam pumice vivo
et levibus tofis nativum duxerat arcum.   (3.157–60)

In the most distant corner of the valley is a sylvan grotto, produced by no art: nature by its own power had simulated art; for
it had shaped a natural arch of living pumice and smooth tufa.

The stream which runs through the cave makes this a grotto-nympheum, like the one inhabited by Achelous (8.562–64; see Chapter
Three). Here Ovid informs us who was responsible for the artifice: it
is not man, but nature itself. What an extraordinary form of statement—"nature by its own power had simulated art"! The words
laboratum and *ingenio* and the syntax of the sentence, with *natura* the
subject of a transitive verb, tend to personify nature, which renders
more plausible the inversion of a familiar relationship. And nature's
role is emphasized by repeating the root of *natura* in *ingenio* and
nativum.[19] The same odd relationship is suggested elsewhere by the
phrase *artifices natura manus admovit* (15.218, "nature used her artful
hands"). To be sure, *artifices* might mean simply "skillful," but in the
context of the poem the juxtaposition with *natura* seems intended
and the notion "artful" justified. The point of view taken by Ovid
brings to mind an exchange from *The Winter's Tale*, where the discussion is about parti-colored flowers and how they are produced:

> *Perdita.*   For I have heard it said
> There is an art which in their piedness shares
> With great creating nature.
> *Polixenes.*   Say there be;
> Yet nature is made better by no mean
> But nature makes that mean. So, over that art
> Which you say adds to nature, is an art
> That nature makes. . . .
>   This is an art
> Which does mend nature—change it rather—but
> The art itself is nature.   (4.4.86–92, 95–97)

Perdita raises the question of art's role in what is considered natural.
In his reply Polixenes denies the antithesis of art and nature: art, he
claims, is itself finally nature. Ovid too erases the antithesis, but by
the opposite move!

The description of Diana's grotto is one of the most important passages in the *Metamorphoses*. It states most clearly the poem's unique
view of how art is related to nature.[20] This is not, to be sure, the only
work of Ovid's to which the theme of art is central. The *Ars Amatoria*

is concerned with it also, though it takes a different view. The notion that dominates in the *Ars* is that art is deception, and the ideal lover is instructed to be an artist/deceiver. Yet there too another notion is found, which adumbrates that of our poem. In speaking of the recognition which art bestows, Ovid advances this extreme claim:

> *si Venerem Cous nusquam posuisset Apelles,*
> *mersa sub aequoreis illa lateret aquis.*   (*Ars* 3.401–2)

If Apelles in Cos had never painted Venus, she would be unknown, sunk beneath the waters of the sea.

Referring to a famous painting of Venus' birth in her temple at Cos, he tells us it is the artist who makes things real: were it not for Apelles, Venus would not have been born, would not have come into existence. Here, as later in the *Metamorphoses*, art is not the imitator but the definer and creator of reality.[21]

Metamorphosis, as a form of art, plays the same role. Several phrases at the start of the poem open this perspective on its central subject. After a short preface Ovid begins with a brilliant description of the primeval chaos out of which the world will evolve. The chaos, the very first thing to be transformed, Ovid terms a *pondus iners* (1.8), which is a pun, meaning "a mass" that is both "inert" or "sluggish" and "inartistic" (from *in-ars*).[22] A little further on, the unpeopled earth is called *rudis et sine imagine* (1.87, "crude and without recognizable appearance"); as we saw earlier, the words are regularly applied to works of art.[23] The language here, tellingly placed, suggests that as the world became recognizable in form and occupied increasingly by animals, plants, and objects whose names and characteristics are known to us, it was evolving in the direction of greater artfulness. Through metamorphosis creatures pass from the realm of nature, which they inhabited before, and enter the higher realm of art. The only discernible movement in the poem is the greater number of clear embodiments to be found in the world, as it becomes populated with more metamorphosed figures.

Fundamentally this evolution is an advance in perception. We are invited to see metamorphosis as not only clarifying a character, activity, or emotion, but also by that effort encapsulating and defining it. The wolf shows us the essence of Lycaon and at the same time so clearly embodies ferocity as to define ferocity for us—and so with Arachne, the spider, and weaving, or the Lycian peasants, frogs, and boorish truculence, to the same effect. Art/metamorphosis transmutes what was personal or individual into a monument for all, and these monuments give us our bearings, identifying and representing and even creating for us notions such as ferocity. Without art, Ovid says in effect, the world would be not so much unlovely as unintelligible. Henri Matisse expresses this leading role of art in similar terms: "It is the painters who, by creating images, allow the objects and scenes of nature to be seen. Without them we could distinguish objects only by their different functions of utility or comfort."[24] With this Ovid would agree, for in the *Metamorphoses* art is "poetic" rather than mimetic: it creates reality, it does not solely imitate it.

The visual arts, moreover, are regularly analogues to the arts of language—poetry, story-telling, rhetoric. *Imago*, we have seen, can be used for sound as well as sight. Implicit in the poem's view of the relation between art and nature is an equally remarkable view of the relation between language and experience. Language too, far from distorting or merely reflecting reality, in fact creates it. Words create reality in that they make it possible to discriminate and identify phenomena. As Isidore declares at the start of his encyclopedia, "if you do not know the name, the knowledge of things is lost" (*Etym.* 1.7.1). Actaeon, unable to speak his own name, loses his identity, and soon his existence. The movement that marks several artworks as virtually alive is the movement of the mouth: *adapertaque velle / ora loqui credas* (5.193–94, "you would think his opened mouth wishes to speak"), says Ovid of one of Perseus' victims.[25] More generally, speech is the principal tool by which characters try to shape themselves and the world around them: the largest example may be the alternative remakings of the Trojan War (and therefore of themselves) presented in the speeches of Ajax and Ulysses. It is not surprising that the verbal artifacts far outnumber the visual in the poem.

The Figure of the Artist

THE DEMIURGE

In this view the artist becomes a supremely important figure: he is the creator of what sense and order there is. An important hint of this is given, once again, near the opening of the poem. To explain how original chaos was changed into cosmos, Ovid invokes a creator god. He is, however, studiously vague in identifying him. "God and better nature" are the subject of one verb (1.21); that the verb is singular may imply the second term is only a restatement of the first. More clearly evasive is the phrase *quisquis fuit ille deorum* (32, "who-

ever of the gods it was").[26] Instead of naming the god Ovid refers to
him as *mundi fabricator* (57, "maker of the world") and *ille opifex rerum*
(79, "that artisan of the universe"). A little of the language in the
passage is Epicurean—for example, *semina* (9, "seeds")—and some
of the ideas, including that of the creating demiurge, which Ovid
seems to refer to here, resemble those of Plato and the Porch, in
particular the neo-Stoicism of Posidonius.[27] Nevertheless, since several philosophies seem mixed together and since no poet can be
imagined to whom philosophy was more uncongenial than to Ovid,
it is difficult to believe that he was aiming at a particularly philosophical portrayal of the Creation. The choice of terms suggests
rather that the creator of the world is an artist himself; not only the
first metamorphoses in the universe but, presumably, the others that
follow as well are the handiwork of the Great Artist. Moreover, by
nearly defining this god as "better nature" and calling him "the origin of a better world" (79), the poet indicates that the development
here begun takes a certain direction: the world, in becoming more
art-filled, becomes clearer and therefore better.

PYGMALION

The greatest, or nearly the greatest, artist in the poem is Pygmalion.
His story follows that of the Propoetides, the women who after becoming the first prostitutes were changed into stone (10.238–42).
Reacting with disgust to them, Pygmalion sculpts an ivory statue,
with which he then falls in love. He prays to Venus that he may have
a wife like the ivory statue, and upon returning home he finds that it
grows warm at his touch and quickens to life, becoming his bride
(10.243–97). As is often the case, the story forms various patterns
with a number of others nearby, offering contrasts and parallels to
them. It is the reverse of the one directly preceding: the Propoetides
are turned from flesh to stone, Pygmalion's creation from ivory to
flesh. Like the tale of Iphis, which closes Book Nine (666–797), it
includes a miraculous transformation, bestowed by a goddess upon
one who was blameless and pious.[28] It is recounted not by Ovid
directly, but by Orpheus, another artist whose powers were great
enough to bring his spouse to life.

Nonetheless, comparison of this version with its Greek source
shows how, in making it over, the poet gave it a new subject and
reconceived it so powerfully that it became a paradigm for later ages.
Philostephanus of Cyrene, a pupil or friend of Callimachus, wrote
what appears to be the original account; Philostephanus' work is

lost, but two later writers have preserved notice of it.[29] That version makes Pygmalion, there a king of Cyprus, so possessed by the beauty of a cult statue of Aphrodite that in his lust he has sexual relations with it. Ovid has kept the idea of love for a statue; he devotes a good number of lines to describing the tender words, gifts, and attentions Pygmalion bestows on his ivory statue.[30] But he has turned Pygmalion from an iconophile king into the sculptor himself, and by this invention—for so it is universally agreed to be—made him the exemplar of the artist's power. He has substituted artistic force for political. The opposing views of art conveyed by the poem meet here, and the dominance of one of them over the other gives the story a special significance.

The tale falls into two parts of nearly identical length, Pygmalion's creating of the statue and falling in love with it (243–69) and the animating of the statue (270–97). Successive lines early in the account, ending with the contrasting words *arte* and *nasci* (247, 248), announce the terms of the argument: this is a story about the relation between art, that which is made by human skill, and nature, that which is born.

In the first half Pygmalion is the talented sculptor who carves an extremely lifelike woman. The statue is outstanding both morally and physically. The modesty and chastity which were the first impulse to its creation are found in the statue, with its becoming, maidenly bashfulness (251), and later in the living woman, who blushes upon feeling her first kiss (293). Much more is made of its pulchritude, for the statement that "he conceived a love for his own work" (249) directly follows upon mention of its beauty, and throughout the passage emphasis is laid on its physical, not to say sexual, attractiveness. Pygmalion's sculpture is successful because it imitates nature so faithfully: "the appearance is that of a real maiden: you would believe she was alive and, if not prevented by modesty, eager to move" (250–51). By calling the ivory a *simulatum corpus* (253, "a simulated body"; cf. *simulacra*, 280), Ovid reminds us that art can only strive towards an (unattainable) imitation of nature.

In a famous, witty sentence the poet tells us that art is not only the means of achieving this but also the means of concealing its achievement: *ars adeo latet arte sua* (252, "to such an extent is art hidden by its own art"). The word *sua* is crucial to the epigram, for over that art which imitates nature is an art which art serves. It is extremely interesting that the doctrine derives from the precepts of rhetoric.[31]

Yet at the same time, still in the first half and less conspicuously, Ovid also suggests the other view, that art is superior to nature. "By

his miraculous art" (247) Pygmalion *formamque dedit, qua femina nasci /
nulla potest* (248–49, "gave to the ivory a beauty such as no woman
can be born with"). The realism of the work, the power of its art, is
carried so far as to reach the point where it surpasses what is real
and natural.

It is that extra measure of ability which produces the statue's extraordinary effect. To appreciate this properly we may recall an anec-
dote that Pliny the Elder tells in his history of painting (*HN* 35.65):

> It is reported that Parrhasius and Zeuxis entered into competi-
> tion. Zeuxis exhibited grapes painted so successfully that birds
> flew up to the wall of the stage. Parrhasius exhibited a linen
> curtain which was painted with such realistic representation that
> Zeuxis, swelling with pride over the birds' verdict, demanded
> that his rival remove the curtain and show the picture. When he
> realized his error, he yielded the victory, frankly admitting that
> whereas he had deceived the birds, Parrhasius had deceived
> Zeuxis himself, a painter.

Ovid in his account has gone this one better: Pygmalion's representation is so persuasive that it deceives not the birds, not a fellow artist,
but the maker himself! The poet elaborates this conceit, somewhat
playfully:

> *saepe manus operi temptantes admovet, an sit
> corpus an illud ebur, nec adhuc ebur esse fatetur.
> oscula dat reddique putat loquiturque tenetque
> et credit tactis digitos insidere membris
> et metuit, pressos veniat ne livor in artus.*   (254–58)

Often he lays upon the work hands that test whether it is flesh
or ivory, nor yet does he concede that it is ivory. He gives it
kisses, and thinks they are returned. He speaks with it and embraces it, believes that his fingers sink into the limbs he
touches, and fears lest by squeezing them he turn them black
and blue.

If the artist himself is so deluded, how extraordinary the work must
be! Imagine, *a fortiori*, its effect on others! This sculpture has no
equal. Since it is the most conspicuous piece of art in the poem, it is
not surprising that Ovid is at pains to draw the parallel between its
creation and the act of metamorphosis. Anderson has demonstrated
that Ovid uses for the statue's creation language that is the standard
vocabulary of metamorphosis.[32] Pygmalion then, the artist/metamor-
phoser, practices what might be called "super-realism."

The second half of the story may appear to dim Pygmalion's glory. The statue is animated in answer to the prayer which the sculptor addresses to Venus. The scene of the goddess's festival is not to be skipped over lightly. Ovid describes the sacrifices offered, Pygmalion's carefully worded prayer, Venus' harkening to it, and the favorable omen which she then gives (270–79). Pygmalion, moreover, when certain of the metamorphosis, renders full and solemn thanks to Venus (290–91). Does this not rob Pygmalion of the credit for bringing the statue to life and confer it instead on Venus? Is not divine intervention the cause rather than artistic power? It cannot be denied that the goddess plays a role in the miraculous awakening; yet a look at the scene in which the ivory becomes flesh shows that Ovid has narrated it so as to call attention once again, and more dramatically, to the artist's own creative power.

The tenor of the passage makes us feel not that the statue has been changed all at once by the waving of a magic wand, as it were, but rather that it is being changed, gradually, under the sculptor's hands:

> *incumbensque toro dedit oscula: visa tepere est.*
> *admovet os iterum, manibus quoque pectora temptat:*
> *temptatum mollescit ebur positoque rigore*
> *subsidit digitis ceditque, ut Hymettia sole*
> *cera remollescit tractataque pollice multas*
> *flectitur in facies ipsoque fit utilis usu.*
> *dum stupet et dubie gaudet fallique veretur,*
> *rursus amans rursusque manu sua vota retractat:*
> *corpus erat, saliunt temptatae pollice venae.*   (281–89)

Lying upon the bed, he kissed the girl: she seemed to be warm. Again he puts his lips to hers, with his hands too he touches her breasts: the ivory, touched, grows soft and, surrendering its stiffness, gives way and yields to his fingers, just as Hymettian wax is softened by the sun and, when worked by the thumb, is turned into many shapes and by use becomes usable. While the lover in his amazement is but doubtfully joyous and fears to be deceived, again and again he works by hand the object of his prayers: she was flesh, and her veins throb under the touch of his thumb.

Many of the details, especially the choice of diction, reinforce the overall impression. To begin with, the rhythm of the passage conveys the sense that the statue awakens in response to Pygmalion's efforts. Three times the same alternation is repeated, in which an action of his is followed by, and therefore appears to cause, a reaction in her. He kisses her: she grows warm (281). He touches her: she grows soft (282–86). He caresses her: she becomes flesh and blood (287–89). Near the beginning the verb *temptare* may mean, as in the first half of the story, both "test" and "touch": Pygmalion treats the statue as if real and at the same time is uncertain whether it is. Moreover, the figure of anadiplosis ("he touches the breasts; having been touched, the ivory . . .") links action and response closely, suggesting a causal relationship.[33] The verb *mollescit* ("grows soft"), it has been claimed, is associated with the sculptor's art.[34] In the simile of the molded wax the association is certainly clear. The thumb that works the wax must be that of a plastic artist; several other times in the poem wax figurines are referred to (3.487–89, 15.169). The neat epigram at the end of the simile—"by use it becomes usable"—can well be applied to the ivory: treated as if it is a body, it becomes a body.[35] Pygmalion not only is the lover but remains still the sculptor as well: he is making the statue for the second time. His caresses, instead of following the act of artistic creation, are the means of that creation.[36] The verb in the next phrase, *sua vota retractat*, picks up *tractata* ("handled") from the simile, emphasizing again the link between Pygmalion and the figurine-maker. *Sua vota* is somewhat unusual. The commentators are surely right to give *vota*, properly "vows," a concrete sense (cf. 1.272, 6.513) and to translate the phrase "he handles again the object of his vows." But perhaps it may also mean "he manages (handles, carries out) his vows," which would suggest that in handling the statue he is himself bringing about what he prayed for.

In the first half of his story Pygmalion is a sculptor whose imitation of nature reaches such a pitch of perfection that it goes beyond imitation and produces a beauty of which nature itself is incapable. His art is superior to nature in its results; in a competition of beauty art comes out ahead. In the second half he brings the inanimate statue to life. The aid rendered by Venus may represent several things: direct divine participation in the creation of art, or an inexplicable superhuman element, or the need for love to be present in addition to skill. In any event, it is clear from Ovid's telling that the power of the artist is chiefly responsible. Here Pygmalion's art is superior to nature in that it usurps what is properly and exclusively the function of nature, the creation of animate life; human existence itself depends on art. What more could Ovid do to establish the priority of art over nature? The story of Pygmalion is crucial to the *Metamorphoses*, for here by a double argument the poet demonstrates most vividly the power of the artist and his art.

OVID

Only one other artist may be held to rank above Pygmalion, and that of course is Ovid himself. A consideration of Ovid in his final capacity, as sovereign creator, brings into focus certain features of him and his work. We have surveyed the many ways in which, breaking with tradition, he obtrudes upon his own narrative and makes himself felt as controlling the world of the poem. But the parallels of the demiurge and Pygmalion remind us that his power extends to the act of ultimate control, the creation of that world. Ovid summons things to life through his extraordinary art, presenting not just one but a large gallery of clear *imagines*. Let us look at him under two aspects: his relation to the other artist figures, and the essentially private, personal nature of his world.

Ovid's work is characterized by attention to visual effects. Not only do its descriptions often represent actual paintings and sculptures—this observation has often been made, and we will return to it shortly—but the narrative, moreover, consists for the most part of static pictures. Both the chief event in the poem and the style of its narration tend towards crystallization; they capture some complexity (character or movement) in a clear and unchanging visual image. Nonetheless, Ovid the artist is different in kind from Pygmalion. His work is literary rather than plastic, words and stories are his medium, and he belongs properly with the other literary artists in the poem. There are, strictly speaking, no writers. Yet we do find great singers (Orpheus, for example) and musicians (Marsyas), who ought to be considered figures of the poet. A much larger group of literary artists is composed of the story-tellers, those who compete with their tales (the Muses and the daughters of Pierus) or simply swap them (Theseus and his companions with Achelous), those who have a particular purpose (Vertumnus) or just want to pass the time (the daughters of Minyas). These are in fact far more numerous than the visual artists.

A certain paradox informs Ovid's creation. It strives for visible clarity and for the public and permanent qualities of a monument. And yet at the same time it remains a feat of triumphant subjectivity. Ovid is keenly aware of the personal and even arbitrary elements that enter into a work of art; it is not easy to know the creator from the creation. The poem's ever-shifting subjects, tones, points of view, and emphases imply that the narrator is not consistent or uniform but rather is himself a changing, willful medium. This shows itself sometimes in regard to the poem's central act too. The plays on words that occasionally link the states before and after metamorphosis evoke the presiding artist, as does also the somewhat arbitrary nature of the changes wrought. Continuity is always present, but who determines which features shall be preserved and in what way? Though the transformed Lycaon reveals the essence of his character, Niobe might have been a monument to pride as well as to maternal grief. The poet's sense of the subjectivity involved in creation can be seen as an extension into the personal sphere of the flux and uncertainty which govern events in the universe. Not yet metamorphosed, he is not simplified and fixed.

The subjectivity of Ovid's monument is also reflected in the *sphragis*, the "seal" or "signature," the closing lines where the poet speaks directly about himself. It is worth quoting in full:

> *iamque opus exegi, quod nec Iovis ira nec ignis*
> *nec poterit ferrum nec edax abolere vetustas.*
> *cum volet, illa dies, quae nil nisi corporis huius*
> *ius habet, incerti spatium mihi finiat aevi:*
> *parte tamen meliore mei super alta perennis*
> *astra ferar, nomenque erit indelebile nostrum,*
> *quaque patet domitis Romana potentia terris,*
> *ore legar populi, perque omnia saecula fama,*
> *siquid habent veri vatum praesagia, vivam.*   (15.871–79)

And now I have finished my work, which neither Jove's wrath nor fire, neither steel nor consuming time can destroy. Let that day which has title over this body alone end the span of my uncertain life whenever it wants: still, by my better part I shall be raised forever above the lofty stars, and my name will be indestructible. Over whichever conquered lands Roman power extends I shall be read aloud by the people, and down through all the ages, because of my fame, if there is any truth in what sages say, I shall live.

The language, sequence, and position of these lines recall unmistakably the poem which closes Horace's first collection of odes, *exegi monumentum aere perennius . . . (Carm.* 3.30, "I have finished a monument more enduring than bronze . . ."). Comparing the passages sheds light on how each one defined what he had accomplished.[37]

In several ways Ovid's claim is grander. He enlarges considerably the extent of his fame in both time and space. Horace predicted his fame would grow so long as Roman religion persisted, "while the Pontifex and Vestal Virgin shall ascend the Capitoline"; Ovid's will continue "through all the ages." The one expected to win renown at least in his native Apulia; the other, throughout the Roman Empire. Ovid's claim, nonetheless, is in every point more private. Horace pictures his achievement as a *monumentum*, a "monument" or "memorial," perhaps a tombstone; the comparison ("loftier than the pyramids") and the forces arrayed in opposition (wind, rain, time) add to the sense of his poetry as a solid and concrete construction. Ovid, by contrast, presents a more abstract notion: he merely terms his poetry an *opus*, "work," while the forces of time which might harm it are divided between the natural (thunder, perhaps lightning) and the human (steel, perhaps fire), with the result that they evoke no one particular image.

At the end of the ode Horace, turning to the Muse, bids her "receive the pride won by her merits" and asks that she crown him with laurel. However conventional it may be, to whatever extent it is a figure of speech, such a reference to divine inspiration is absent from Ovid, who implicitly claims for himself all responsibility for the achievement and who by the cast of his language even suggests that the achievement will make him like a god: his words here, "by my better part (*parte . . . meliore mei*) I shall be raised forever," recall those he used for the apotheoses of Hercules (*parte sui meliore*, 9.269) and Aeneas (*pars optima*, 14.604). Horace, moreover, advances a historical claim, that he is the first to have introduced Greek lyric poetry into Italian meters. And he strengthens his own setting within the historical and political world through an invention the boldness of which has been dimmed by subsequent repetition: the laurel crown that he requests for himself likens the poet to a triumphant general. Horace, though he is a lyric poet, makes his achievement seem objective, nearly impersonal. Ovid's farewell, by contrast, emphasizes the opposite. His feat is wholly private. It originates in him, its sphere is himself, the glory that results will be his alone. Neither the poet nor his poem claims to speak for anything larger than the individual, not divinity or national life, not history or society. The *Metamorphoses* is the very personal creation of Ovid.

The Role of Art

Art may be any number of things. What does it mean in this poem to say that metamorphosis is a form of art? Here art is not cunning or concealment or pretense, as it was in the *Ars Amatoria*. It is not simply beauty or adornment. It is not represented as the product of skill or talent, magic or genius. It is not the vehicle of allegory, symbolism, or any other transcendent meaning. It is not "art for art's sake," whether the autonomy of art is meant by this or the aestheticization of experience. In the *Metamorphoses* art is clarity. It encapsulates, brings out to the surfaces of appearance, and makes plainly visible some human experience, and by this process becomes a monument to that experience. But art does not solely crystallize; it also, as we have seen, defines and creates reality. It enables us, when we look out upon the world, to recognize there such things as love, ferocity, maternal grief, and anger. Ultimately the theme of metamorphosis betokens a concern with perception and understanding. How do we see the universe? What sense can we make of it?

Ovid's view becomes more distinct if it is set in relief against the view of Plato, which is virtually its opposite.[38] (I have in mind the Plato of the *Republic*, where the doctrine of the forms and the role of art are most fully developed.) For Plato this world around us is a world of appearances and for that reason is unreal. Reality must by definition be fixed and unvarying, removed from all contingencies of place and time, perfect. It therefore is abstract and lies outside the realm of the senses. The objects and qualities of this world, because they are material and contingent, are but shadows of what is real. The artist's representation of such things, an imitation of a copy, therefore is two jumps removed from reality. In Ovid precisely the reverse holds. The poet refuses to believe in that which is not open to the senses, particularly to sight. Nothing lies behind or beyond this world. What you see, the surfaces of things, is what is most real.

Despite the differences, the views of Plato and Ovid are rooted in the same fundamental sense: both feel very strongly the chaos and confusion and deceptiveness of the sensible world, the difficulty of finding meaning amid a welter of ever-varied experiences. Plato responds by positing another world, a world of forms accessible only to the intellect, which bestows reality upon this one. Ovid by contrast discovers in this world something which is itself open to the senses and at least makes perception possible: art. Ovid's metamorphosed figures, embodying clearly an emotion like grief or an activity like spinning, somewhat resemble the Platonic forms: each provides a norm by which to recognize the things about us. The direction of movement and the results sought, however, differ sharply. For Plato the abstract and universal form of a bed, or of the Good, is the source of all particular realizations. On Ovid's view the individual Niobe is metamorphosed into a monument of grief and set before mankind retaining traces of her specific character and history. The abstractness of the Platonic system permits a hierarchy of values to be established, and so the system naturally issues in a code of conduct. Morality is altogether absent from Ovid's purpose: far from wanting to state (much less enforce) what ought to be, he simply aims at making clear what is. *Imago* may be used in the sense "deceptive appearance"—but never after metamorphosis.[39]

The background to the world of the poem, in which human experience strives to attain clarity, is not only that experience but also the forms of art which have already communicated it. Direct apprehension of the world not being possible, any concern with apprehension must also take account of those monuments which have previously mediated experience. At many points and in various ways Ovid reminds us that art refers to—art. The art that is metamorphosis, and Ovid's own art, which is analogous to it, are shown to rest very evidently on previous works of art. The evidentness needs to be stressed. It is not simply that both classes of art exist in a tradition, which is undeniable, but that Ovid calls attention to this so conspicuously. He meditates on the fact of artistic tradition.

PAINTING AND SCULPTURE

This is evident in the relation of Ovid's narrative to the visual arts. It has repeatedly been observed that he describes figures just as they were represented in well-known works of painting or sculpture. A river god *innixus cubito* (8.727, "leaning on his forearm"), Europa seated on the bull that is about to carry her off (2.873–75), Niobe's many children slaughtered with a dramatic array of arrow-shots, the latter two groups rendered with detailed attention to the pose of hands, limbs, and torsos—these are a few among many examples.[40] It is not poverty of imagination that leads the poet to rely on such models, nor mere hospitality towards other forms of art, in which he had a particular interest, being a connoisseur of the fine arts. Instead this feature of his style serves as a steady reminder that the world shaped by this poem is indebted to earlier art.

But, it may be objected, do we not find such descriptions elsewhere? To be sure, we do. In the *Aeneid*, for instance, the picture of unholy Furor bound fast within the temple of Janus (1.294–96) reflects a famous painting by Apelles which Augustus had placed in his forum.[41] And the awful scene in which Virgil tells of the death of Laocoon and his sons (2.213–22), whatever its precise relation to the famous statuary group, is certainly influenced by some plastic work.[42] Yet there are important differences. These evocations of already existing works of art are far more common in the *Metamorpho-ses* than in the *Aeneid* or any other poem, and they are scattered about more casually, not reserved for moments of special dramatic intensity. Moreover, the self-consciousness of Ovid's use marks out the phenomenon.

Narcissus admiring himself in the pool was a frequent subject of wall paintings, mosaics, gems, and reliefs. Ovid stresses this by re-peatedly likening his Narcissus to a statue (3.418–93).[43] Elsewhere Apollo engages in a singing contest with Pan and appears in full rig:

ille caput flavum lauro Parnaside vinctus
verrit humum Tyrio saturata murice palla
instructamque fidem gemmis et dentibus Indis
sustinet a laeva, tenuit manus altera plectrum.   (11.165–68)

His golden locks bound with laurel of Parnassus, Apollo swept the ground with his deep-dyed purple mantle. His left hand lifts the lyre, adorned with jewels and ivory, while the other holds the plectrum.

The crown and gown as well as the employment of the hands recall quite precisely the well-known statue type, originated by Scopas, of Apollo Citharoedus.[44] So far this is like the description of the river god; then Ovid adds the ambiguous *artificis status ipse fuit* (169), which may mean "the very pose is that struck by a master per-former" or "that created by a sculptor." The play on words draws attention to the source of the pose. In Book Fifteen, after the Romans have debated whether to bring the worship of Aesculapius to their city, the god reveals himself to one of them at night. The poet de-scribes him as *qualis in aede / esse solet* (15.654–55, "as he is accus-tomed to appear in his temple"); the following verses give the details of the cult statue, a figure holding a snake-entwined staff in his left hand while with the right he strokes his beard. When Aesculapius speaks, though, he announces that he will appear in a different form—as a snake: "I will come, leaving behind my usual appear-ance." Later, upon his actual arrival at Rome, he resumes the guise by which he is recognized (743). Here the resemblance to a statue is completely explicit, and it is only emphasized by the god's temporary assumption of another form. Things which appear real and natural turn out to be modeled on artifacts.

That behind the world of phenomena there lies the world of art is also suggested by an odd use of the word *imago*. Several times we find *imago* with the genitive of a noun ("image of") where we would have expected the noun itself. Perseus, for example, catching sight of Andromeda, is *correptus imagine formae* (4.676, "enraptured by the image of her beauty"), though he could more directly have been "enraptured by her beauty." Here Ovid might have been influenced in his choice of words by the previous verse, in which he compares Andromeda to a statue. Similar turns of expression are *solis imago / evicit nubes* (14.768, "the image of the sun has overcome the clouds") and *aequora me terrent et ponti tristis imago* (11.427, "the seas and the gloomy image of the deep do affright me"); in the latter the parallelism suggests that *"image of* the deep" does not differ much from "seas." More arresting is an instance where *imago* is used in the same way, but without any reference to what can be seen. Minos, learning that Scylla has betrayed her father and city because of her love for him, is: *turbatusque novi . . . imagine facti* (8.96, "perturbed by the image of this novel deed").[45] Repeated recourse to such turns of phrase indicates the poet's view.

We are already familiar with Ovid's intensely visual imagination. We can now add that the *Metamorphoses* is not only the product of such an imagination but also an explication of it. Given that art, which provides the model of reality, is timeless and unchanging, it follows that narrative is likely to be a series of static pictures. Moreover, existing works of visual art enable the poet to envision a scene or a character and what it expresses. It may be that statues of river gods completely defined "river god" for him, as the wolf metamorphosed from Lycaon defined a certain bloodthirstiness.

LITERATURE

Literature, however, has an even higher claim on Ovid's interest than do the visual arts. A contest may be sensed in the *Metamorphoses* between the visual and the verbal, like the great *paragone* enacted in the Renaissance between painting and sculpture. And as Leonardo comes down decisively on the side of painting, so, predictably, does Ovid on the side of literature. Literature forms a more important background to the poem. Ovid is at pains to remind the reader of this body of art which lies behind the world and art of the poem. Both the playing with mythology (almost the sole subject of imaginative literature) and the elimination or drastic truncation of the most famous stories and episodes from particular works suggest that the present telling takes its rise from earlier tellings, not from any particular thematic concerns.

This is implicit in several smaller features as well. Ovid tends to identify characters periphrastically and sometimes not at all, as if the

Metamorphoses directly continues earlier literature and its reader can be expected to follow it with familiarity.[46] Thus Ino is introduced simply as the *matertera* of Bacchus (4.417, "maternal aunt"), while Dido and Pythagoras are not even granted this much. Another fine example can be recalled from Ovid's treatment of the story of Aeneas. Achaemenides, rescued from his miserable life on the island of Polyphemus, is described thus:

> *iam non hirsutus amictu,*
> *iam suus et spinis conserto tegmine nullis.*   (14.165–66)

Now no longer did he have a shaggy cloak or clothing sewn with thorns, now he had returned to himself.

The temporal reference is made not to any earlier moment in the *Metamorphoses*—this is Achaemenides' first appearance—but rather to the *Aeneid*, where Virgil had described him as unkempt and ragged (3.590–94; cf. esp. 594, *consertum tegimen spinis*, "his clothing sewn with thorns"). By playfully attaching his own poem to Virgil's Ovid reminds us how closely literature is made from literature.

Other passages are also so self-conscious as to be probative; these cluster towards the end, where perhaps the Roman setting gives greater opportunity. At a council of the gods called to debate the apotheosis of Romulus, his father Mars argues with Jupiter:

> *tu mihi concilio quondam praesente deorum*
> *(nam memoro memorique animo pia verba notavi)*
> *"unus erit quem tu tolles in caerula caeli"*
> *dixisti.*   (14.812–15)

Once upon a time in the presence of a divine assembly you said to me (for I remember it, and with remembering mind noted your sacred words): "One there shall be whom you will raise to the blue of heaven."

The emphasis on exact recollection only sharpens the wit of the remark, for Mars is quoting a verse from Ennius' *Annals*![47] His past history proves to be earlier literature. A similar parenthetic note on memory is put in the mouth of Pythagoras. Offering himself as an illustration of metempsychosis, the philosopher recalls—*nam memini* (15.160, "for I remember")—that at the time of the Trojan War he was Euphorbus, a warrior slain by Menelaus. Again the mention of his memory stirs ours: what Pythagoras is remembering is the *Iliad* (17.43–60). And this literary allusion is rendered more piquant through its juxtaposition with a concrete piece of historical reality: Pythagoras adds that he has just seen the shield Menelaus stripped from him hanging as a dedication in the Argive temple of Juno, where in fact it was still to be seen in Ovid's day.[48]

Later Pythagoras recalls something else from his days as Euphorbus, the prophecy Helenus had given to Aeneas: *quantumque recordor, / dixerat Aeneae . . . Helenus* (15.436–38, "as far as I can recollect, Helenus had said to Aeneas . . . "). Naturally, what he actually has in mind is the *Aeneid* again (3.374–462). As if to underline his source, Pythagoras begins his version with the same words as Virgil's Helenus: *nate dea* (439, "O goddess-born"), and then adds, self-consciously: *si nota satis praesagia nostrae / mentis habes* (439–40, "if my prophecies are sufficiently well known to you").[49] Indeed they are! Elsewhere, to assure his audience that bees really are born from the putrefying carcasses of oxen, the philosopher states that *cognita res usu* (365, "the fact has been learned by experience"). Yes, but the experience proves to be that of reading the *Georgics*, where the same story is retailed (4.538–47). And again Ovid reinforces the link with an echo of Virgil's language (cf. 15.364 with 4.538). These passages are different from literary allusions such as we are accustomed to meet in the *Aeneid*. These do not complicate or otherwise enhance their meaning by evoking contexts from earlier literature: rather, they point to the fact that such literature has helped to create them. With especially sharp wit these passages remind us that literary art is a principal background to the poem.

ECPHRASES

This sense is confirmed by the three ecphrases in the poem. In view of the prominence of art it is surprising that so few ecphrases are found: the *Aeneid* can show fully as many.[50] The explanation probably lies in the large number of stories narrated within the poem, which serve the same purpose of self-reflection.[51] If we confine ourselves to the visual arts, the contrast between Virgil and Homer on the one hand and Ovid on the other makes clear what is distinctive. The chief characteristic in Ovid's descriptions of works of art is the unrelenting consciousness that they are works of art. The earlier poets' handling of ecphrasis has been well described thus: while Virgil, like Homer, "professes to be describing a work of art and even (unlike Homer) alludes to technique in the appropriate use of metals, his pictures come to life before his eyes and transcend the limitations of art: the scenes become scenes of action, with movements and circumstances which art could not represent."[52] This is precisely what is absent from Ovid. His scenes never break away from their frame and take on a life of their own. All three descriptions are brief and dry, nearly a catalogue, and they never allow us to forget that they are artifacts.

The first is the doors of the Sun's palace, worked by Vulcan with representations of the land, sea, and air. The description opens with the fabulous materials out of which the doors are constructed: gold, silver, ivory, and an alloy of gold with bronze. But, Ovid says, *materiam superabat opus* (2.5, "the workmanship was even greater than the material"). This is a kind of argument *a fortiori*, emphasizing the artisan's skill. A group of the Naiads *nare videtur* (11), which can mean either "are seen to swim" (by the spectator Phaethon) or "appear to swim," which reminds us that this is only a fictitious work. A pair of familiar words at the end of the passage does the same, an ambiguous meaning being involved in each case: the *caeli fulgentis imago* (17, "the image of the gleaming sky"), where the modifier reflects equally well the light of the stars represented or of the silver employed; and, on each of the panels, the six *signa* (18), which are both "constellations" and "sculpted figures." The reader is not allowed to lose sight of the work's artifice.

The longest ecphrasis is actually a pair, the two webs woven by Minerva and Arachne for their contest (6.70–128). Both parts include tell-tale words: *imago* (74, 103, 110, 122), *videri* (100, 105), *simulare* (80). Since Arachne's subject is gods in disguise who raped women, Ovid can again use *imago* in a double sense. The Jupiter who carried off Europa is an *imago* in that he was disguised as a bull in the story and also in that he is now represented on a work of art (103; similarly in 110 and perhaps 74). Ovid applies a revealing phrase to Minerva's tapestry. The twelve chief gods were, as we might say, recognizable by their attributes. The poet puts it thus: *sua quemque deorum / inscribit facies* (73–74, "his appearance identified each of the gods"). The word *inscribit*, however, properly means "inscribe, write," and Haupt and Ehwald correctly explain its odd use here: "*inscribit*: 'labels,' as clearly as if the name were written beside, as is often found on ancient vases and wall-paintings." Pictorial art is implicitly likened to the art of writing.

The last of the ecphrases in the poem, a bronze mixing bowl given to Aeneas (13.685–99), also compares the sculpted to the written. The artist has carved a city with seven gates, of which Ovid says, *hae pro nomine erant et, quae foret illa, docebant* (686, "they were in place of a name and told which city it was," meaning Thebes). The description falls into nearly equal halves (685–91, 692–99). In the first there is an interesting progression in the cognitive status of the representa-

tion. As Ovid moves along he states different relations between the
scenes and the viewer/reader's understanding of them. The gates
"tell" (*docebant*) which city it was. Next pyres and funeral mounds
"signify" (*significant*) grief. The nymphs then "appear" (*videntur*) to
weep. And finally the subject is described immediately: the trees are
bare of leaves, the goats nibble at the rocks. The stages are: absolute
declaration of meaning; qualified declaration, one thing standing for
or pointing to another; approximation to reality; and reality appre-
hended directly. This steady movement from interpretation to reality
leads us to feel that now the work of art will take off, its figures come
to life, as happens with Homer and Virgil. The second half, however,
defeats such an expectation. Syntactically it is a single sentence, with
the verb *facit* (692, "he makes, represents") governing a series of
accusatives with infinitive: *facit . . . / hanc . . . dare vulnus* (692–93,
"he represents this woman as dealing wounds"), and so forth. The
construction is extremely rare with pictorial representations, and nowhere else in Latin is it so extensive as here.[53] We ought to note how
the construction usual for reporting discourse is transferred to reporting images. Ovid employs it because it marks most clearly the
subordinate nature of the scenes portrayed on the bowl. In this novel
way he again reminds us that art is artifice, and also suggests either
that the visual and verbal arts are almost interchangeable or that
the visual can ultimately be translated into the verbal. This, like the
other ecphrases, conveys the sense that in the background of art
there lies other art.

Metamorphosis, we may say in conclusion, is a phenomenon in
which two domains meet, art and experience. Where does the balance lie between them? Does metamorphosis chiefly encapsulate
some human experience, or does it echo art itself? Ovid both acknowledges the claims and is aware of the limitations of each. His
interest is directed to the ways in which the two interpenetrate one
another. Our experiences of ordinary life are endlessly varied, complex, unique, and to some extent mysterious. Mythological narratives, literary structures, artistic works of any sort, are inadequate for
capturing experiences in their fullness; they necessarily falsify them.
Yet at the same time no experience is unmediated; art, visual or literary, is itself an inextricable part of experience and has already shaped
our perception of it.

It is on these grounds that Ovid is skeptical towards the possibilities of art and yet disposed to have faith in it as a means, limited but
indispensable, for making sense of experience. As for Ovid's own

literary art, though subject to the same restrictions, it is at least less liable to misrepresent or mislead: it is more self-conscious and more open. And of course it is also true that as the poem has itself come to occupy an important place in Western tradition, and not only the Latin and literary traditions, it too in turn has played a large role in shaping our perceptions of art and experience. Even now, twenty centuries after Ovid composed it, the *Metamorphoses* remains a source of enjoyment, enlightenment, and liberation.

NOTES

Where neither title nor page references are cited for a modern author, the reader may generally assume that I am referring to that author's commentary. Commentaries on the *Metamorphoses* cited in this book are listed in the Bibliography; commentaries on other classical works are simply credited to their authors by last name, as are collections of fragments to their editors.

INTRODUCTION

1. At least two other efforts have borne this title, an essay by Wilkinson and a seminar given by R. J. Tarrant. Cf. also Friedrich, "Der Kosmos Ovids."
2. See the excellent bibliography by Elliott; also Hofmann.
3. For references to this and the other books mentioned by author consult the Bibliography.
4. Altieri, 33.
5. *Ovid Recalled*, 144–240.
6. This is the opinion of Tarrant himself, 342 n. 1.

CHAPTER ONE

1. "Cupid and Venus."
2. "Mythos und Geschichte."
3. *Struktur und Einheit.*
4. *Ovid as an Epic Poet.*
5. Ludwig, 26–31.
6. Otis, 128–65.
7. "The game of structural analysis is a legitimate and valid one, and I am sure that Ovid expected his readers to play it, each in his own way, but the point is that there is no single correct or final solution" (Curran, 74).
8. Books Seven and Fourteen also begin with *iamque*, Book Five with *dumque*.

9. On this difference between Ovid and Virgil see Ludwig, 85. On book divisions in Ovid see Tolkiehn, "Bucheinteilung," who attributes Ovid's practice to the desire for suspense.

10. "Ovids Humor: ein Schlüssel zur Interpretation der Metamorphosen." Still more revealing is the title under which the essay was reprinted: "Ovids Humor und die Einheit der Metamorphosen." "Unity" appears in the titles of works about the poem as often as "world," and for the same reason.

11. See Guthmüller, *Aufbau*, who gives a good history of the study of the question too.

12. The title is unquestionably ancient, attested for the first time in Seneca the Elder, *Contr.* 3.7.

13. For example, Kenney, "Style," 146 n. 15, and Galinsky, *Introduction*, 3, who emphasizes that the poem is "not about metamorphosis." Cf. Lafaye, 75: "Once and for all let us put aside whatever in the poem has to do with the metamorphoses, properly called, since despite the title they are really only an accessory." This follows a section of more than sixty pages on the history of metamorphosis as a theme for writers! See, however, Viarre, 39, and Frécaut, 260.

14. The phrase is also a programmatic allusion to the kind of poetry which had been rejected by Callimachus, the *hen aeisma diēnekes* (frag. 1.3 Pfeiffer, "one continuous poem"). On the whole preface see Kenney, "Ovidius Prooemians."

15. The story of Syrinx, set within that of Io, is parallel to both also, in its general subject (a god pursuing a mortal girl) as well as its language (cf. 487 and 695, 678 and 709, 698 and 588).

16. Despite his denial, the evidence adduced in Hollis's introductory note to the story (pp. 128–33) serves to show that Callimachus' was the version Ovid had in mind: discrepancies from it indicate not another source but a different purpose.

17. See the fine comparison of the two versions by Diller, 324–28.

18. I have regularly asked students in my classes to analyze a particular story, suggesting they might consider others insofar as it seemed worthwhile. My experience of their essays has been that nearly all did do this and discovered networks of thematic links.

19. Ludwig, 77–80.

20. Lafaye, 89–90.

21. On the inclusion of all literary genres within the poem see Saint-Denis, 113; Barsby, 31; and most especially Kraus, 114–16. Norwood, 170–74, also notes the variety of genres but believes the poem is unified by themes like fire and water, the royal house of Thebes, snakes, man in competition with god, and Hercules, among others.

22. See Lafaye, 141–59.

23. Murphy ad loc.

24. Lanham, 12.

25. Cf. *Am.* 1.1.25; Prop. 1.10.30, *Am.* 1.1.26. Other echoes: cf. 505–6 with *Ars* 1.117, 2.363; 512 with Prop. 2.7.19, Tib. 4.13.3, *Ars* 1.42; 527 with *Am.* 2.5.44, *Ars* 1.533; 530 with *Ars* 1.126.

26. See Copley, 134–39.

27. With Heinsius I read *abductas* in 677.

28. Cf. 679 with *Ecl.* 1.79; perhaps also 682–83 with *Ecl.* 9.51–52.

29. Haupt and Ehwald's notes collect many echoes of Theocritus and Virgil.

30. Callimachus' *Aetia* may also be said to include these two kinds of epigrams: the lock of Berenice speaks as a dedicatory offering (frag. 110 Pfeiffer), and the poet Simonides addresses us in a sepulchral inscription (frag. 64). But both are so long as to destroy any illusion of being actual inscriptions.

31. Kraus, 116. Haupt and Ehwald compare Nep. *Alc.* 11.4.

32. Griffiths, "Theocritus' *Hymn to the Dioscuri*," argues that in that poem the author combines hymn, bucolic, mime, epic, and encomium. He looks back to Hesiod as the model of the discontinuous style, the precedent for the mixing of genres.

33. See Sheets, "Ennius Lyricus."

34. See Jannacone, 59–76, on the dissolution of literary genres in the development of Ovid's work.

35. On this see Chapter Five.

36. Stitz, 17–18, has drawn attention to the frequency of *tamen* in the *Metamorphoses*: it is about six times as common as in the *Aeneid* and is often found combined with a negative, as it almost never is by Virgil. This use of adversative relationship as the logical connection between two events reflects, Stitz observes, the intellectual nimbleness fostered by Ovid's rhetorical training. Haupt and Ehwald ad 15.745 give other examples of *tamen* found in transitions.

37. Altieri, 34. He remarks on the similarly deceptive notion of a story: "a plot is also a trick" (38).

38. Grimal, 247–48, argues that there are two Atlases, representing two different stages of the legend: one, the Titan, is a Hesiodic conception, whereas the other, a human of gigantic size, is more recent and rationalized. He concludes that Ovid has made no chronological error. This does not persuade me.

39. Ludwig, 56; see also Wilkinson, "World," 234. I feel that most of what follows 11.193 is also atemporal.

40. For these and more examples see Chapter Three.

41. Ovid toys here with the reader's recollection of the *Aeneid* too. Virgil,

who, it is agreed, had invented the figure of Achaemenides, introduced him into the narrative at the moment when the Trojans came upon him and rescued him. The Achaemenides of the *Metamorphoses* recounts his story only later, when his old companion Macareus catches up with him and inquires about his experiences. In Achaemenides Virgil had created a novel perspective on the Cyclops episode; Ovid in turn varies the Virgilian angle.

42. Again Ovid explicitly and without other motivation denies the account of his model: Circe and her maids, he tells us, were not weaving (cf. 14.264–65 with *Od.* 10.221–24).

43. Besides much that is unknown to the *Iliad* (for instance, the story of how Ulysses unmasked Achilles, who was shirking his calling by hiding among women, 13.162–80), each of the two speeches contains a fact that contradicts the *Iliad*: Ulysses' father, it is implied, was Sisyphus, not Laertes (26), and Dolon is said to have been slain by Ulysses instead of by Diomedes (244–45). But of course it is Ajax who makes the former claim, seeking to associate his opponent with a notorious trickster, whereas the latter is alleged by Ulysses himself! The reader who catches these errors is reminded that stories do not reach him as privileged, impersonal truths, but rather are mediated by a narrator, who can alter them as he wishes. This is true of the poet-narrator too.

44. For a detailed discussion of the simile, complementing the argument here, see Chapter Five.

45. Cf. Anderson's review of Bernbeck, 354: "Even single stories may be composed in a variety of tones, mixing the playful and the serious and leaving the audience in a state of ambivalence." I would only add that "playful" and "serious" do not form the only set of terms useful for describing the tones of the poem.

46. Lanham, 16–17.

47. Altieri, 33.

48. On the studiously vague creating agent see Chapter Six.

49. Eduard Fraenkel, in what may be his only published remark on Ovid, says parenthetically: "I consider the *Metamorphoses* one of the most perfect poems of antiquity" (247). I am curious what his reasons would be. I wonder whether they would agree with a very pertinent general remark made by Yeats: "Only that which does not teach, which does not cry out, which does not condescend, which does not explain, is irresistible" (*The Irish Review*, September 1911, 327).

CHAPTER TWO

1. Anderson, *Commentary*, 501.

2. Peters, 96, citing several other examples.

3. It does not matter to us where the story of Myrrha is laid. Ovid leaves this uncertain: since Cinyras was born on Cyprus (297–98) we presume his daughter was too, but several references seem to locate the story in the East, in Arabia or the fabled isle of Panchaea nearby (309, 316, 478, 480).

4. Cf. Virg. *Aen.* 1.546–47, however, which is cited for this very reason by Isid. *Etym.* 1.34.9. Verse 305, it should be noted, is omitted or added between the lines by some manuscripts, and several editors delete it.

5. Fränkel, 220 n. 70.

6. On the transitions see especially Steiner, 229–30, and Altieri, 34.

7. Other examples: 2.676–79, 4.1–4, 6.421, 7.162, perhaps also 1.449–51 and 11.266–68.

8. Another example is 3.131–32.

9. Kraus, 113.

10. Not all that is memorable is epigrammatic. Horace, for instance, is often memorable without being epigrammatic: consider *neque semper arcum tendit Apollo* (*Carm.* 2.10.19–20). The matching of a word more to an image than to another word may give the Horatian tags their special quality.

11. For the antithesis of *dulcis* and *asper* cf. Sen. *Nat.* 3.2.1: *aliae* (sc. *aquae*) *dulces sunt, aliae varie asperae.*

12. At least the *Thesaurus Linguae Latinae* gives no other instances of this pairing.

13. Stitz, 12.

14. See Bömer ad loc.

15. *Restare* with indirect discourse is otherwise unexampled in Latin; I suppose we must understand *dicere* or something such.

16. On this aspect of parentheses see von Albrecht, *Die Parenthese*, 193–215, esp. 209–15.

17. For instance, Ovid's use of apostrophe and of the particle *tamen*, if carefully studied, might also prove to be signs of the narrator.

18. On Philomela's entrance and the simile see the good remarks by Anderson ad loc.

19. An exception is *Aen.* 9.337–38, where Virgil, as on other occasions, expresses sympathy for characters who die young.

20. The imperfect subjunctives here and in the next examples express past potential, strictly speaking. Even if this is to be regarded as somewhat different from contrary-to-fact, my point still stands.

21. Some additional examples: 4.673–75, 11.15–18, 11.241–42.

22. Other examples: 1.504, 4.415, 10.811. 12.75–76.

23. Other examples: 3.158, 6.12, 6.680, 6.758, 8.627.

24. Other examples: 1.55, 2.222, 2.342, 7.369–70; with future passive participle, 2.366, 8.211–12.

25. On the inserted apposition see Solodow, "*Raucae, tua cura, palumbes.*"

26. Other examples: 1.94, 1.97, 1.450, 2.219, 4.688, 5.66, 6.418, 9.17,

14.789; also 8.305, 8.316. The only precedents I know are found in Callimachus (*Art.* 244–45, *Del.*48–49, *Dem.* 24), who also strives to make himself
apparent to his readers; but cf. Virg. *Aen.* 12.134–35.

27. On Ovid's assumption that the material is already familiar to the
reader see Bernbeck, 47–54; on 105–106 he contrasts Ovid's aetiologies with
those of Callimachus, Apollonius of Rhodes, and Virgil.

28. I find only three comparable phrases in the *Aeneid*. Two refer to Juno's
pain and unslaked anger towards the Trojans (1.25–26, 5.608); one of Virgil's
principal themes, her hostility is resolved within the poem, and indeed her
reconciliation, foretold from the beginning (1.279–82), directly precedes and
makes possible the poem's end. The third instance comes from the description of Cleopatra at the Battle of Actium (8.696–97); here the poet's fore-
knowledge is rendered objective in a work of art, the shield which Vulcan
forges for Aeneas.

29. See Bernbeck, 32, who discusses 4.520 excellently; another example is
13.900–903.

30. This makes me less inclined to heed in regard to this passage von
Albrecht's reminder (in Haupt and Ehwald, ad 4.145) that *ab* with the ablative need not imply personification, but may instead be merely a feature of
poetic diction.

31. A good overview of such phrases in ancient poetry is given by Norden, ad *Aen.* 6.14; but when discussing those in Virgil that express actual
distrust he does not distinguish what is said by the poet (e.g., 6.173, discussed below) from what is said by a figure in the poem (3.551, 8.140).
Stinton, " 'Si credere dignum est'," offers a much fuller treatment, subtle and
thoughtful. Though valuable, his essay devotes relatively little space to the
Latin poets and, when it comes to Ovid, dwells on the *Fasti* more than the
Metamorphoses; it does not recognize the extent of such expressions in the
latter and analyzes no passage except the speech of Pythagoras.

32. Servius glosses it as *oppressum insidiis*; Donatus explains it through a
simile, *ut feram venabulo*.

33. Cf., however, Pind. *Ol.* 9.2–40, Apoll. Rh. 1.154–55, 4.984–85, 4.1381–
82. Galinsky, *Introduction,* 176, lists these passages but is tendentious in
drawing a distinction between them and the *Metamorphoses*.

34. This is pointed out by Galinsky, *Introduction,* 176, whose treatment of
the narrator's self-ironic remarks (172–79) is helpful.

35. The effect is no doubt different when Ovid speaks similar phrases in
exile (*Trist.* 1.2.81, 4.10.129).

36. Those who know Anna Russell's hilarious retelling of Wagner's *Ring*
will recall in this connection her flawlessly timed, indignant exclamation:
"I'm not making this up, you know!"

37. See Heinze, 370–74, on the limited ways that Virgil is present in the
Aeneid.

38. Compare the similar lines *Aen.* 7.4 (on which see above) and 9.446–49.

39. Mine is what I take to be the usual understanding of this passage, that Aristotle praises Homer for saying very little in his own person (examples would be the brief proems or the renewed invocation of the Muse before the Catalogue of Ships). But serious consideration is also merited by the different view of Else, 619–21, who argues that Aristotle praises Homer for composing a narrative of which a large portion is direct discourse rather than reported action. The strength of Else's position lies in his observing that Aristotle here uses several technical terms from the theater and in pointing out that he likens Homer elsewhere to a dramatist. I find a weakness, however, at a crucial point. "Homer, he says, uses straight narrative only for a brief prologue, then immediately 'brings on stage' a 'character' (who then takes over and speaks for himself)." But then when the character ceases to speak, is it anyone other than the poet who once again takes up the narrative? Else's view fails to distinguish between Homer speaking and Homer speaking in his own person, and in the *Iliad* and *Odyssey*, unlike the *Metamorphoses*, this distinction is sharp.

40. Altieri, 34.

41. Spitzer, 69. When he adds that Cervantes is always subordinate to God and the Church, on the grounds that only God does not have multiple perspectives, he points to an important difference between the Spaniard and the Roman: for Ovid even this distant finality does not exist.

CHAPTER THREE

1. This distinction was drawn in antiquity by Hyginus (apud Gell. 10.16), who on the one hand considered it acceptable for Virgil to know that the place in Italy where Aeneas made land was (later) called Lavinium (*Aen.* 1.2) or that Cumae was (later) the site of a Chalcidian colony (6.17), but on the other hand thought Virgil at fault when one of his characters, Palinurus, was aware that the coast his body lay on was going to be known as Velia (6.366). Hyginus called this *prolēpsis historiae*, which is one species of anachronism. Servius (ad *Aen.* 3.703) makes the same distinction as Hyginus. Norden (ad *Aen.* 6.2) has showed that criticism of this sort was derived from earlier commentaries on Greek poets, e.g., the A and T scholia on *Il.* 21.362 or the scholia on Eur. *Phoen.* 6 or Apoll. Rh. 4.553.

2. We might note in passing that among Ovid's quasi-anachronistic similes a number are drawn from contemporary spectacles. From the dragon teeth sown by Cadmus, for instance, men rise head first, just as in the Roman theater the figure painted on the curtains arises out of the floor (3.111–14); a cypress tree is compared to the turning posts of the circus (10.106); Orpheus is pursued like a stag hunted in the amphitheater (11.25–27); Achilles, frus-

trated in his attack on Cygnus, resembles a bull in the ring that has been enraged by a red cloth (12.102–104). Not only do these by their novelty suggest the poet's intense modernity, but they also signal his characteristic interest in the act of viewing.

3. To make finer distinctions than this seems hardly worthwhile. It would be a fruitless exercise to worry whether or not it is anachronism if at the time of the Flood, in the prehistoric era of mythology itself, we hear of "sacred objects" (1.287), or if the god of prophecy tells Daphne how laurel is going to be employed in Augustan Rome (1.560–63).

4. Some examples are Servius ad *Aen.* 1.182, commenting on biremes (this comes from Varro); 1.213, boiled meat (Servius attempts to explain this away by saying that the water mentioned by Virgil was used for washing hands, not cooking meat; the attempt reveals his discomfort with anachronisms); 3.703, Gela and Agrigentum not yet founded; 4.367, tigers. The Homeric scholia had also drawn attention to this; cf., e.g., schol. ad *Il.* 15.679, 21.362, 24.480–82. See also n. 1 above.

5. Though found occasionally in earlier Latin (Lucil. 219 Marx; *Rhet. Her.* 4.43), *sarisa* appears not to have been an altogether familiar word. Livy, Ovid's contemporary, twice explains the term before using it (37.42.4, 38.7.12); and where, because the context is a discussion of Alexander the Great and the Macedonian army, he uses it without explanation, the gloss *id est hastae* has crept into most of the manuscripts (9.19.7). On the *sarisa* see Gomme and Sandbach, 499, 744.

6. Marrou, 222, 265–66, 274. Bonner, 135–36, presents evidence that in Martial's day (about seventy-five years after Ovid's) coeducation did exist, but it seems to me conclusive only for the second level of study.

7. Ovid describes at *Fast.* 2.315 a cave like Achelous' and constructed of the same materials. He refers to artificial grottoes at *Met.* 3.157–60 and 10.691–92.

8. Pliny the Elder, *HN* 36.154, attests the use of such clumps in simulating caves. Actual examples of all the features mentioned are to be found in Neuerburg, esp. 92–94.

9. A nearly identical anachronism is found in Callimachus, frag. 261 Pfeiffer.

10. Wilkinson, *Ovid Recalled*, 167.

11. Alcon is mentioned at *Culex* 67 and Athen. 11.469a.

12. Additional instances of anachronism: epigraph on a tomb (2.326), trumpet (3.535, 10.652; cf. *Aen.* 5.113, where Servius remarks that this is *Romano more*), slingstones and a spear fitted with a throwing strap (7.777, 788), royal palace decorated with spoils (8.154), purple awnings drawn over a white marble atrium (10.595–96, spoken by Venus; contrast 5.389, a simile), temple built *ex voto* (10.686–87).

13. To be sure, Pliny, *HN* 36.11–12, seems to put the first marble sculpture around 775; but this date is calculated in a very dubious manner and conflicts with a much later date given at the beginning of the same book.

14. See Papadopoulos, 15–63, who quotes scores of passages. Since, however, she confines herself to those in which the word *xoanon* is used—a curious limitation—she misses a number of clear references in Greek literature to ancient images of wood, and all those in Latin: e.g., Apoll. Rh. 1.1117–19; Paus. 1.27.1; Plut. frag. 158 Sandbach; Clem. *Protr.* 4, p. 40P; Cic. *Ver.* 2.4.7; Prop. 4.2.60; Ov. *Met.* 10.693–94; Plin. *HN* 34.34; Plin. *Epist.* 9.39.4.

15. Rosivach, "Latinus' Genealogy," argues that Virgil is ambiguous about whether this building is a temple or royal palace. Ovid locates his marble statue in an *aedes sacra* (14.315, 316): did he at least understand Virgil to have been describing a temple?

16. Though opinions differed in detail, scholars of Virgil's time were unanimous in attributing these institutions to the early regnal period. *Fasces*: Romulus (Liv. 1.8.3), Romulus or Tarquinius Priscus (Dion. Hal. 3.62.3), Tullus Hostilius (Macr. *Sat.* 1.6.7). *Ancile*: Numa (Ov. *Fast.* 3.361–82; Dion. Hal. 2.71.1; Luc. *Bell. Civ.* 9.477–80; Plut. *Num.* 13; Serv. ad *Aen.* 7.188, 8.644; Non., p. 554M; that Varro was interested in the question is shown by *Ling.* 7.43). *Lituus*: Romulus (Cic. *Div.* 1.30; Plut. *Rom.* 22.1, *Cam.* 32.5), Numa (Liv. 1.18.7, by implication). *Trabea*: Romulus (Isid. *Etym.* 19.24.8), Numa (Dion. Hal. 2.70.2). The adjective *Quirinalis*, applied by Virgil to the *lituus* (7.187) and to the *trabea* (7.612), reminds us that these were used by Quirinus, who was either Romulus or Mars; see Rosivach, 150.

17. The combination of literary and archaeological evidence shows that even the temple of Jupiter Capitolinus, built centuries later and considered extremely splendid (cf. Liv. 1.55.7–56.2), had but twenty columns; for reference to reconstructions see Ogilvie's commentary on Livy ad loc.

18. Contrast the utterly fantastic buildings of the *Metamorphoses*: the palace of the Sun (2.1–4), for instance, or the temple guarded by Baucis and Philemon (8.700–702).

19. See Kroll, 178–84, an excursus on anachronism which is impaired by its assumption that all later poets followed the practice of Virgil.

20. There are, to be sure, instances without either of these justifications. In the passage just discussed, "beaks torn from ships" (7.186) are among the trophies mounted on the temple's walls. A ship's beak should be an anachronism in this period, unless, as Conington and Nettleship suggest, Virgil believed that it was warranted by Hector's threat to cut off the *korymba* of the Greek ships (*Il.* 9.241). (The meaning of the phrase is taken to be "high-pointed sterns" today, but in antiquity it was disputed, as we see from Aristophanes, frag. 222 Edmonds.)

21. Peters, 79: "the entire coloring of the feelings and the stories is Roman."

22. In Virgil this is never the case; instead *triumphus* either is a metonym for "victory" (2.578, 4.37, 11.54), or it appears appropriately in passages that, looking beyond the heroic age in which the poem is set, predict the future (6.626, 6.814, 8.714).

23. This resembles the gentle joke at 8.668–69, where, after telling us that all Baucis and Philemon's pots and dishes were ceramic, the poet speaks of "a mixing-bowl of the same silver," that is, as much a silver vessel as the others were: not at all.

24. Additional instances of Romanization: the morning greeting of Aeacus recalls a *salutatio* (7.665–67); Hymenaeus is dressed in a dark yellow cloak, like a Roman bride (10.1); a festival of Ceres has several Roman touches (10.431); *submittere cannas* is modeled on *submittere fasces* (11.171; despite Bömer's objections); the trial of Myscelus is conducted according to Roman procedure (15.36–38).

25. The latter is the suggestion of Bömer, who notes that Ovid makes the chamber marble (*marmoreo . . . recessu*, 177).

26. See Bernbeck, 92–93, on this passage.

27. It seems likely, as several commentators have said, that this passage of the *Aeneid* was in fact a model for Ovid. He takes over unaltered the phrase *conciliumque vocat* (*Aen.* 10.2; *Met.* 1.167) and echoes others.

28. It is improbable that the phrase suggested a precise place to Virgil's readers. Procopius informs us that the temple of Janus in Rome had doors at either end, facing east and west (*Goth.* 1.25.21; cf. Stat. *Silv.* 4.1.11), but he adds that it was only large enough to accommodate the statue; so this place would be too small for any meeting. Vitruvius (3.2.8), a contemporary of Virgil's, describes a kind of temple with doors at both ends, but goes on to declare that there are no examples in Rome.

29. Servius and modern commentators have seen in this escort accorded to Jupiter a Roman practice by which people conducted a magistrate or someone of equal dignity to his home (see also Cic. *Sen.* 63; Liv. 3.26.11, 23.23.7; Ov. *Pont.* 4.4.41; Val. Max. 2.1.9; Sen. *Dial.* 9.11.11; Tac. *Hist.* 3.86). It is difficult, however, to understand *ad limina* as meaning "to the threshold (of his home)": except perhaps for 7.579 I know of no passage in the *Aeneid* where without the support of a modifier or the immediate context *limen* refers to a house; at 2.321 and 3.347, and maybe 7.579 as well, *limen* indicates the threshold of a city gate. It is preferable, therefore, to think of the threshold of the hall in which the meeting is held. Consequently, the Romanness of this detail is doubtful.

30. See Serv. ad *Aen.* 6.244; Plaut. *Curc.* 108; Val. Fl. 2.610.

31. For the superiority of a hairdresser over other servants cf. *Am.* 1.11.1–2.

32. It is curious how Ovid urges upon us the thought of this most essential and most virtuous household duty of a woman, first by stating that Circe and her maids were *not* weaving, then by having her examine (or distribute) *pensas . . . herbas* (14.270, "weighed-out herbs"): *pendo* in the literal sense is not common, and the participle *pensas* may suggest the noun *pensum*, "amount of wool to be woven."

33. Haupt and Ehwald note the differences from Homer's Circe, who lives in "a house constructed of smooth stone," has but four servants, and herself opens the door to the strangers (*Od.* 10.210–31).

34. The *loci classici* are *Ars* 3.101–28 and *Medic.* 1–30. Stitz, 118, remarks on the presence of Roman social usages in the poem and particularly on the attention to *cultus*; she cites inter alia the toilette scene between Scylla and Galatea (13.737–39) and Polyphemus' absurd attempts to make himself look smart (13.764–67).

35. Bernbeck, 14–15; see also his more general discussion, 91–94.

36. Bothe, cited by Haupt and Ehwald ad 13.123.

37. On Thebes we have the direct testimony of the geographer Strabo (9.2.5), Ovid's contemporary; cf. Paus. 9.7.6. For Athens see Judeich, 96–97. Since the time of Heinsius many scholars have rejected these lines together with a varying assortment of surrounding verses as spurious, chiefly because of the anachronism. But Jahn in his edition of the poem (Leipzig, 1832) answered the objections, and today the general view seems to be that the verses are genuine. This I am certain is correct. To go no further than the same speech, Pythagoras reports that Tyre was no longer an island (288), and mentions two cities which sank into the sea (293)—though these changes were not effected until the years 332 and 373, respectively! The lines on Thebes and Athens recall a passage from the *Aeneid* (6.773–76) in which Anchises foretells to Aeneas the rise of Gabii, Fidenae, and other towns of the Prisci Latini. By Virgil's day these had all died again; yet Anchises cannot be accused of a historical error like Pythagoras', since he does not specify when they will arise. (An apter comment, however, may be Norden's, that the faded glory of these towns was already touched up by Augustan romanticism.)

38. See, e.g., Galinsky, *Introduction*, 168: Ovid has "virtually limited the deities to human behavior, without restoring the compensatory aspect of their majestic or ideal role." See also n. 39 below.

39. Lamacchia, 320: "The queen of the gods, who in the Virgilian tradition served as the supernatural mover and cause of the war, takes on in Ovid the role of a simplistic mortal, an antagonist of Aeneas, of the same sort as Turnus, only perhaps more powerful."

40. Haupt and Ehwald appositely quote the verses of Homer: "the Achaeans were stunned with fear by Hector and father Zeus" (*Il.* 15.636–37). This too is a striking expression. But, couched in the passive and with a verb less

physical than *fero*, it seems less audacious, and the implied parallelism between god and man is echoed nowhere else. The T scholia on the *Iliad* interestingly remark that the poet exalts the hero by mentioning him together with the god. Ovid, it seems to me, does the very opposite.

41. Some examples: Alcman frag. 2; Theoc. *Id.* 17.1; Virg. *Ecl.* 3.60; even Ovid himself, *Fast.* 5.111; Stat. *Silv.* 1.praef. (referring to Domitian!). For a long list see Gow ad Theocr. loc. cit.

42. Very similar is a turn in the monologue of Scylla, who is wrestling with her desire to betray her father to an enemy with whom she is in love: *di facerent, sine patre forem! sibi quisque profecto / est deus: ignavis precibus Fortuna repugnat* (8.72–73, "Would that the gods had made me fatherless! Surely everyone is a god to himself: Fortune spurns the prayers of those who do not help themselves"). Again casual mention of the gods is the pivot of thought, again the gods are rationalized, here as self-help.

43. These passages are well analyzed by Doblhofer, 230–31.

44. There is no point in listing the many studies that have addressed this question. Let me refer only to the superb discussion by Bernbeck, 80–91, which not only analyzes well Ovid's humanization of the gods but also, through careful comparisons with Homer, Virgil, and especially Apollonius, sets this in the perspective of literary history.

45. The best discussion of this is by Doblhofer, 83–91, who sees in it the poet's general concern with the question of *Ichspaltung*, or "split identity."

46. The difference is subtle but clear between this and a Virgilian phrase like *o Thybri tuo genitor cum flumine sancto* (*Aen.* 8.72, "o father Tiber with thy sacred stream"), where any gap between the personal and the natural is so effaced as to be nearly invisible. Ovid, by contrast, accentuates it.

47. On Ovid's tendency to personify topographic features see Richardson, 162.

48. There is another joke here too. The constellation of the Bears is the only one which is always visible and therefore appears never to set into the waters: in this sense, the water is "forbidden" to them. Ovid's story of Callisto (2.401–530) gives a fanciful aetiology of this.

49. This is based on Lamacchia, 311–12. Though I agree with her on many matters, I consider it misleading to speak about Ovid's narrative as "rational" and "bourgeois," unless by the latter term one means merely "not heroic." Bömer too uses this word unfairly.

50. But consider 4.246–51, the description of Mount Atlas, which remains, however, an isolated instance in Virgil.

51. More examples of this feature are collected by Bernbeck, 98–99: 2.454, 2.526, 5.250–51 (cf. 5.46), 12.614.

52. Bernbeck's book is an outstanding analysis of one such sequence, the story of Ino (4.416–542).

53. Quoted in Price, 62.

CHAPTER FOUR

1. The other chief links: the Greeks use a wooden horse to enter and take Troy (Book Two); a horse indicates the place of Carthage's founding and later becomes the city's symbol, a sign of war prowess (1.444–45); Anchises interprets horses seen on the Italian shore as an omen of war (3.537–40); King Latinus sends Aeneas a present of horses (7.274–83); and in a simile Turnus is compared, appropriately enough, to a horse (11.492–97).

2. Contrast a description of Iris by Virgil: *ergo Iris croceis per roscida pinnis / mille trahens varios adverso sole colores / devolat (Aen.* 4.700–702, "dewy Iris with her saffron wings flew down, trailing a thousand different colors through the sun-lit sky"). Neither dewiness nor wings are particularly human.

3. It is possible that a sense of this wavering tone prompted Seneca's famous remarks on the scene. He complained that Ovid had marred the scene by adding the detail of the wolves swimming among the sheep (*Nat.* 3.27.13–14). In part his complaint is mere cavil ("Is it possible to swim in such a flood, which carries one off?"), and he is well answered by Fränkel, 173. But Seneca's remarks are mainly directed at the indecorous tone of the passage, at the discrepancy between the sober theme and the playful treatment: "It is not satisfactorily sober to be playful when the world has been destroyed." It is not easy to see why Seneca finds the detail of the wolf and the sheep playful. It may have suggested to him the Golden Age (cf. Virg. *Ecl.* 4.22 and, in a similar context, 5.60; also Theoc. *Id.* 24.86, which is an interpolation, but an early one—see Gow ad loc.), and the Golden Age would sound a wrong note in the Flood. Yet the wolf with the sheep was often a mere *adynaton*, among the Greeks (Diogenian. 5.96; Apostol. 14.96) as well as the Romans (Hor. *Epod.* 15.7, 16.33). And in describing another kind of natural catastrophe Virgil could add this same detail without arousing complaint (*Geor.* 3.537–38). Thus Seneca's judgment remains puzzling. A passage of Horace's which Ovid evidently had in mind while composing his own (*Carm.* 1.2.5–12) provoked a remarkably similar judgment from Porphyrio (ad loc.).

4. See Bernbeck, 106, on the effect of this and other grotesque scenes.

5. Bernbeck, 13, shows similarly that Ovid's description of the Underworld at 4.432–63 lacks terror.

6. Cf. van Ooteghem, 447: "Ovid shows no pity for the poor human victims of the disaster. Virgil would have treated the subject altogether differently: he would have described at length the scenes of anxiety, disturbance, suffering, and grief which the subject called for. . . . It might be said that the poet was more interested in the animals than the men."

7. Bömer gives 291–92 to the second, as do Haupt and Ehwald implicitly by their paragraphing; Lee gives them to the third. The epigrammatic nature of 291 may suggest that the verse marks the end of a paragraph. But the

imperfect tenses make the lines read better as the background to 293ff. than as the conclusion to the preceding passage. The initial *iamque* of 290 need not bind the lines to the previous section: Books Three and Fourteen open with the word *iamque*; cf. also 7.404 and 14.581.

8. See Bernbeck, 10–11.

9. See Bernbeck, 28–29.

10. See Bernbeck, 16–17.

11. See Bernbeck, 6.

12. On parades of Cybele's worshipers see *Real-Enzyklopädie der Altertums-wissenschaft*, 21:1949–50.

13. See Stitz, 108.

14. See Bernbeck, 10–11.

15. The adjective *Berecyntius* is used almost exclusively of Cybele in Latin.

16. *Mulciber* is found a few times before Ovid, but he is the first to use it in the sense of "fire."

17. Among the extant works of Latin literature Astraeus is named for the first time in this passage.

18. See Bernbeck, 44–47.

19. Coleridge might almost have been describing the difference between Virgil and Ovid when he observed: "The antithesis of Junius is a real antithesis of images or thought; but the antithesis of Johnson is rarely more than verbal" (*Table Talk*, 3 July 1833). See also Bernbeck, 39, 78.

20. See Bernbeck, 44–47, 54–55.

21. Note the zeugma in applying *eversam* ("overthrown") to both (physical) walls and (abstract) hope.

22. Stitz's suggestion, 64, that *evicere* means simply "avoided" and that the Trojans are to be understood as having sailed all around Sicily, is proved wrong by Ovid's use of *evincere* in precisely the same context at 15.706 and in a closely similar one at *Trist.* 1.10.33.

23. See Putnam, 130–34.

24. This is also true on the level of syntax. Independent clauses usually represent primary events, subordinate clauses secondary. "The ship, having lost its pilot, sails past Ischia" (see 14.88–89) makes the sailing past the principal fact and subordinates to it the loss of the pilot. To say "The ship, while sailing past Ischia, loses its pilot" would subordinate the sailing to the loss. This example is plain; more interesting ones come up later.

25. Klingner, 204–6.

26. The most elaborate instance is found in Book Five, where the narrative consists of four boxes one inside another. Within (1) the framework of a conversation between the Muses and Minerva, one of the Muses recounts (2) their singing competition with the daughters of Pierus. She briefly reports (3) the song of the Pierides, which itself contains (4) allusions to a number of

stories. Then she tells at length (3) the song her sister Calliope sang, which was about Ceres and the rape of her daughter Proserpina; within this tale in turn are set (4) the stories of Cyane, Ascalaphus, the Sirens, and Arethusa.

27. The general situation is the same, and verses 3.608–9 recall 2.74–75. It is also significant that verse 3.612 has been transferred to 2.76 in several manuscripts.

28. Altieri, 38.

29. Varro apud Servius Danielis ad *Aen.* 2.636; see Stitz, 25–26.

30. This might be considered a kind of zeugma, in which things not evidently commensurable are nevertheless linked as parallel or equal. This is a device by which Ovid often lowers some high concept. Several more examples appear later. It would be useful to contrast Ovid's with Virgil's employment of zeugma, a fine study of which is found in Mack, 89–94.

31. Ovid uses the same phrase at *Fast.* 1.527.

32. We might also note that though his identity is clearly alluded to in the phrase *Cythereius heros* and in the epithet *pius*, Aeneas is not named here at the start of his story proper (see Bernbeck, 44–47). His name in fact does not appear until 681, almost sixty verses later. In Virgil's poem, it is true, Aeneas is not named until the ninety-second verse, but then that is also the first moment that he takes a part in the narrative. Ovid may be downplaying the "central" figure.

33. See Stitz, 36.

34. In straining the use of *Iovem* Ovid may be drawing attention to his altered explanation. *Iuppiter*, the name of the sky god, is often used for the sky itself, according to a familiar synecdoche. Nowhere else, however, so far as I know, must *Iuppiter* be taken in the sense of "weather" or "climate." The word *caelum* regularly bears this meaning, so Ovid may have in mind some string of associations like this: *caelum*, "climate"; *caelum*, "sky"; *Iuppiter*, "sky"; *Iuppiter*, "god of sky."

35. See Bömer, "Ovid und die Sprache Vergils."

36. Cf. Tib. 3.3.8 *dives . . . Orcus*; also Cic. *N.D.* 2.66, which cites the parallel of the Greek *Ploutōn*, from *ploutos*.

37. Lamacchia, 319.

38. Note the pointless epigram: Ajax' crime is not that of dragging like away from like.

39. Haupt and Ehwald point out the two "corrections." Servius too noticed the latter and was bothered by it.

40. See Lanham, 60.

CHAPTER FIVE

1. See Stitz, 39.

2. Otis, 205; Büchner, 219.

3. Diller compared the two versions in a fine essay, "Die dichterische Eigenart von Ovids Metamorphosen." His comparison is refined and extended by Büchner, 206–20. Worthwhile remarks are added by Galinsky, "Ovid's Metamorphosis of Myth."

4. Hollis notes the verbal parallels between the two (cf. 739–40 and *Aen.* 7.648, 8.7), as also between their children, both deserving of better parents (cf. 874 and *Aen.* 7.653–54); the reminiscence of Laocoon's attack upon the Trojan horse (cf. 757–58 and *Aen.* 2.50–53), which appeared to be another violation of a sacred object, hints at the same.

5. For a lengthy list see Segal, 278–79.

6. Alfonsi, 265–66.

7. Several distinctive phrases recur (cf. 15.104 with 1.32, 15.194 with 1.21). The mention of the Golden Age (96–110, 260–61) and, in general, the discussions of time (186–213) and the four constituent elements of the universe (239–51) recall the Creation in Book One. Swanson observes that the sequence of subjects at 15.176–251—time, living forms, elements—is reversed from the corresponding passage in Book One.

8. Cic. *N.D.* 1.27, *Sen.* 78; see Saint-Denis, 120–21.

9. Fränkel, 108–9, suggests the possibility. For Sotion's influence on Seneca see *Epist.* 108.17–22.

10. Hor. *Epod.* 15.21, *Serm.* 2.6.63, for instance; see Segal, 280–82.

11. Boillat, 34–39, demonstrates, moreover, that the poem is not Pythagorean. Where comparison is possible, Pythagoras' explanations of metamorphosis do not agree with Ovid's.

12. For the reading *animans* see Clausen.

13. Johnson, 139, remarks that the length is part of the joke.

14. Contrast Ovid's own account, 1.89–112.

15. On the Golden Age in Pythagoras' speech see Johnson, 141–43.

16. Similarly, Pythagoras pictures a bull just before it is to be sacrificed as "seeing between its horns the very grain it helped to grow" (133–34, a reference to the *mola salsa* of Roman sacrifices), and calls the oxen "your farmers" (142).

17. Contrast with this expression the one Ovid had used somewhat earlier: *mollia quae nobis vestras velamina lanas / praebetis* (15.118–19, "[you sheep,] who offer us your wool as soft coverings").

18. For a partial list of Lucretian echoes see Haupt and Ehwald ad 67ff., 150ff., 244, 340.

19. Segal, 284–86.

20. Cf. verse 433 with *Aen.* 1.33, and 447 with *Aen.* 1.272.

21. See Segal, 288.

22. Here are all the references to stories in which *poena* is applied to a metamorphosis: 1.209, 1.735, 2.467 (and 521), 2.564, 2.833, 5.200, 5.501, 5.668, 6.137 (and 150), 6.215, 9.372, 10.154, 10.232 (and 234), 10.303, 10.698; the four made by Ovid himself are 1.735, 2.467 and 521, 2.833, 5.200. The distribution of these instances—concentrated in the first six books and absent from the last five—is probably without significance. I find little merit in either of two explanations that might be offered: that Ovid's notion of metamorphosis evolved during the composition of the poem, or that metamorphosis as punishment becomes increasingly rare as the gods withdraw from the scene.

23. Others are Callisto (2.474–75), Actaeon (3.189–93), Ascalaphus (5.542), and the women who killed Orpheus (11.67–70).

24. The imagery of the fields is continued in the phrase *sterilem sperando nutrit amorem* (496, "with his hopes he nourishes a sterile love").

25. Ovid, to be sure, does not mention the fox's insuperability. It is fair to assume, though, that this was evident to readers, since the story was well known: see Nic. frag. 97 (from Pollux 5.38); Eratosth. *Cat.* frag. 33; Paus. 9.19.1; Apollod. 2.4.6–7; Ant. Lib. 41.10.

26. Ovid's wondering about this point may be a polemic directed against those who firmly asserted that Jupiter was responsible—Eratosthenes, the sources of Apollodorus, and Antoninus Liberalis (see n. 25 above).

27. As Friedrich, 367, says: "Apart from life and death, apart from survival and destruction, there exists a third possibility—metamorphosis. Ovid himself at least says as much." See also Segal, 266.

28. Compare a passage in which metamorphosis, though stated to be a punishment, is nonetheless a compromise between a too harsh and a too mild form of punishment: Venus is deliberating the fate of the Cerastae: *exilio poenam potius gens inpia pendat / vel nece vel siquid medium est mortisque fugaeque. / idque quid esse potest, nisi versae poena figurae?* (10.232–34, "Let the impious race rather pay the penalty through exile, or extinction, or something in the middle between death and flight. And what can that be but the punishment of a changed form?").

29. *Lurent* is Housman's conjecture for *lucent*; see Lee's critical notes ad loc.

30. Other examples: 2.706, 4.561, 4.602, 4.750, 4.802, 5.677, 6.374 (see Anderson ad loc.), 7.467, 7.656, 7.855, 9.226, 9.664, 11.144.

31. *Stephen Hero*, 218.

32. Ancient writers sometimes make Procne the swallow and Philomela the nightingale, sometimes vice versa. For Ovid's version this question is not important, although, by specifying their abodes as birds, he seems to indicate that Philomela was the nightingale.

33. In this very passage Ovid himself makes the comparison, 712–13; see also *Fast.* 4.111; Tib. 1.1.64.

34. Ovid, to be sure, mentions the discrepant social status of the pair (698–99) and introduces the nurse into his story too (703–704), but neither does the nurse's role have any consequence in the tale nor is it suggested that anything other than character explains the girl's disdain for Iphis.

35. This addition to the story is probably an invention of Ovid's, as Haupt and Ehwald remark.

36. Again, comparison with other versions suggests that Ovid has innovated here in order to achieve his aim. Both Apollodorus (3.9.2) and Hyginus (*Fab.* 185) set the outrage in a grove of Jupiter, in which case the lions do not convey anything of their former selves. Servius ad *Aen.* 3.113 knows a version that sets it in a grove of Cybele (not a temple), but it serves to explain something quite different.

37. In Nicander's version, as recorded by Antoninus Liberalis (10), the sisters are changed into three different birds all of which avoid the light; but no reason is given for why they do so, nor is any other link established between the women and the birds they become.

38. Voit, 135–49.

39. Verse 657 may be spurious: see Tarrant, 359.

40. Ovid's account probably refers to the reputation of the Aeginetans as successful businessmen; see *Der Kleine Pauly*, 1:160–62. Strabo 8.6.16 gives a different historical interpretation of the story (the Aeginetans had to excavate and spread their poor soil, as ants do), yet he also mentions the inhabitants' skill at trade.

41. For *latus* used of ships see *Thesaurus Linguae Latinae* 7.1:1028.8–13.

42. "Wandlung und Dauer." I am indebted to this fine essay for help in reaching my own interpretation of metamorphosis, which nevertheless differs somewhat.

43. Frag. 96 (Edelstein and Kidd), from Stobaeus *Ecl.* 1.8.42.

44. A description of the rainbow at 6.63–67 is very similar. Other examples of in-between states: 14.93–94 (men changed into monkeys), 12.464–65 (a warrior between manhood and old age, without metamorphosis).

45. That Ovid has a deep interest in "wavering identity" was brought out by Fränkel, esp. 79–89, through numerous examples; see also Doblhofer, 227–28. This state, we can add, is brought to an end by metamorphosis.

46. Other examples of speechlessness: Cadmus (4.586–89), Niobe (6.306–7), Myrrha (10.506), Hecuba (13.569).

47. Altieri, 35.

48. Riddehough, 205.

49. Even Dörrie, 108–9, speaks of "a descent into the bestial."

50. Fränkel, *Early Greek Poetry and Philosophy*, 146.

51. Anderson, *Commentary*, ad loc.

52. See also the comments on Aeneas in the previous chapter.

53. The most recent and, on account of its full notes, most useful edition is that by Papathomopoulos.

54. A later Greek work, Longus' pastoral novel *Daphnis and Chloe*, probably from the second century A.D., includes a version of the Echo story (3.23), which, though quite different from Ovid's, resembles it at least in that the nymph's metamorphosis preserves her chief quality.

55. Servius proposes both interpretations without stating a preference.

56. Servius Danielis favors the latter, commenting that "the phrase is considered a strained substitute for the color white."

57. Dante reveals his awareness of Ovid in Canto Twenty-Five of the *Inferno*, where he boasts that his own (quite remarkable) description of a metamorphosis has no rival in his predecessor's work.

58. Skulsky has written an intriguing study of metamorphoses in western literature, from Homer to Virginia Woolf.

59. See the ancient scholia on this passage; Demetr. *Eloc.* 7; Heraclitus (*Alleg.* 37) and Cornutus (*Theol. Graec.* 12), both allegorists of the first century A.D.; and also modern commentators, such as Leaf and Ameis and Hentze.

60. Virgil describes *Fama*, or Rumor, in a like manner (4.173–91). Ovid, when essaying the same subject (12.29–64), meets the challenge which this passage presents through novel means: saying scarcely a word about Rumor herself, he catalogues her minions and allies and conducts the reader on a tour of her house. Hesiod had simply mentioned the house of Sleep (*Theog.* 758), and no one before Ovid, so far as we know, had described the abode of an allegorical figure. This forms the centerpiece in his portrayal of Rumor, though it is an element in the other three as well. The knack for imagining a setting appropriate to his figures is one of his gifts.

61. I venture to print my own conjecture here. The readings of the manuscripts have been emended in a dozen ways by editors.

62. Dickie, "Ovid, *Metamorphoses* 2.760–764."

63. It is especially appropriate that Envy's house is said to be *ignavi plenissima frigoris* (763). As the commentators point out, *ignavum* here means *quod facit ignavum*, that is, the adjective is transferred from the effect to the agent. But such shift of meaning is not remarkable in Latin: see also, for example, 1.147 *lurida aconita*, "aconite, which turns people yellow" (and Lee ad loc.); *caecus* in the sense of "making blind" (see Bömer ad 3.490).

CHAPTER SIX

1. Viarre, *Image et pensée*, 40–43, has interesting remarks on *imago*, along lines somewhat different from mine. Daut, *Imago*, is a helpful study but, as the author says, does not cover all meanings of the word, and in fact it

touches upon none of the meanings dealt with in this chapter.

2. Similarly Juno declares to Ino's companions, before changing them into stones, "I shall make you outstanding monuments (*monumenta*) of my rage" (4.549–50).

3. Ovid may have intended a pun in verse 225, where he makes Perseus say, "I shall grant you what I can grant you, what amounts to a great gift to one who is *iners*." The word may have one of its ordinary meanings here, "cowardly," and at the same time, with reference to what Phineus is to become, hint at its etymological sense, "without art." The same possibilities exist for *inertia* in 175.

4. Other examples: 5.229, 6.305, 12.23, 13.714.

5. *Simulamen*, to be sure, is found only here in Latin and may well have been coined by Ovid, who was fond of formations in -*men*, which are metrically convenient. But the word is in effect a variant on *simulacrum*, perhaps somewhat more abstract than it.

6. Though this imitates a passage from Euripides' *Andromeda* (frag. 125), the contrary-to-fact condition is typically Ovidian.

7. See Viarre, 45–68, on metamorphosis as related to sculpture and, 69–96, to painting.

8. Callimachus had called Niobe "a marble stone in place of a woman" (*Apol.* 24), which hardly draws attention to continuity between the two. Nonnus later, though he imitated Callimachus, was perhaps influenced by Ovidian notions too, for he called her "a statue" (*Dion.* 12.81).

9. See Anderson ad 7.791.

10. A comparison of the word *imago* in Virgil is instructive. Of these uses from the *Metamorphoses*, only two are found in the *Aeneid*: "dream-vision" (1.353, 2.773, 4.353, and often elsewhere) and "reflection" (8.23). And whereas Ovid very often emphasizes the special connotation the word has for him by joining it with others such as *deceptus*, *falsus*, or *mendax*, Virgil does so but twice and even then with adjectives that are less unequivocal: *cava sub imagine formae* (6.293, "under the hollow image of appearance") and *levis . . . imago* (10.663, "light image").

11. Petronius, for instance, who like Ovid is keenly aware of the role literature plays in shaping our actions and perceptions, in a single passage about the beautiful Circe reproduces both views of the relationship between art and nature. The narrator Encolpius describes her as having *osculum quale Praxiteles habere Dianam credidit* (*Sat.* 126.16, "a mouth such as Praxiteles believed that Diana had"), but he also says about the whiteness of her skin that *Parium marmor extinxerat* (126.17, "it outshone Parian marble"), and he terms her in general *mulierem omnibus simulacris emendatiorem* (126.13, "a woman more flawless than all statues").

A passage in Propertius may imply the primary nature of art: *sed facies aderat nullis obnoxia gemmis, / qualis Apelleis est color in tabulis* (1.2.21–22, "their complexion was indebted to no jewels; it was like the color in paintings by Apelles"). The second verse judges natural beauty (here, that of legendary women from the past) in the light of the artificial. And yet the whole context within the poem, as expressed in the first half of this couplet, exalts natural, unadorned beauty. Propertius' intention remains obscure.

12. To demonstrate this Bömer aptly cites *Met.* 3.20 and Val. Fl. 4.405–6. *Parva* does not need alteration.

13. I adopt Bühler's punctuation and interpretation as best despite their difficulties.

14. Ovid may have been thinking of the statue of Cyllarus, a horse belonging to Castor or Pollux and represented in their temple at Rome: see Stat. *Silv.* 1.1.53–54. Very similar to what Ovid says is an isolated statement of Euripides: "she showed breasts and a chest that were very beautiful, as if of a statue" (*Hec.* 560–61). A comparison from the *Aeneid* may also appear similar. Venus sheds grace on her son at the moment he first appears before Dido: *quale manus addunt ebori decus aut ubi flavo / argentum Pariusve lapis circumdatur auro* (*Aen.* 1.592–93, "such beauty as artisans add to ivory, or when silver or Parian marble is encircled by tawny gold"). But the point of this simile, as of its model in the *Odyssey* (6.232–35 = 23.159–62), is that normal beauty is enhanced by art, which is a quite different matter.

15. See Chapter Two for discussion of a similar comment made at 6.454. That Ovid is intent on art here is suggested by the phrase *laudaret faciem Livor quoque* (10.515, "even Envy would praise his appearance"), which recalls one he had earlier used for another artistic creation, Arachne's arras: *non illud carpere Livor / possit opus* (6.129–30, "Envy could not find fault with that work"). Aeschylus has the phrase *prepousa tōs en graphais* (*Agam.* 241, "standing out as in a picture"); but the meaning, as Fraenkel shows, is that Iphigenia is conspicuous against the background, not that she is outstandingly lovely.

16. This was an extremely contemporary comparison for Ovid to use, since clear glass had been developed just recently: see Forbes, 166. Perhaps the reference to clear glass exalts the skill of the artist, since the statue is seen undistorted, that is, very lifelike.

17. Immobility alone is the point when Catullus says the deserted Ariadne is *saxea ut effigies bacchantis* (64.61, "like the stone statue of a bacchant"): her beauty is not mentioned in the context.

In the *Metamorphoses* Perseus and Narcissus are further linked through the repeated phrase *visae correptus imagine formae* (3.416, 4.676, "enraptured by the picture of the beauty he had glimpsed"), applied to the one catching sight of Andromeda and the other of his own reflection. The phrase implies the power of images.

18. Murphy well remarks ad loc.: "Note the sophistication of the editorial parenthesis. . . . The way in which Ovid, like a connoisseur of landscape

gardening, measures up the relative influence of *natura* and *ars*, deciding on balance in favour of *ars*, is characteristically mannered." He also observes: "It is 'ars' rather than 'natura' which is the back-cloth for the *Metamorphoses*."

19. *(G)natus*, from which *natura* and *nativum* derive, includes the zero degree of *gen-*.

20. Lefèvre, "Plinius-Studien I," claims that at *Epist.* 5.6.13 Pliny attests the same view, recognizing the beauty of the landscape only insofar as nature satisfies the conditions of a work of art. But as Sherwin-White points out ad loc., the key words *formam pictam* refer to a map, not a painting: *descriptio* in the next clause and the similar use of *forma* at 9.39.5 make it certain that he is right.

21. On the notions of art in the earlier poem see Solodow, "Ovid's *Ars Amatoria*," 121–27.

22. For other examples of the pun, from Ovid and other authors, see Solodow, "Ovid's *Ars Amatoria*," 123 and n. 29; also n. 3 above.

23. *Rudis* is used in verse 7 also; cf. 1.406 and *Trist.* 1.7.22.

24. From a radio interview recorded in *Matisse on Art*, 91.

25. See also 10.256 and (assuming the manuscripts' reading, *latrare*, is right) 7.791.

26. This clause, repeated after a fashion at 15.104, has sometimes been taken as belonging to the language of cult, a blanket form of expression used in prayer; thus Norden, 391 (to the examples he gives, 144–47, add Firm. Mat. 5.praef.3). Bömer is right in rejecting this, on the grounds that there is no question here of addressing a god.

27. For the creator god Cicero employs both *fabricator* (*Tim.* 6) and *opifex* (*N.D.* 1.18).

28. Otis, 189.

29. Clem. Alex. *Protr.* 4, p. 51 P; Arnob. *Adv. Nat.* 6.22.

30. The eroticism emerges for the most part in subtle ways. In the phrase *saepe manus operi temptantes admovet* (254, "often he laid upon the work *temptantes* hands") the participle means "testing" and is construed with the indirect question following ("whether it was flesh or ivory"), yet it also suggests "feeling, fondling." After telling how the sculptor adorned the statue with clothing and jewelry the narrator says: "nor did she seem less lovely when nude" (266). This coy remark hints at a repeated dressing and undressing. Less indirect is the notice that he put her in a bed and called her "the sharer of his couch" (267–69).

31. See, for example, Quint. 1.11.3, 4.2.127; cf. Stroh, 580 n. 43.

32. Anderson, "Multiple Changes in the *Metamorphoses*," 26 (with a study of metamorphosis vocabulary, 2–5).

33. Cf. for example Ter. *And.* 398: *accepi: acceptam servabo.*

34. Fränkel, 95 and n. 60, quoting *Fast.* 3.832, where the sculptor is de-

scribed as "you who with skillful hand make rocks soft" (*mollia*). Cf. also *Met.* 1.401–2 (*molliri . . . mollitaque*) and *Aen.* 6.847 (*mollius*).

35. Elsewhere too Ovid describes pretense passing over into reality: *Ars* 1.615–18; *Rem.* 497–98, 504; see Solodow, "Ovid's *Ars Amatoria*," 120–21.

36. In the first part of the story too Ovid had used, prospectively, language which identified caressing with creating: *manus operi . . . admovet* (254, "he put his hands to the work") indicates physical contact, but also connotes artistic creation (cf. 15.218; Plin. *HN* 35.133).

37. This is treated most fully by Paratore, 193.

38. An extremely interesting comparison of Plato and Ovid, focused on the play of rhetoric and seriousness, may be found in Lanham, chapters 1 and 2.

39. A misunderstood pair of lines from Book Fourteen may appear to constitute the sole exception. One of Circe's maids points out to Macareus the transformed Picus: *forma viro quam cernis erat: licet ipse decorem / adspicias fictaque probes ab imagine veram* (14.322–23, "the man had the form you see: you may perceive his handsomeness for yourself, and from the fictitious picture appreciate the true"). The "true picture" is his original form (*imago* is used thus at 3.331 and 14.415 also), the "fictitious" his metamorphosed form: the latter is an imperfect version of the former. The sense is "you now, who are present after the metamorphosis, can see what he looked like before," which emphasizes the continuity between before and after states. I am unsure about the force of *forma*: is it the same as *imago ficta*, or is it a neutral term? However that may be, *imago* here does not imply that the transformed shape is in any way deceptive, because the original shape is equally termed an *imago* and the maid is in fact describing not the woodpecker but a marble statue of it.

40. For more see Buccino, Bartolomé, and Laslo.

41. Servius Danielis tells us this.

42. On this, as on the other passage, see Austin's commentary for informed, concise, helpful discussion.

43. The words suggesting the likeness are *imago* (416, 434, 463), *marmore signum* (419), *eburnea* (422), *simulacra* (432), *marmoreis* (481), and *cerae* (488).

44. We might observe in passing the advantages enjoyed by the literary artist. Only he can make it clear that the hair is golden, the laurel comes from Parnassus, the mantle is colored purple with Tyrian dye, and the fretwork or inlay is ivory from India: to express color, origin, or material does not lie within the sculptor's province.

45. I do not agree with Anderson's view that *imago* emphasizes the aspect of the novel deed, which wore a different face to the king than to its perpetrator.

46. See Bernbeck, 44–47, 51–55, who describes and illustrates these fea-

tures, carefully comparing Ovid's usage with that of other poets; see also Chapter Four.

47. Frag. 65 Vahlen. Ovid makes the same joke at *Fast.* 2.487–88. Both times he gives a twist to the borrowing by dropping a word from Ennius, who had said "the blue regions of heaven," and thus making *caerula* into a noun. For similar alteration by Ovid of a verse see Sen. *Contr.* 71.127. Cf. Due, 28–29.

48. Its presence was attested even later by Pausanias (2.17.3).

49. Here too Ovid gives a twist by changing the setting of this prophecy; see Chapter Four.

50. The friezes on the temple of Juno (*Aen.* 1.466–94), the sculpted doors to Apollo's temple at Cumae (6.20–33), and the shield of Aeneas (8.630–728).

51. I agree with Leach, who takes this as the premise of her study.

52. Fordyce ad *Aen.* 8.626ff.

53. See Draeger, 418; also *Thesaurus Linguae Latinae* 6.1:117.82–118.28. The example closest in size is *Aen.* 8.630–34.

BIBLIOGRAPHY

Albrecht, M. von. "Ovids Humor: ein Schlüssel zur Interpretation der Metamorphosen." *Der altsprachliche Unterricht* 6, no. 2 (1963) 47–72. Reprinted in von Albrecht and Zinn, 405–37.

———. *Die Parenthese in Ovids Metamorphosen und ihre dichterische Funktion.* Spudasmata, 7. Hildesheim, 1964.

———, and Zinn, Ernst, eds. *Ovid.* Wege der Forschung, 92. Darmstadt, 1968.

Alfonsi, L. "L'inquadramento filosofico delle Metamorfosi ovidiane." In Herescu, 265–72.

Altieri, C. "Ovid and the New Mythologists." *Novel: A Forum on Fiction* 7, no. 1 (Fall 1973) 31–40.

Anderson, W. S. "Multiple Changes in the *Metamorphoses.*" *Transactions of the American Philological Association* 94 (1963) 1–27.

———. Review of Bernbeck. *American Journal of Philology* 90 (1969) 352–55.

———, ed. and comm. *Metamorphoses, Books 6–10.* Norman, Okla., 1972.

———, ed. *Metamorphoses.* Bibliotheca Teubneriana. Leipzig, 1977.

Barsby, J. *Ovid.* Greece and Rome: New Surveys in the Classics, 12. Oxford, 1978.

Bartolomé, H. *Ovid und die antike Kunst.* Leipzig, 1935.

Bernbeck, E. J. *Beobachtungen zur Darstellungsart in Ovids Metamorphosen.* Zetemata, 43. Munich, 1967.

Boillat, M. *Les Métamorphoses d'Ovide: thèmes majeurs et problèmes de composition.* Publications universitaires européennes, Série 15: Philologie et littérature classiques, 8. Berne and Frankfort-am-Main, 1976.

Bömer, F. "Ovid und die Sprache Vergils." *Gymnasium* 66 (1959) 268–87. Reprinted in von Albrecht and Zinn, 173–202.

———, comm. *Metamorphosen.* 6 vols. Heidelberg, 1969–86.

Bonner, S. F. *Education in Ancient Rome.* Berkeley and Los Angeles, 1977.

Buccino, C. *Le opere d'arte nelle Metamorfosi di Ovidio.* Naples, 1913.

Buchheit, V. "Mythos und Geschichte in Ovids Metamorphosen I." *Hermes* 94 (1966) 80–108.

Büchner, K. "Ovids Metamorphosen." In *Humanitas Romana: Studien über Werke und Wesen der Römer,* 203–28. Heidelberg, 1957. Partially reprinted in von Albrecht and Zinn, 384–92.

Clausen, W. V. "Ovid, *Met.* 15.90." *American Journal of Philology* 100 (1979) 247–49.

Copley, F. O. *Exclusus Amator: A Study in Latin Love Poetry.* Baltimore, 1956.

Curran, L. C. "Transformation and Anti-Augustanism in Ovid's *Metamorphoses.*" *Arethusa* 5 (1972) 71–91.

Daut, R. *Imago: Untersuchungen zum Bildbegriff der Römer.* Bibliothek der klassischen Altertumswissenschaften, N.F., ser. 2, vol. 56. Heidelberg, 1975.

Dickie, M. W. "Ovid, *Metamorphoses* 2.760–764." *American Journal of Philology* 96 (1975) 378–90.

Diller, H. "Die dichterische Eigenart von Ovids Metamorphosen." *Humanistisches Gymnasium* 45 (1934) 25–37. Reprinted in von Albrecht and Zinn, 322–39.

Doblhofer, E. "Ovidius Urbanus: Eine Studie zum Humor in Ovids Metamorphosen." *Philologus* 104 (1960) 63–91, 223–35.

Dörrie, H. "Wandlung und Dauer: Ovids Metamorphosen und Poseidonios' Lehre von der Substanz." *Der altsprachliche Unterricht* 4, no. 2 (1959) 95–116.

Draeger, A. *Historische Syntax der lateinischen Sprache,* vol. 2. 2nd ed. Leipzig, 1881.

Due, O. S. *Changing Forms: Studies in the Metamorphoses of Ovid.* Classica et Medievalia, Dissertationes, 10. Copenhagen, 1974.

Elliott, A. G. "Ovid's *Metamorphoses*: A Bibliography 1968–78." *Classical World* 73 (1979–80) 385–412.

Else, G. F. *Aristotle's Poetics: The Argument.* Cambridge, Mass., 1967.

Forbes, R. J. *Studies in Ancient Technology,* vol. 5. Leiden, 1957.

Fraenkel, Eduard. "Carattere della poesia augustea." *Maia* 1 (1948) 245–64. Reprinted in *Kleine Beiträge zur klassischen Philologie,* 2:209–29. Rome, 1964.

Fränkel, H. *Ovid: A Poet Between Two Worlds.* Sather Classical Lectures, 18. Berkeley and Los Angeles, 1945.

———. *Early Greek Poetry and Philosophy.* Translated by M. Hadas and J. Willis. New York and London, 1973.

Frécaut, J.-M. *L'esprit et l'humour chez Ovide.* Grenoble, 1972.

Friedrich, W.-H. "Der Kosmos Ovids." In *Festschrift Franz Dornseiff,* edited by H. Kusch, 94–110. Leipzig, 1953. Reprinted in von Albrecht and Zinn, 362–83.

Galinsky, G. K. "Ovid's Metamorphosis of Myth." In *Perspectives of Roman Poetry: A Classics Symposium,* 108–14. Austin, 1974.

———. *Ovid's Metamorphoses: An Introduction to the Basic Aspects.* Oxford, 1975.

Gomme, A. W., and Sandbach, F. H. *Menander: A Commentary.* Oxford, 1973.

Goold, G. P. *See* Miller.

Griffiths, F. T. "Theocritus' *Hymn to the Dioscuri.*" *Harvard Studies in Classical Philology* 80 (1976) 297–300.

Grimal, P. "La chronologie légendaire dans les *Métamorphoses* d'Ovide." In Herescu, 245–57.

Guthmüller, H.-B. *Beobachtungen zum Aufbau der Metamorphosen Ovids.* Marburg, 1964.

Haupt, M., and Ehwald, R., eds. and comms. *Metamorphosen.* Corrected and enlarged by M. von Albrecht. 2 vols. 9th and 5th eds. (respectively). Dublin and Zurich, 1966.

Heinze, R. *Virgils epische Technik.* 3rd ed. Leipzig and Berlin, 1915.

Herescu, N. F., ed. *Ovidiana: recherches sur Ovide.* Paris, 1958.

Hofmann, H. "Ovids 'Metamorphosen' in der Forschung der letzten 30 Jahre (1950–1979)." In *Aufstieg und Niedergang der römischen Welt*, edited by H. Temporini and W. Haase, II.31.4:2161–2273. Berlin and New York, 1981.

Hollis, A. S., ed. and comm. *Metamorphoses, Book VIII.* Oxford, 1970.

Jannacone, S. *La letteratura greco-latina delle metamorfosi.* Messina and Florence, 1953.

Johnson, W. R. "The Problem of the Counter-classical Sensibility and its Critics." *California Studies in Classical Antiquity* 3 (1970) 123–51.

Joyce, J. *Stephen Hero.* Edited by T. Spencer, revised by J. J. Slocum and H. Cahoon. London, 1960.

Judeich, W. *Topographie von Athen.* 2nd ed. Munich, 1931.

Kenney, E. J. "The Style of the *Metamorphoses.*" In *Ovid*, edited by J. W. Binns, 116–53. London, 1973.

———. "Ovidius Prooemians." *Proceedings of the Cambridge Philological Society* 202, n.s. 22 (1976) 47–53.

Klingner, F. "Catulls Peleus-Epos." In *Studien zur griechischen und römischen Literatur*, 156–224. Zurich and Stuttgart, 1964.

Kraus, W. "Ovidius Naso." In *Real-Enzyklopädie* XVIII.2:1910–86. Reprinted in revised form in von Albrecht and Zinn, 67–166.

Kroll, W. *Studien zum Verständnis der römischen Literatur.* Stuttgart, 1924.

Lafaye, G. *Les Métamorphoses d'Ovide et leurs modèles grecs.* Paris, 1904. Reprinted Hildesheim and New York, 1971.

Lamacchia, R. "Ovidio interprete di Virgilio." *Maia* 12 (1960) 310–30.

Lanham, R. A. *The Motives of Eloquence: Literary Rhetoric in the Renaissance.* New Haven and London, 1976.

Laslo, N. "Riflessi d'arte figurata nelle Metamorfosi di Ovidio." *Ephemeris Dacoromania* 6 (1935) 368–440.

Leach, E. W. "Ekphrasis and the Theme of Artistic Failure in Ovid's *Metamorphoses.*" *Ramus* 3 (1974) 102–42.

Lee, A. G., ed. and comm. *Metamorphoses, Book I.* Cambridge, 1953.

Lefèvre, E. "Plinius-Studien I: Römische Baugesinnung und Landschaftsauffassung in den Villenbriefen (2,17; 5,6)." *Gymnasium* 84 (1977) 519–41.

Ludwig, W. *Struktur und Einheit der Metamorphosen Ovids.* Berlin, 1965.

Mack, S. *Patterns of Time in Vergil.* Hamden, Conn., 1978.

Marrou, H. I. *A History of Education in Antiquity.* Translated by G. Lamb. London and New York, 1956.

Martini, E. "Ovid und seine Bedeutung für die römische Poesie." In *Epitymbion Heinrich Swoboda dargebracht,* 165–94. Reichenberg, 1927. Reprinted as an appendix to the reprint of his *Einleitung zu Ovid.* Darmstadt, 1970.

Matisse, H. *Matisse on Art.* Edited by J. D. Flam. New York, 1978.

Miller, F. J., ed. and trans. *Metamorphoses.* Loeb Classical Library. Revised by G. P. Goold. 2 vols. 3rd and 2nd eds. (respectively). Cambridge, Mass., and London, 1977, 1984.

Murphy, G. M. H., ed. and comm. *Metamorphoses, Book XI.* Oxford, 1972.

Neuerburg, N. *L'architettura delle fontane e dei ninfei nell'Italia antica.* Memorie dell'Accademia di Archeologia, Letteratura e Belle Arti di Napoli, 5. Naples, 1965.

Norden, E. *Agnostos Theos.* Stuttgart, 1913.

Norwood, F. "Unity in the Diversity of Ovid's *Metamorphoses.*" *Classical Journal* 59 (1964) 170–74.

Ooteghem, J. van. "Le déluge d'après Ovide." *Les études classiques* 25 (1957) 444–48.

Otis, B. *Ovid As an Epic Poet.* 2nd ed. Cambridge, 1970. (1st ed., 1966.)

Papadopoulos, J. *Xoana e Sphyrelata: testimonianza delle fonti scritte.* Studia Archeologica, 24. Rome, 1980.

Papathomopoulos, M., ed. *Antoninus Liberalis: Les Métamorphoses.* Budé. Paris, 1968.

Paratore, E. "L'evoluzione della 'sphragis' dalle prime alle ultime opere di Ovidio." In *Atti del Convegno internazionale ovidiano,* 1:173–203. Rome, 1959.

Peters, H. *Symbola ad Ovidii artem epicam cognoscendam.* Göttingen, 1908. Reprinted together with Lafaye, 1971.

Price, L. *Dialogues of Alfred North Whitehead.* Boston, 1954.

Putnam, M. C. J. *The Poetry of the Aeneid.* Cambridge, Mass., 1966.

Richardson, J. "The Function of Formal Imagery in Ovid's *Metamorphoses.*" *Classical Journal* 59 (1964) 161–69.

Riddehough, G. B. "Man-into-Beast Changes in Ovid." *Phoenix* 13 (1959) 201–209.

Rosivach, V. J. "Latinus' Genealogy and the Palace of Picus." *Classical Quarterly* 74, n.s. 30 (1980) 140–52.

Saint-Denis, E. de. "La génie d'Ovide d'après le livre XV des *Métamorphoses*." *Revue des études latines* 18 (1940) 111–40.

Segal, C. "Myth and Philosophy in the *Metamorphoses*: Ovid's Augustanism and the Augustan Conclusion of Book XV." *American Journal of Philology* 90 (1969) 257–92.

Sheets, G. "Ennius Lyricus." *Illinois Classical Studies* 8, no. 1 (1983) 22–32.

Skulsky, H. *Metamorphosis: The Mind in Exile*. Cambridge, Mass., and London, 1981.

Solodow, J. B. "Ovid's *Ars Amatoria*: The Lover as Cultural Ideal." *Wiener Studien* 90, n.s. 11 (1977) 106–27.

———. "*Raucae, tua cura, palumbes*: Study of a Poetic Word Order." *Harvard Studies in Classical Philology* 90 (1986) 129–53.

Spitzer, L. "Linguistic Perspectivism in the *Don Quijote*." In *Linguistics and Literary History: Essays in Stylistics*, 42–85. Princeton, 1948.

Steiner, G. "Ovid's *Carmen Perpetuum*." *Transactions of the American Philological Association* 89 (1958) 218–36.

Stephens, W. "Cupid and Venus in Ovid's *Metamorphoses*." *Transactions of the American Philological Association* 89 (1958) 286–300.

Stinton, T. C. W. " 'Si credere dignum est': Some Expressions of Disbelief in Euripides and Others." *Proceedings of the Cambridge Philological Society* 202, n.s. 22 (1976) 60–89.

Stitz, M. *Ovid und Vergils Aeneis: Interpretation Met. 13,623–14,608*. Freiburg, 1962.

Stroh, W. "Ein missbrauchtes Distichon Ovids." In von Albrecht and Zinn, 567–80.

Swanson, R. A. "Ovid's Pythagorean Essay." *Classical Journal* 54 (1958) 21–24.

Tarrant, R. J. "Editing Ovid's *Metamorphoses*: Problems and Possibilities." *Classical Philology* 77 (1982) 342–60. Review of Anderson's Teubner edition.

Tolkiehn, J. "Die Bucheinteilung der Metamorphosen Ovids." *Jahresberichte des philologischen Vereins zu Berlin* 41 (1915) 315–19.

Viarre, S. *L'image et la pensée dans les "Métamorphoses" d'Ovide*. Paris, 1964.

Voit, L. "Die Niobe des Ovid." *Gymnasium* 64 (1957) 135–49.

Wilkinson, L. P. *Ovid Recalled*. Cambridge, 1955.

———. "The World of Ovid's *Metamorphoses*." In Herescu, 231–44.

INDEX OF PASSAGES CITED

This index first lists passages from the *Metamorphoses*, then all others, including those from other works by Ovid. In the part of the index dealing with the *Metamorphoses*, parenthetic additions indicate the story narrated in a passage. When a story as a whole is discussed in the text, references to it are given directly after these parenthetical additions.

GENERAL INDEX

For characters and stories in the *Metamorphoses*, this index gives their location in the poem, which may then be followed up in the Index of Passages Cited. For ancient authors, the same index should be consulted along with this one.

WITHDRAWN

Printed in the United States
5110

9 780807 854341